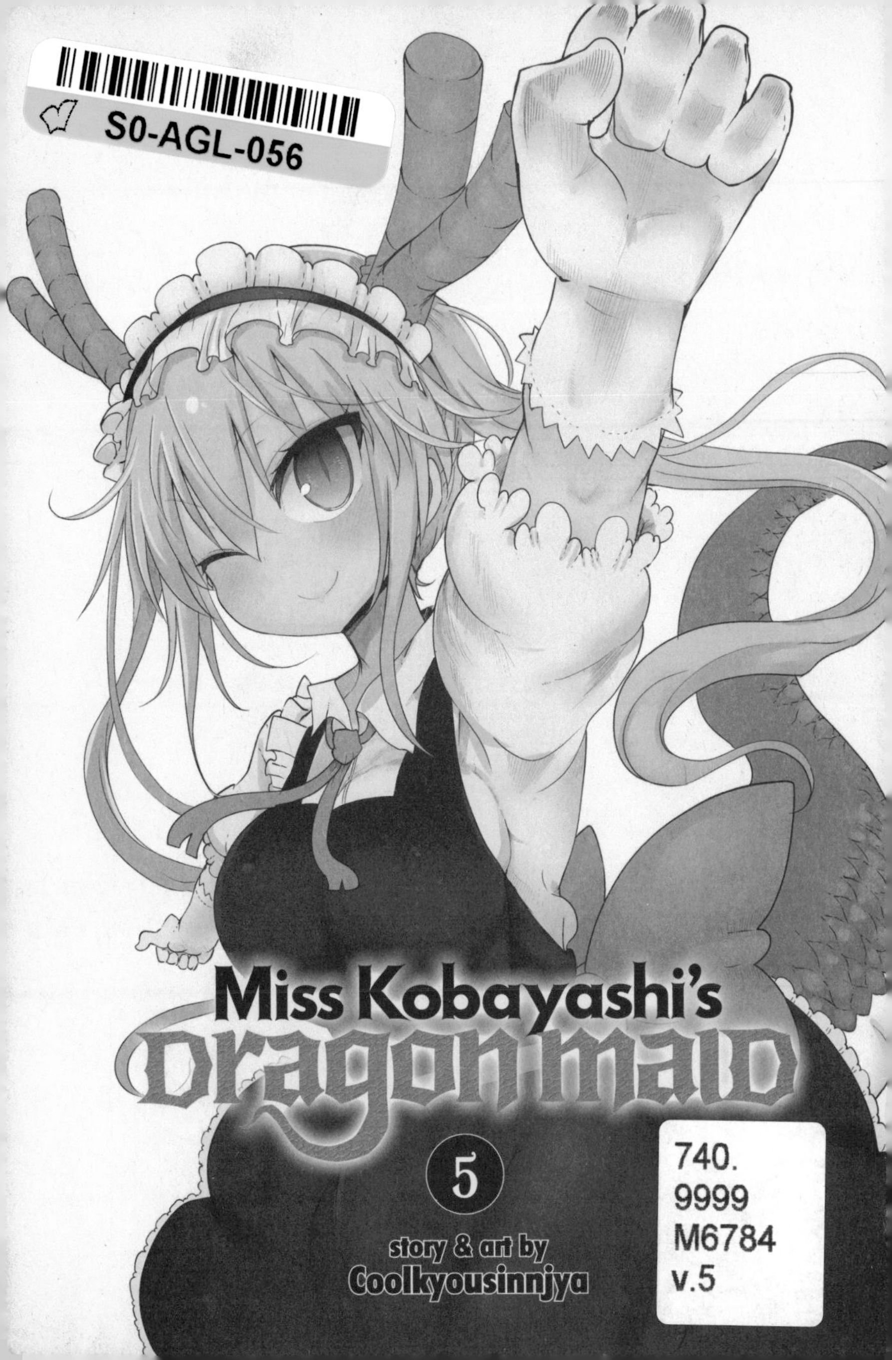

Miss Kobayashi's Dragon Maid

5

story & art by
Coolkyousinnjya

SEVEN SEAS ENTERTAINMENT PRESENTS

Miss Kobayashi's DRAGON MAID VOL.5

story and art by **coolkyousinnjya**

TRANSLATION
Jenny McKeon

ADAPTATION
Shanti Whitesides

LETTERING
Jennifer Skarupa

LOGO DESIGN
KC Fabellon

COVER DESIGN
Nicky Lim

PROOFREADING
Brett Hallahan

ASSISTANT EDITOR
Jenn Grunigen

PRODUCTION ASSISTANT
CK Russell

PRODUCTION MANAGER
Lissa Pattillo

EDITOR-IN-CHIEF
Adam Arnold

PUBLISHER
Jason DeAngelis

First published in Japan in 2016 by Futabasha Publishers Ltd., Tokyo.
English version published by Seven Seas Entertainment, LLC.
Under license from Futabasha Publishers Ltd.

ISBN: 978-1-626926-74-5

Printed in Canada

First Printing: November 2017

10 9 8 7 6 5 4 3 2 1

FOLLOW US ONLINE: ***www.gomanga.com***

READING DIRECTIONS

This book reads from ***right to left***, Japanese style. If this is your first time reading manga, you start reading from the top right panel on each page and take it from there. If you get lost, just follow the numbered diagram here. It may seem backwards at first, but you'll get the hang of it! Have fun!!

1
2
3
4
5
6
7
8
9

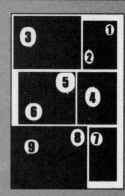

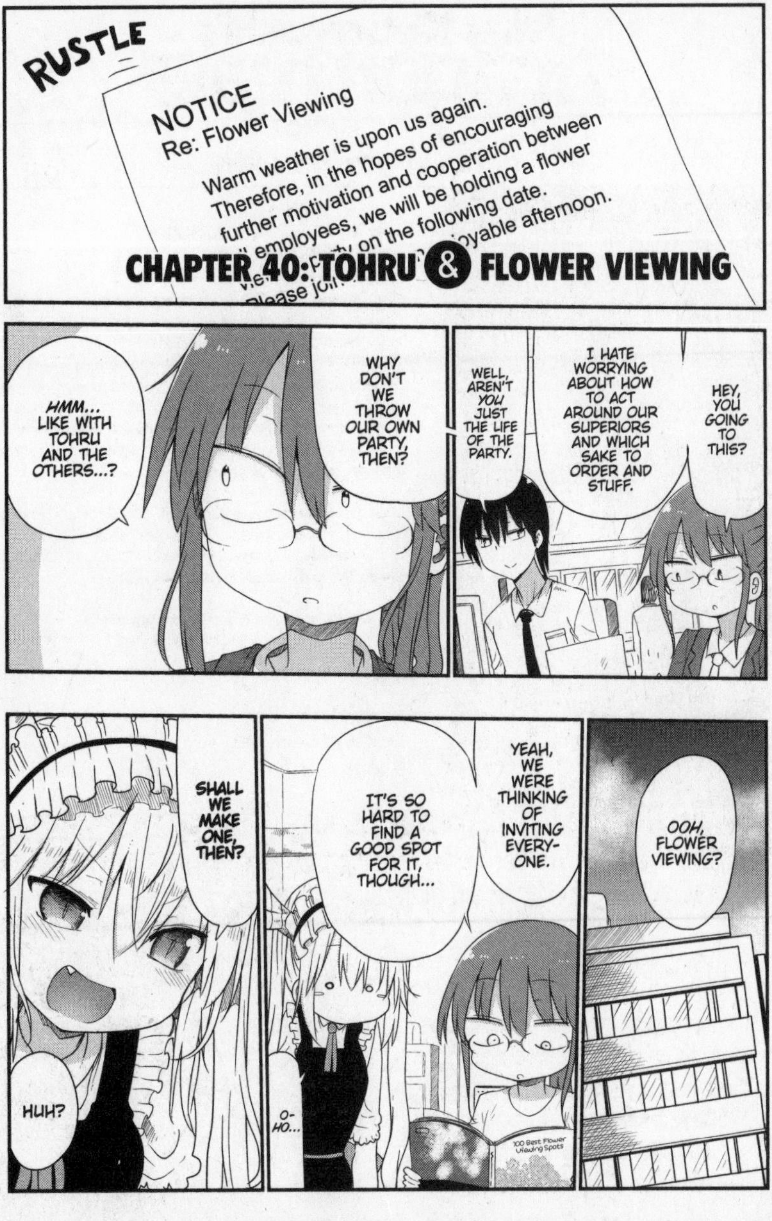
RUSTLE
NOTICE
Re: Flower Viewing
Warm weather is upon us again. Therefore, in the hopes of encouraging further motivation and cooperation between employees, we will be holding a flower on the following date.
joyable afternoon.
CHAPTER 40: TOHRU & FLOWER VIEWING
HEY, YOU GOING TO THIS?
I HATE WORRYING ABOUT HOW TO ACT AROUND OUR SUPERIORS AND WHICH SAKE TO ORDER AND STUFF.
WELL, AREN'T YOU JUST THE LIFE OF THE PARTY.
WHY DON'T WE THROW OUR OWN PARTY, THEN?
HMM... LIKE WITH TOHRU AND THE OTHERS...?
OOH, FLOWER VIEWING?
YEAH, WE WERE THINKING OF INVITING EVERY-ONE.
IT'S SO HARD TO FIND A GOOD SPOT FOR IT, THOUGH...
O-HO...
100 Best Flower Viewing Spots
SHALL WE MAKE ONE, THEN?
HUH?

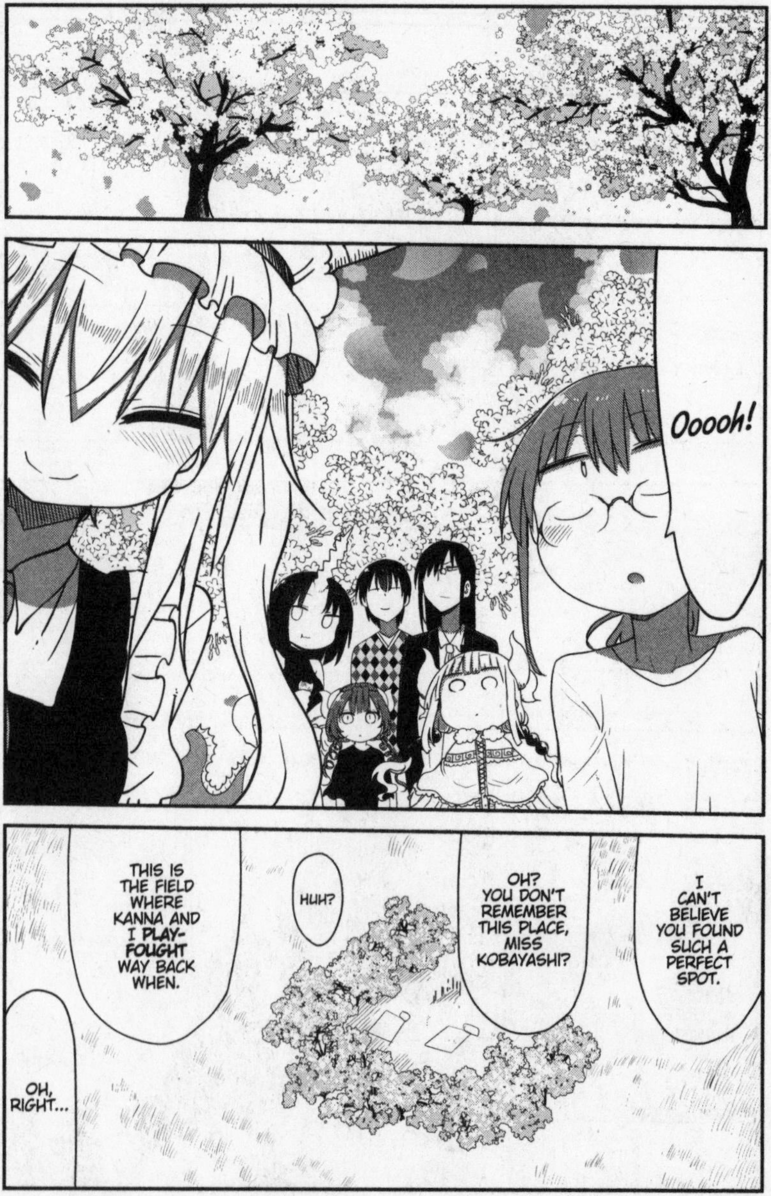
Ooooh!
I CAN'T BELIEVE YOU FOUND SUCH A PERFECT SPOT.
OH? YOU DON'T REMEMBER THIS PLACE, MISS KOBAYASHI?
HUH?
THIS IS THE FIELD WHERE KANNA AND I PLAY-FOUGHT WAY BACK WHEN.
OH, RIGHT...

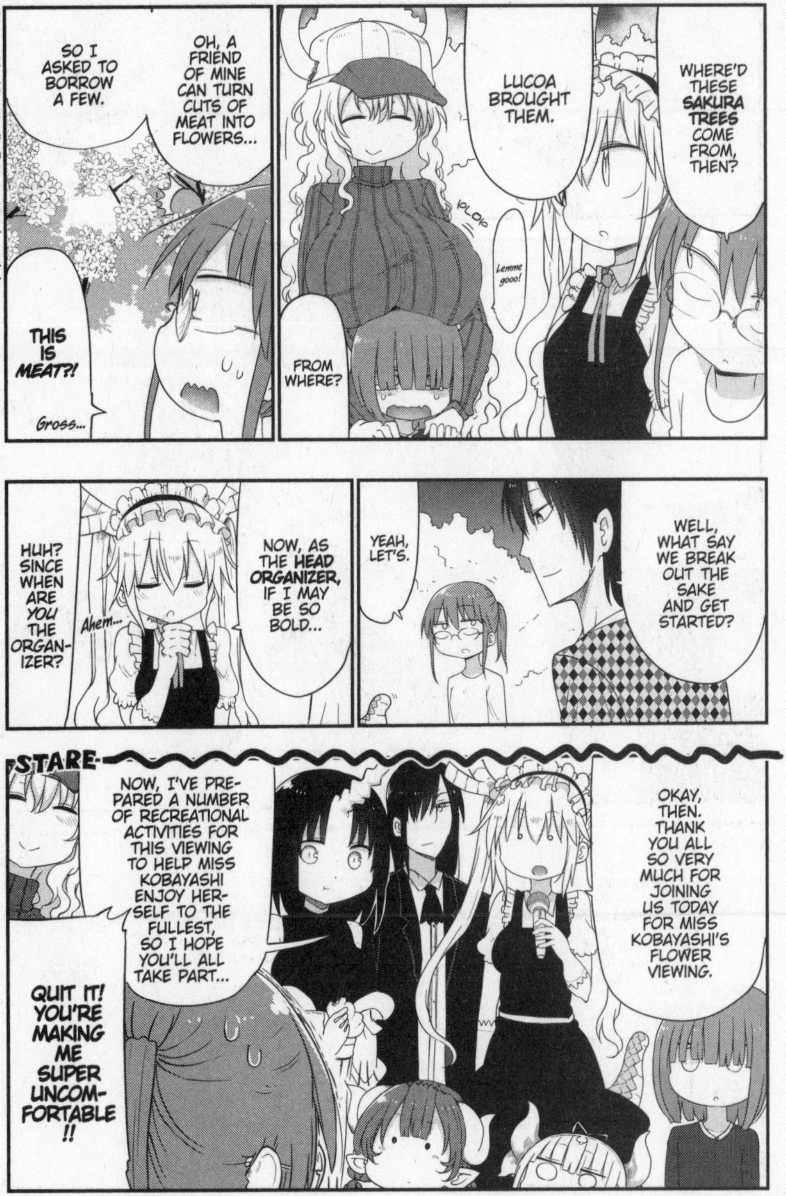
WHERE'D THESE SAKURA TREES COME FROM, THEN?
LUCOA BROUGHT THEM.
Lemme gooo!
FROM WHERE?
OH, A FRIEND OF MINE CAN TURN CUTS OF MEAT INTO FLOWERS...
SO I ASKED TO BORROW A FEW.
THIS IS MEAT?!
Gross...
WELL, WHAT SAY WE BREAK OUT THE SAKE AND GET STARTED?
YEAH, LET'S.
NOW, AS THE HEAD ORGANIZER, IF I MAY BE SO BOLD...
Ahem...
HUH? SINCE WHEN ARE YOU THE ORGANIZER?
OKAY, THEN. THANK YOU ALL SO VERY MUCH FOR JOINING US TODAY FOR MISS KOBAYASHI'S FLOWER VIEWING.
NOW, I'VE PREPARED A NUMBER OF RECREATIONAL ACTIVITIES FOR THIS VIEWING TO HELP MISS KOBAYASHI ENJOY HERSELF TO THE FULLEST, SO I HOPE YOU'LL ALL TAKE PART...
STARE
QUIT IT! YOU'RE MAKING ME SUPER UNCOMFORTABLE!!

(Name: Xochiquetzal's Prunus x yedoensis.)

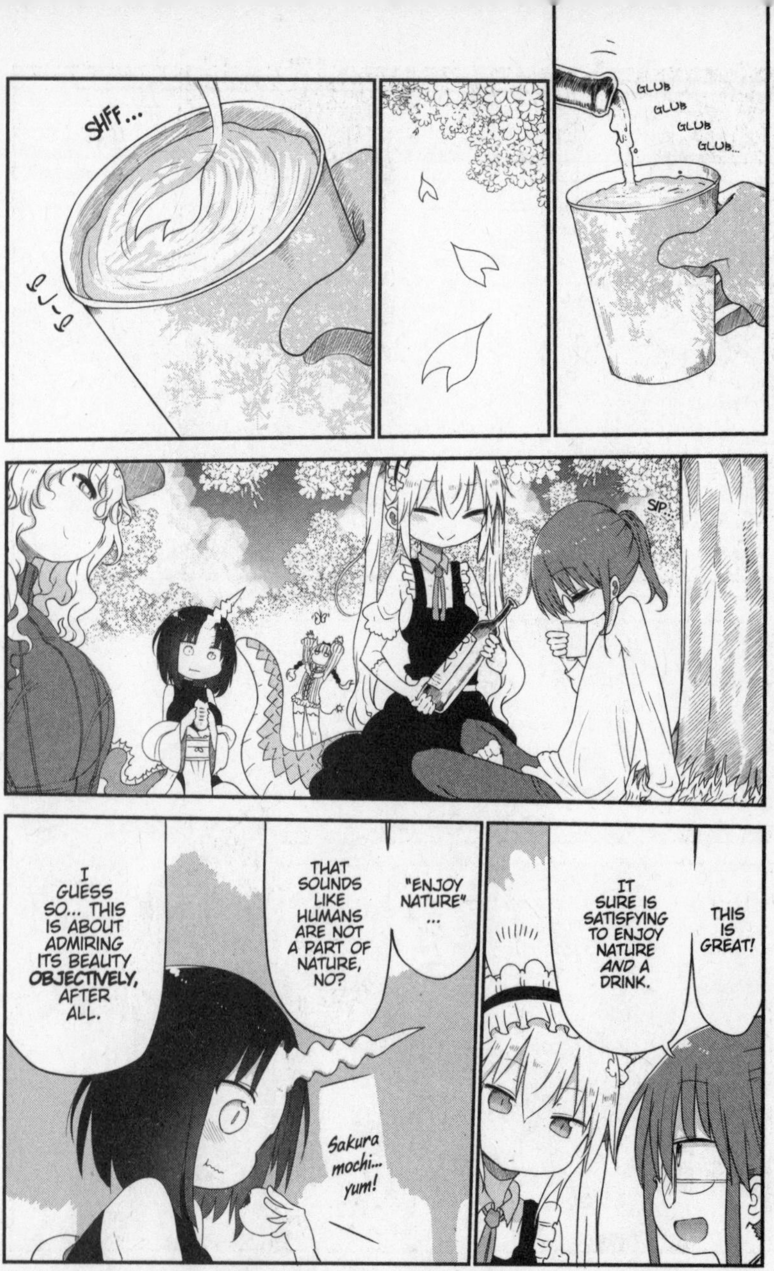

GLUB GLUB GLUB GLUB...
SHFF...
SIP
THIS IS GREAT!
IT SURE IS SATISFYING TO ENJOY NATURE AND A DRINK.
"ENJOY NATURE" ...
THAT SOUNDS LIKE HUMANS ARE NOT A PART OF NATURE, NO?
I GUESS SO... THIS IS ABOUT ADMIRING ITS BEAUTY OBJECTIVELY, AFTER ALL.
Sakura mochi... yum!

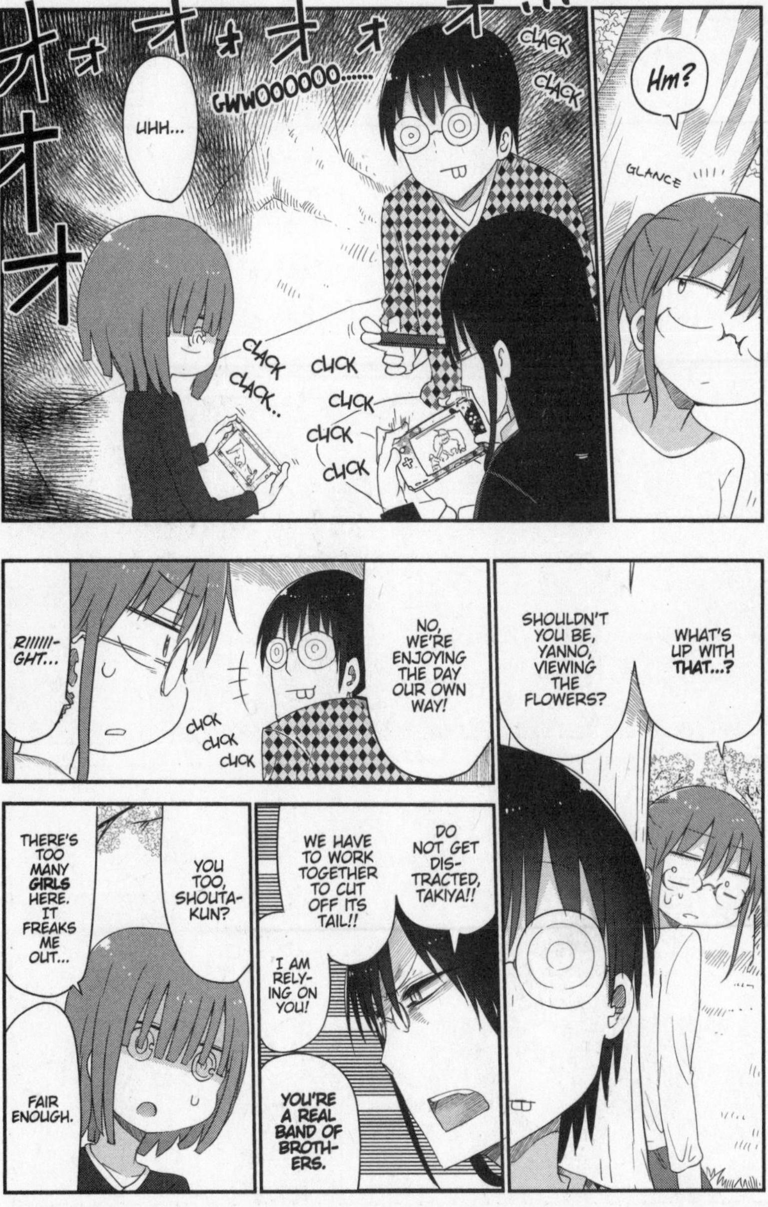
Hm?
GLANCE
オォォォォォォォ……
GWWOOOOOO.......
UHH...
CLACK
CLACK
CLICK
CLICK
CLICK
CLICK
CLACK
CLACK...
WHAT'S UP WITH THAT...?
SHOULDN'T YOU BE, YANNO, VIEWING THE FLOWERS?
NO, WE'RE ENJOYING THE DAY OUR OWN WAY!
CLICK CLICK CLICK
RIIIIII-GHT...
DO NOT GET DIS-TRACTED, TAKIYA!!
WE HAVE TO WORK TOGETHER TO CUT OFF ITS TAIL!!
I AM RELY-ING ON YOU!
YOU'RE A REAL BAND OF BROTH-ERS.
YOU TOO, SHOUTA-KUN?
THERE'S TOO MANY GIRLS HERE. IT FREAKS ME OUT...
FAIR ENOUGH.

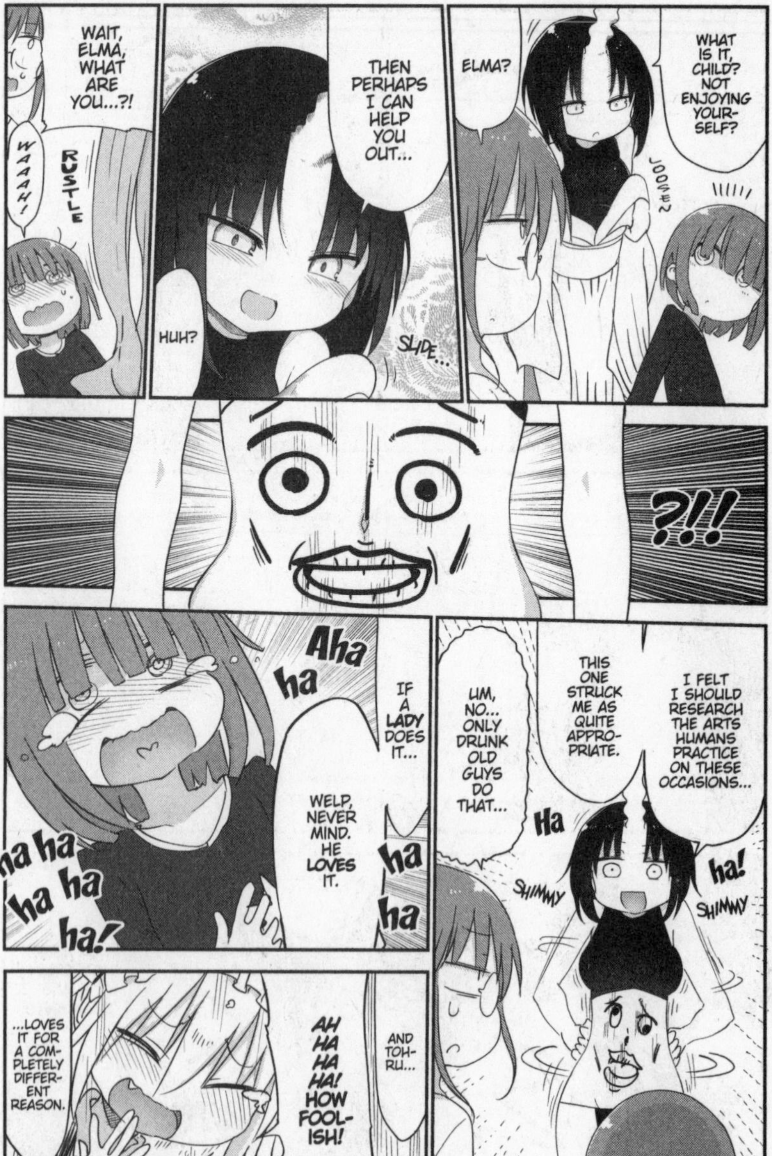
WHAT IS IT, CHILD? NOT ENJOYING YOURSELF?
ELMA?
LOOSEN
THEN PERHAPS I CAN HELP YOU OUT...
HUH?
SLIDE...
WAIT, ELMA, WHAT ARE YOU...?!
RUSTLE
WAAAH!
?!!
I FELT I SHOULD RESEARCH THE ARTS HUMANS PRACTICE ON THESE OCCASIONS...
THIS ONE STRUCK ME AS QUITE APPROPRIATE.
UM, NO... ONLY DRUNK OLD GUYS DO THAT...
Ha ha!
SHIMMY
SHIMMY
IF A LADY DOES IT...
WELP, NEVER MIND. HE LOVES IT.
Aha ha
ha ha ha ha ha!
ha ha
AND TOHRU...
AH HA HA HA! HOW FOOLISH!
...LOVES IT FOR A COMPLETELY DIFFERENT REASON.

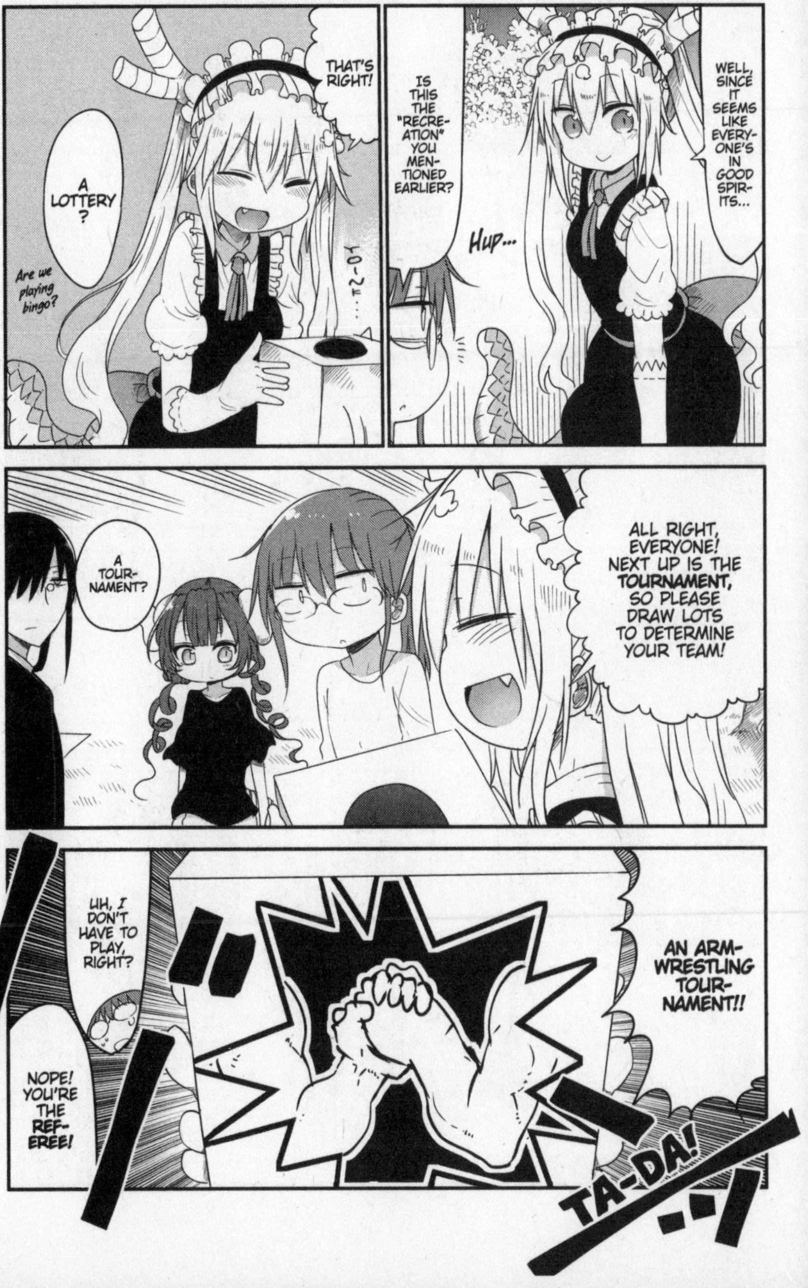
WELL, SINCE IT SEEMS LIKE EVERYONE'S IN GOOD SPIRITS...
Hup...
IS THIS THE "RECREATION" YOU MENTIONED EARLIER?
THAT'S RIGHT!
YOINK...
A LOTTERY?
Are we playing bingo?
ALL RIGHT, EVERYONE! NEXT UP IS THE **TOURNAMENT**, SO PLEASE DRAW LOTS TO DETERMINE YOUR TEAM!
A TOURNAMENT?
AN ARM-WRESTLING TOURNAMENT!!
TA-DA!
UH, I DON'T HAVE TO PLAY, RIGHT?
NOPE! YOU'RE THE REFEREE!

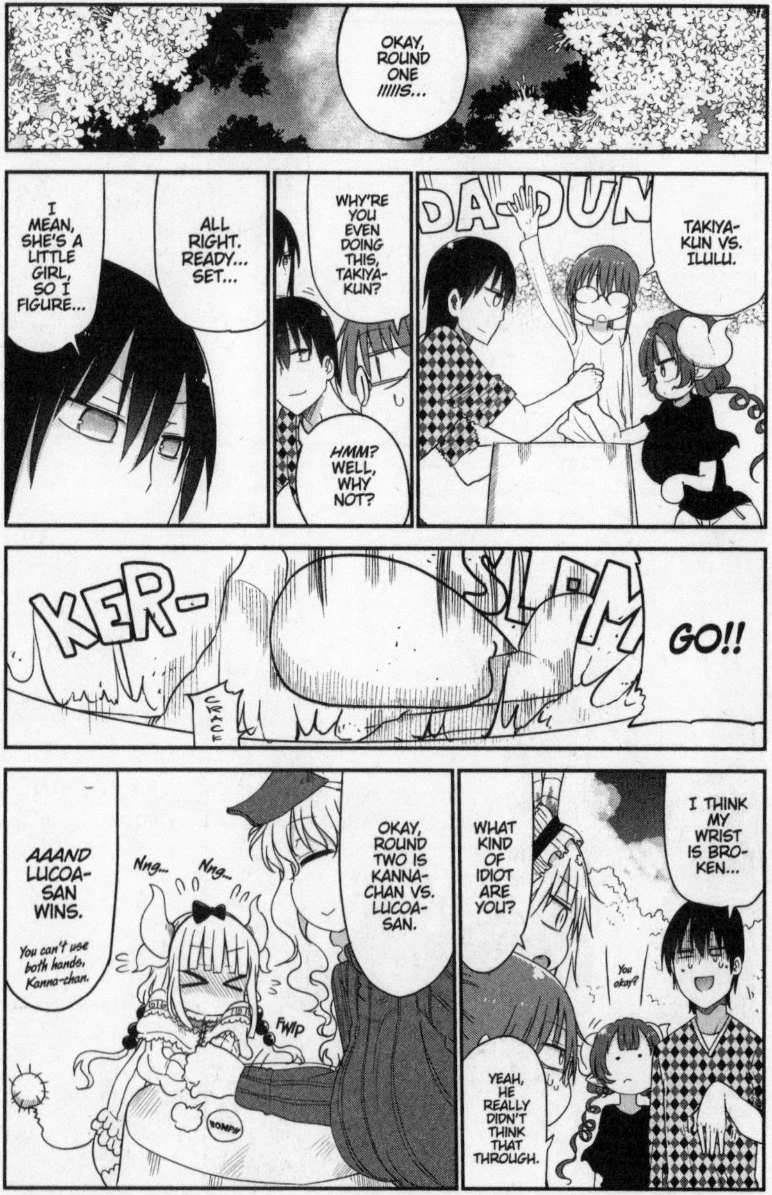
OKAY, ROUND ONE IIIIIS...
DA-DUN
TAKIYA-KUN VS. ILULU.
WHY'RE YOU EVEN DOING THIS, TAKIYA-KUN?
HMM? WELL, WHY NOT?
ALL RIGHT. READY... SET...
I MEAN, SHE'S A LITTLE GIRL, SO I FIGURE...
GO!!
KER-
CRACK
I THINK MY WRIST IS BRO-KEN...
WHAT KIND OF IDIOT ARE YOU?
You okay?
YEAH, HE REALLY DIDN'T THINK THAT THROUGH.
OKAY, ROUND TWO IS KANNA-CHAN VS. LUCOA-SAN.
Nng... Nng...
FWIP
BOMPH
AAAND LUCOA-SAN WINS.
You can't use both hands, Kanna-chan.

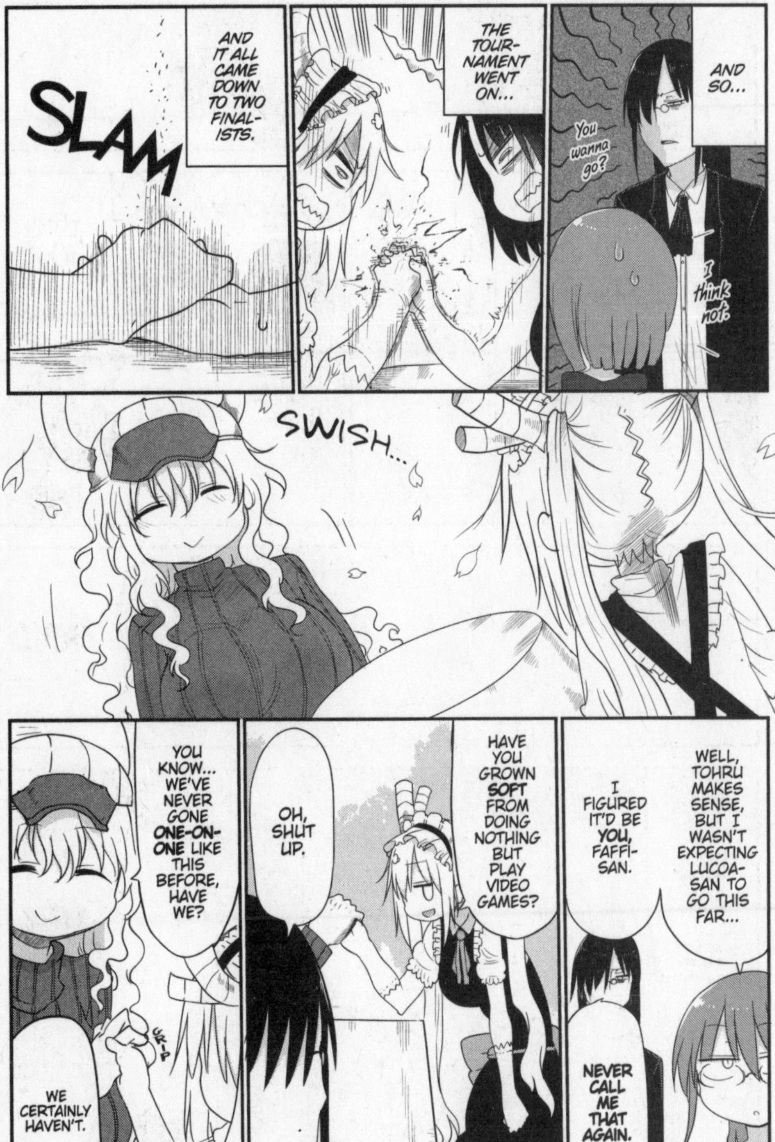
AND SO...
You wanna go?
I think not.
THE TOURNAMENT WENT ON...
AND IT ALL CAME DOWN TO TWO FINALISTS.
SLAM
SWISH...
WELL, TOHRU MAKES SENSE, BUT I WASN'T EXPECTING LUCOA-SAN TO GO THIS FAR...
I FIGURED IT'D BE YOU, FAFFI-SAN.
NEVER CALL ME THAT AGAIN.
HAVE YOU GROWN SOFT FROM DOING NOTHING BUT PLAY VIDEO GAMES?
OH, SHUT UP.
YOU KNOW... WE'VE NEVER GONE ONE-ON-ONE LIKE THIS BEFORE, HAVE WE?
GRIP
WE CERTAINLY HAVEN'T.

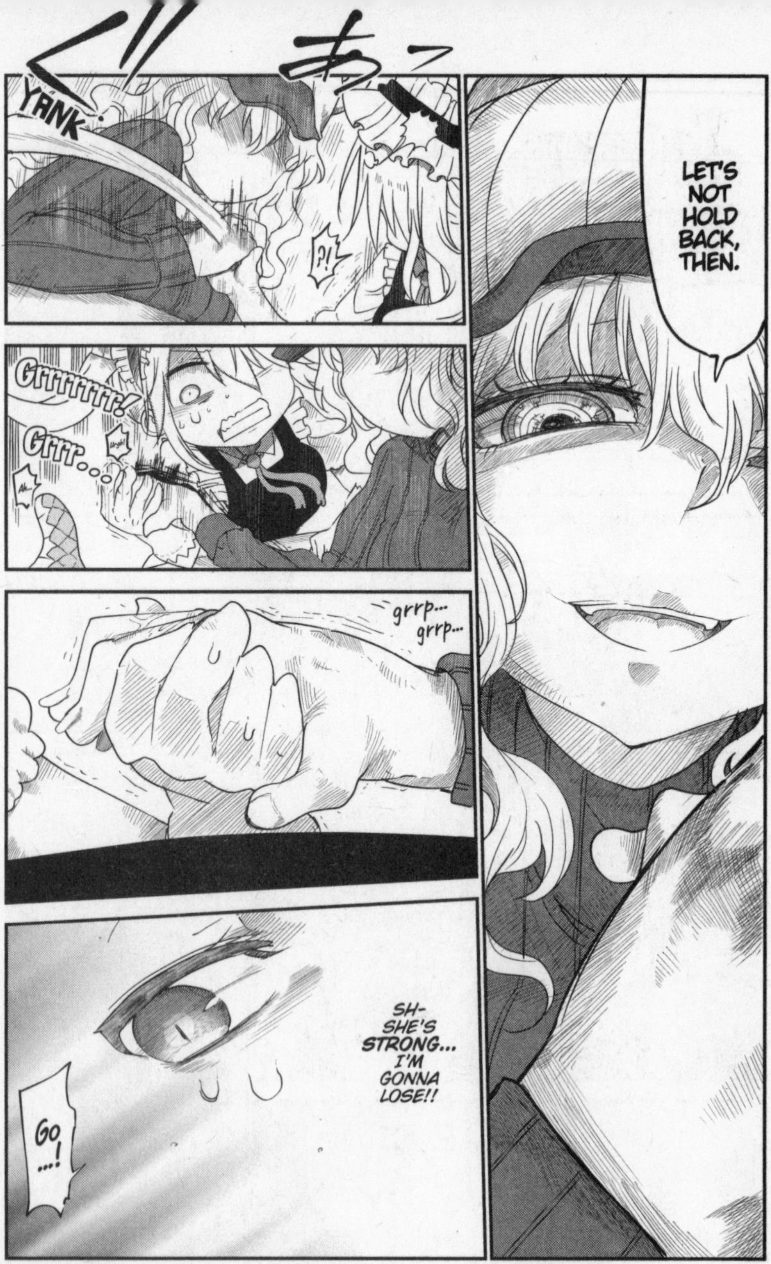
LET'S NOT HOLD BACK, THEN.
くい
あっ
YANK
?!
Urgh!
Grrrrrrrr!
Grrr...
Ah...
grrp... grrp...
SH-SHE'S STRONG... I'M GONNA LOSE!!
GO...!

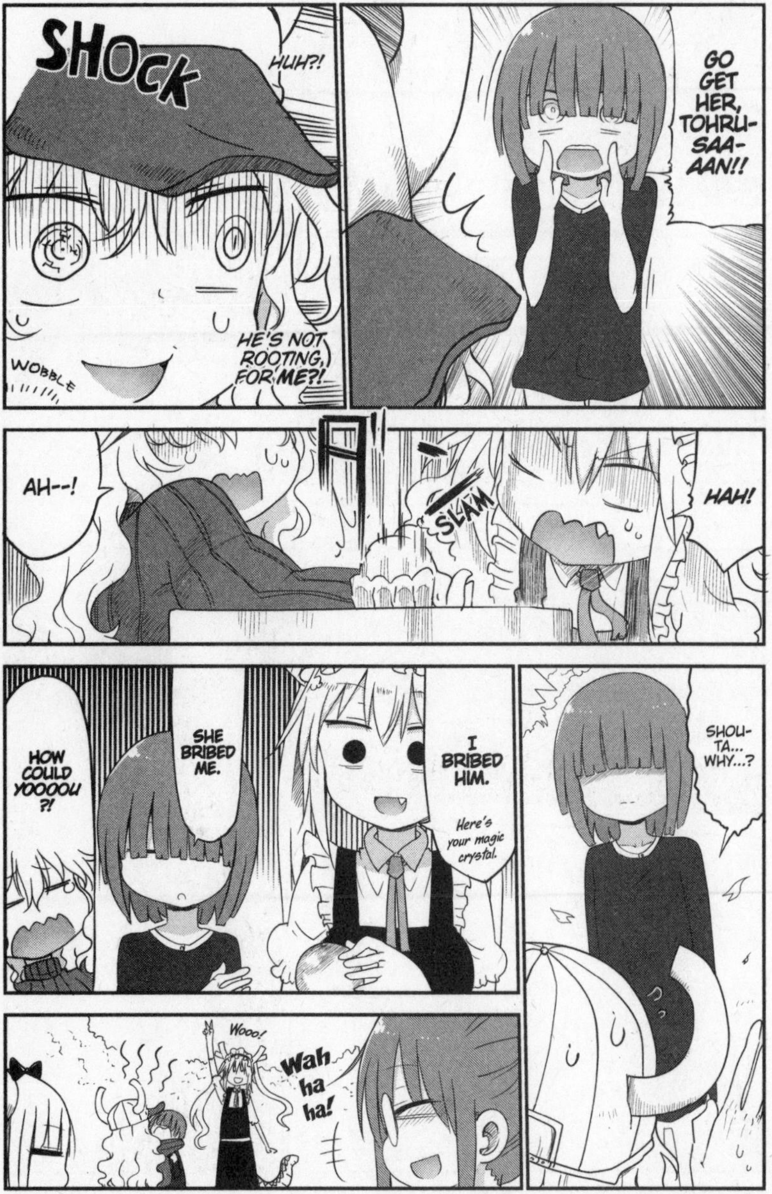
GO GET HER, TOHRU-SAAA-AAN!!
SHOCK
HUH?!
HE'S NOT ROOTING FOR ME?!
WOBBLE
HAH!
SLAM
AH--!
SHOU-TA... WHY...?
I BRIBED HIM.
Here's your magic crystal.
SHE BRIBED ME.
HOW COULD YOOOOU?!
Wooo!
Wah ha ha!

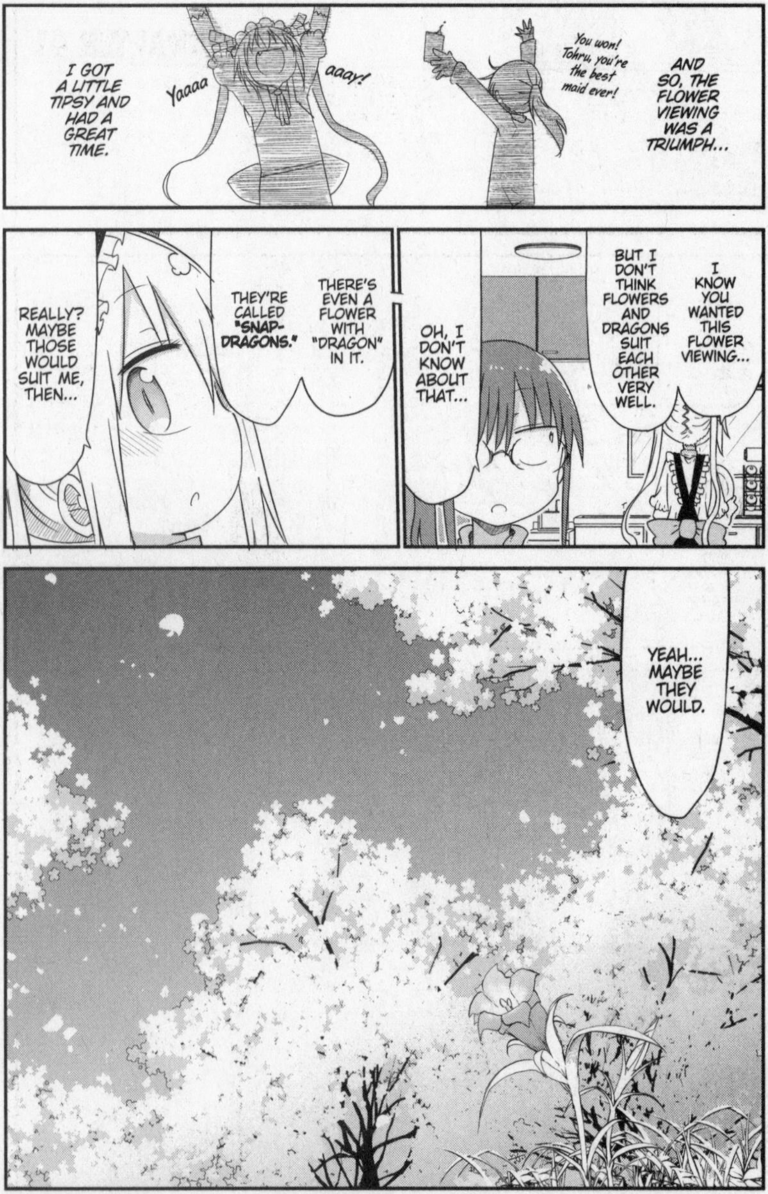
AND SO, THE FLOWER VIEWING WAS A TRIUMPH...
You won! Tohru, you're the best maid ever!
Yaaaa aaay!
I GOT A LITTLE TIPSY AND HAD A GREAT TIME.
I KNOW YOU WANTED THIS FLOWER VIEWING...
BUT I DON'T THINK FLOWERS AND DRAGONS SUIT EACH OTHER VERY WELL.
OH, I DON'T KNOW ABOUT THAT...
THERE'S EVEN A FLOWER WITH "DRAGON" IN IT.
THEY'RE CALLED "SNAP-DRAGONS."
REALLY? MAYBE THOSE WOULD SUIT ME, THEN...
YEAH... MAYBE THEY WOULD.

CHAPTER 40/END

CHAPTER 41

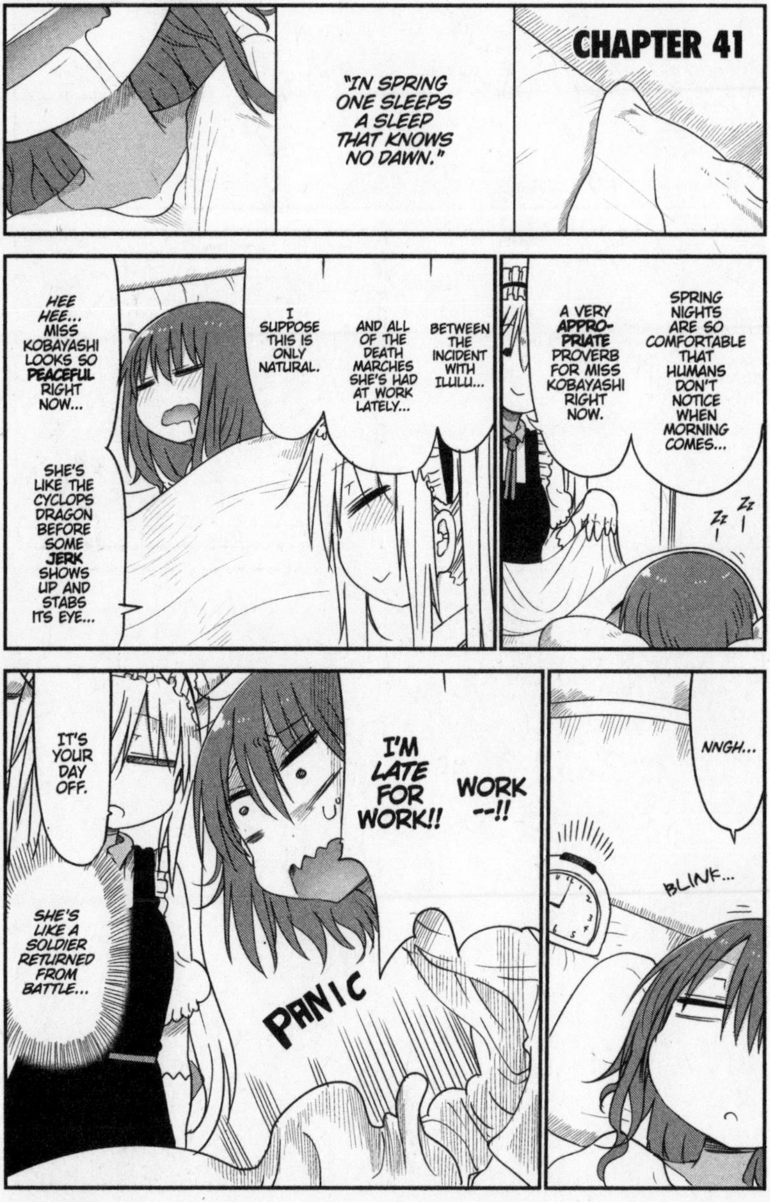
"IN SPRING ONE SLEEPS A SLEEP THAT KNOWS NO DAWN."
SPRING NIGHTS ARE SO COMFORTABLE THAT HUMANS DON'T NOTICE WHEN MORNING COMES...
A VERY APPROPRIATE PROVERB FOR MISS KOBAYASHI RIGHT NOW.
Zz Zz
BETWEEN THE INCIDENT WITH ILULU...
AND ALL OF THE DEATH MARCHES SHE'S HAD AT WORK LATELY...
I SUPPOSE THIS IS ONLY NATURAL.
HEE HEE... MISS KOBAYASHI LOOKS SO **PEACEFUL** RIGHT NOW...
SHE'S LIKE THE CYCLOPS DRAGON BEFORE SOME **JERK** SHOWS UP AND STABS ITS EYE...
NNGH...
BLINK...
I'M LATE FOR WORK!!
WORK--!!
PANIC
IT'S YOUR DAY OFF.
SHE'S LIKE A SOLDIER RETURNED FROM BATTLE...

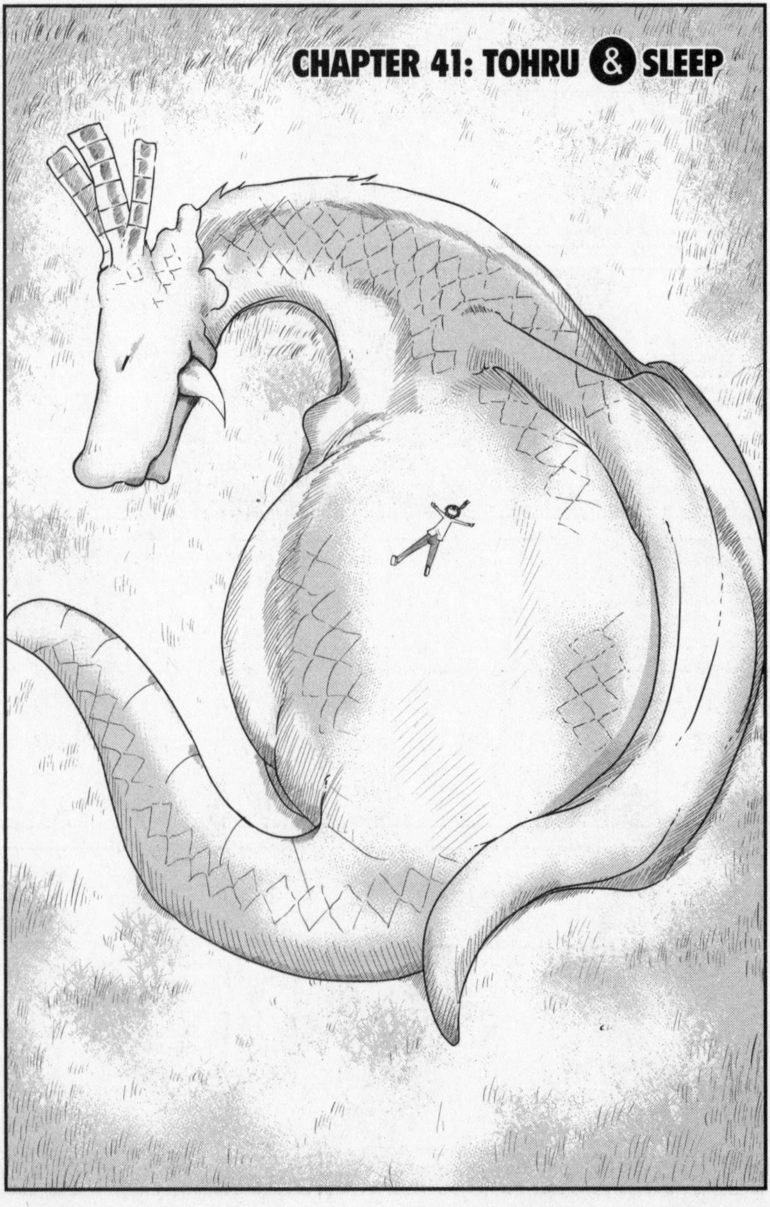
CHAPTER 41: TOHRU & SLEEP

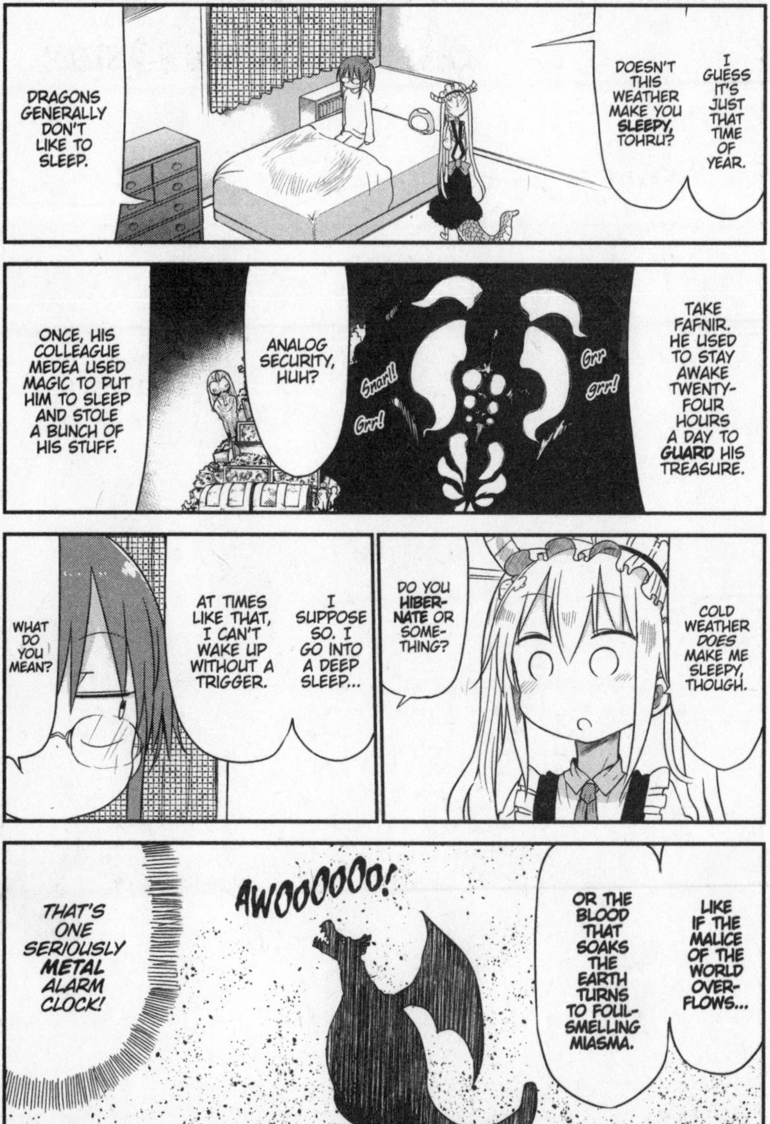
I GUESS IT'S JUST THAT TIME OF YEAR.
DOESN'T THIS WEATHER MAKE YOU SLEEPY, TOHRU?
DRAGONS GENERALLY DON'T LIKE TO SLEEP.
TAKE FAFNIR. HE USED TO STAY AWAKE TWENTY-FOUR HOURS A DAY TO GUARD HIS TREASURE.
Grr grr!
Snarl!
Grr!
ANALOG SECURITY, HUH?
ONCE, HIS COLLEAGUE MEDEA USED MAGIC TO PUT HIM TO SLEEP AND STOLE A BUNCH OF HIS STUFF.
COLD WEATHER DOES MAKE ME SLEEPY, THOUGH.
DO YOU HIBERNATE OR SOMETHING?
I SUPPOSE SO. I GO INTO A DEEP SLEEP...
AT TIMES LIKE THAT, I CAN'T WAKE UP WITHOUT A TRIGGER.
WHAT DO YOU MEAN?
LIKE IF THE MALICE OF THE WORLD OVERFLOWS...
OR THE BLOOD THAT SOAKS THE EARTH TURNS TO FOUL-SMELLING MIASMA.
AWOOOOOO!
THAT'S ONE SERIOUSLY METAL ALARM CLOCK!

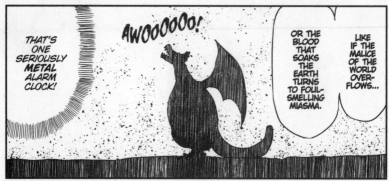

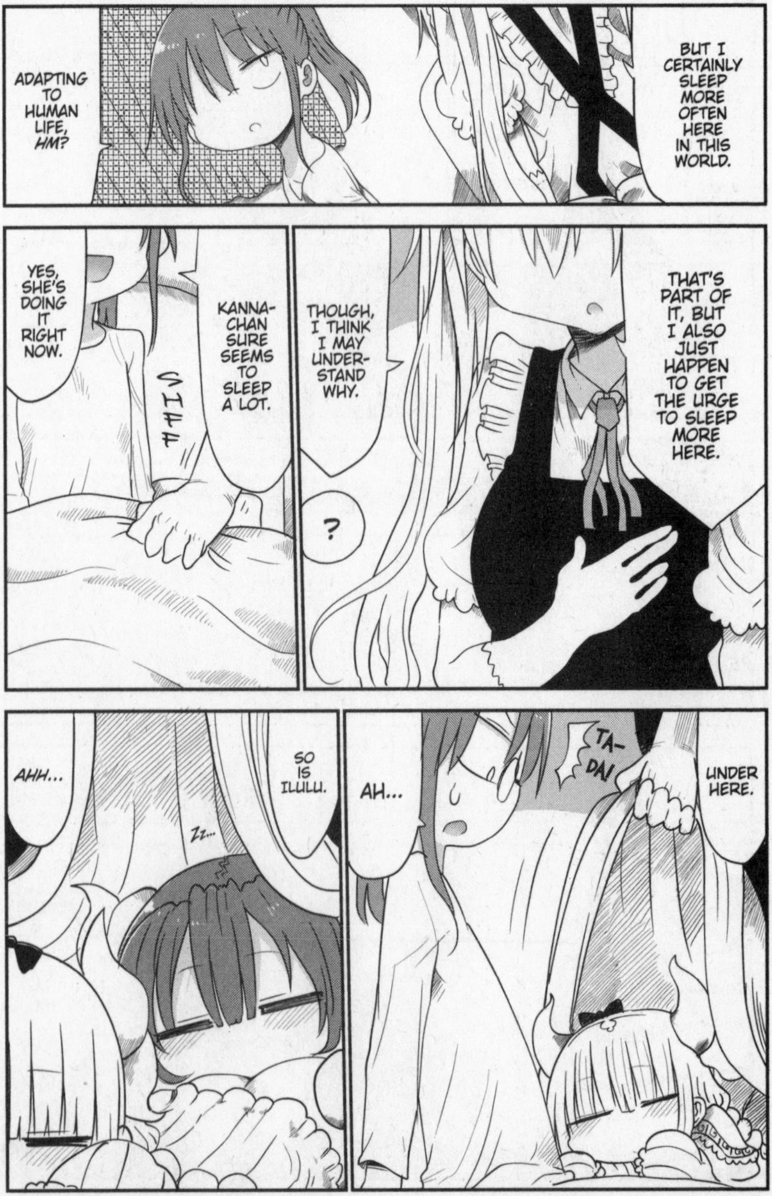
BUT I CERTAINLY SLEEP MORE OFTEN HERE IN THIS WORLD.
ADAPTING TO HUMAN LIFE, *HM?*
THAT'S PART OF IT, BUT I ALSO JUST HAPPEN TO GET THE URGE TO SLEEP MORE HERE.
THOUGH, I THINK I MAY UNDERSTAND WHY.
?
KANNA-CHAN SURE SEEMS TO SLEEP A LOT.
SHFF
YES, SHE'S DOING IT RIGHT NOW.
UNDER HERE.
TA-DA!
AH...
SO IS ILULU.
Zz...
AHH...

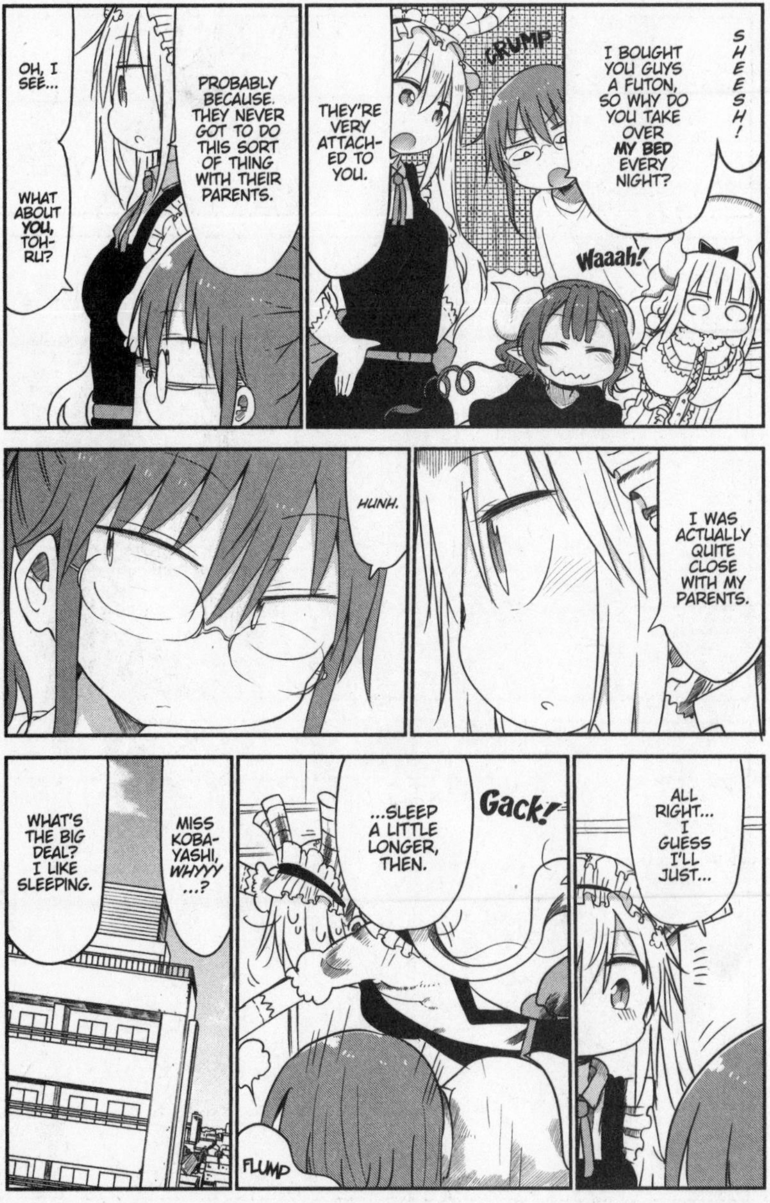
SHEESH!
I BOUGHT YOU GUYS A FUTON, SO WHY DO YOU TAKE OVER **MY BED** EVERY NIGHT?
CRUMP
Waaah!
THEY'RE VERY ATTACHED TO YOU.
PROBABLY BECAUSE. THEY NEVER GOT TO DO THIS SORT OF THING WITH THEIR PARENTS.
OH, I SEE...
WHAT ABOUT **YOU,** TOHRU?
I WAS ACTUALLY QUITE CLOSE WITH MY PARENTS.
HUNH.
ALL RIGHT... I GUESS I'LL JUST...
Gack!
...SLEEP A LITTLE LONGER, THEN.
FLUMP
MISS KOBAYASHI, *WHYYY*...?
WHAT'S THE BIG DEAL? I LIKE SLEEPING.

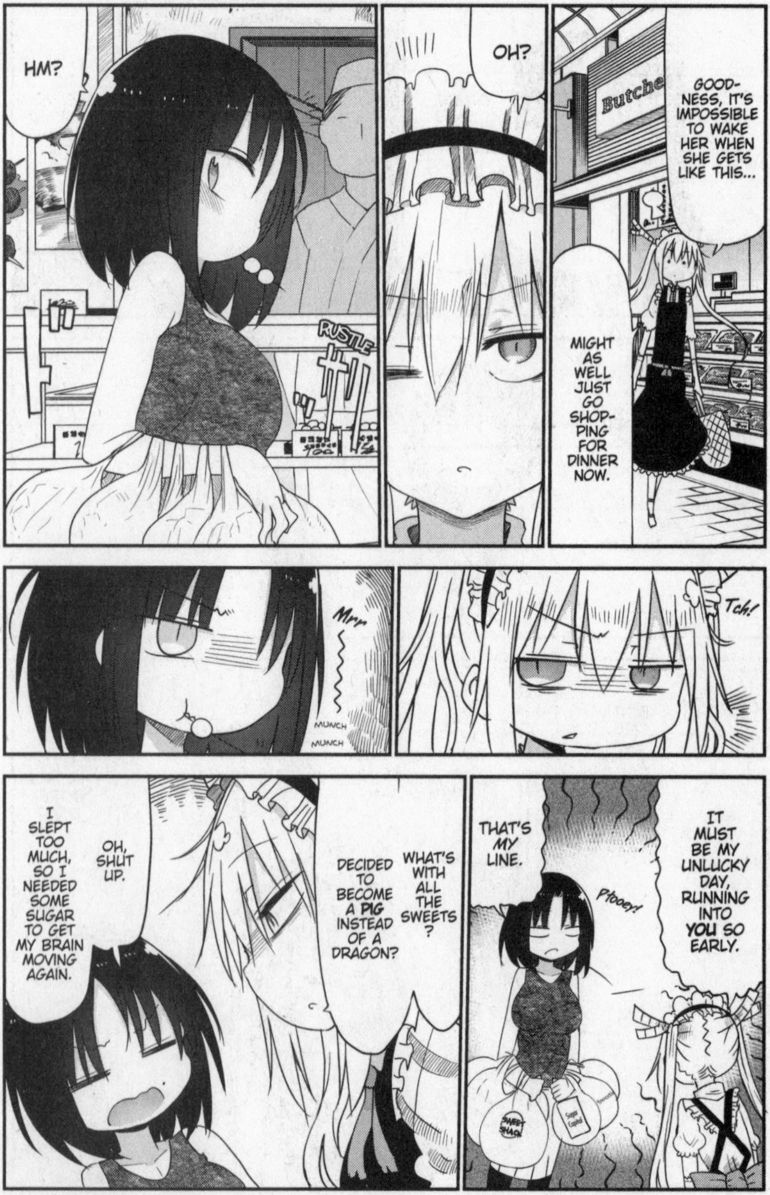
Butche
GOODNESS, IT'S IMPOSSIBLE TO WAKE HER WHEN SHE GETS LIKE THIS...
MIGHT AS WELL JUST GO SHOPPING FOR DINNER NOW.
OH?
HM?
RUSTLE
Tch!
Mrr
MUNCH MUNCH
IT MUST BE MY UNLUCKY DAY, RUNNING INTO YOU SO EARLY.
THAT'S MY LINE.
Ptooey!
SWEET SHACK
Sugar Capital
WHAT'S WITH ALL THE SWEETS?
DECIDED TO BECOME A PIG INSTEAD OF A DRAGON?
OH, SHUT UP.
I SLEPT TOO MUCH, SO I NEEDED SOME SUGAR TO GET MY BRAIN MOVING AGAIN.

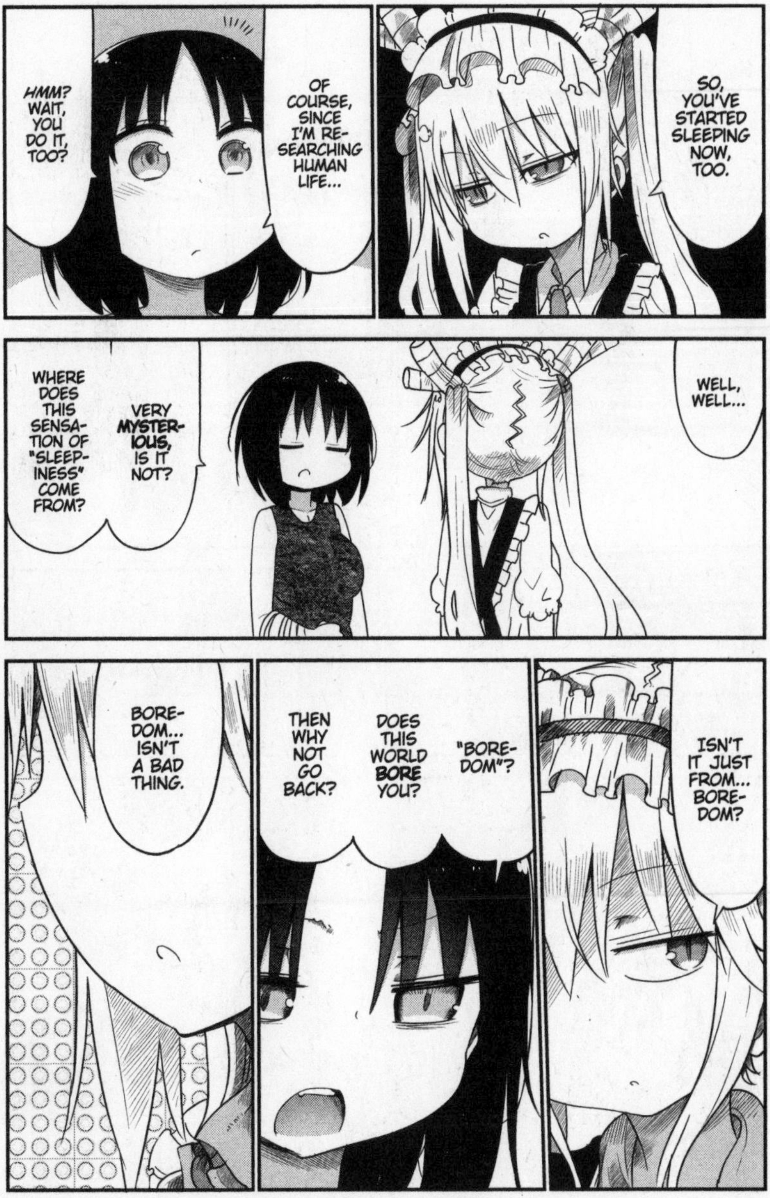
SO, YOU'VE STARTED SLEEPING NOW, TOO.
OF COURSE, SINCE I'M RE-SEARCHING HUMAN LIFE...
HMM? WAIT, YOU DO IT, TOO?
WELL, WELL...
WHERE DOES THIS SENSATION OF "SLEEPINESS" COME FROM?
VERY MYSTERIOUS, IS IT NOT?
ISN'T IT JUST FROM... BORE-DOM?
"BORE-DOM"?
DOES THIS WORLD BORE YOU?
THEN WHY NOT GO BACK?
BORE-DOM... ISN'T A BAD THING.

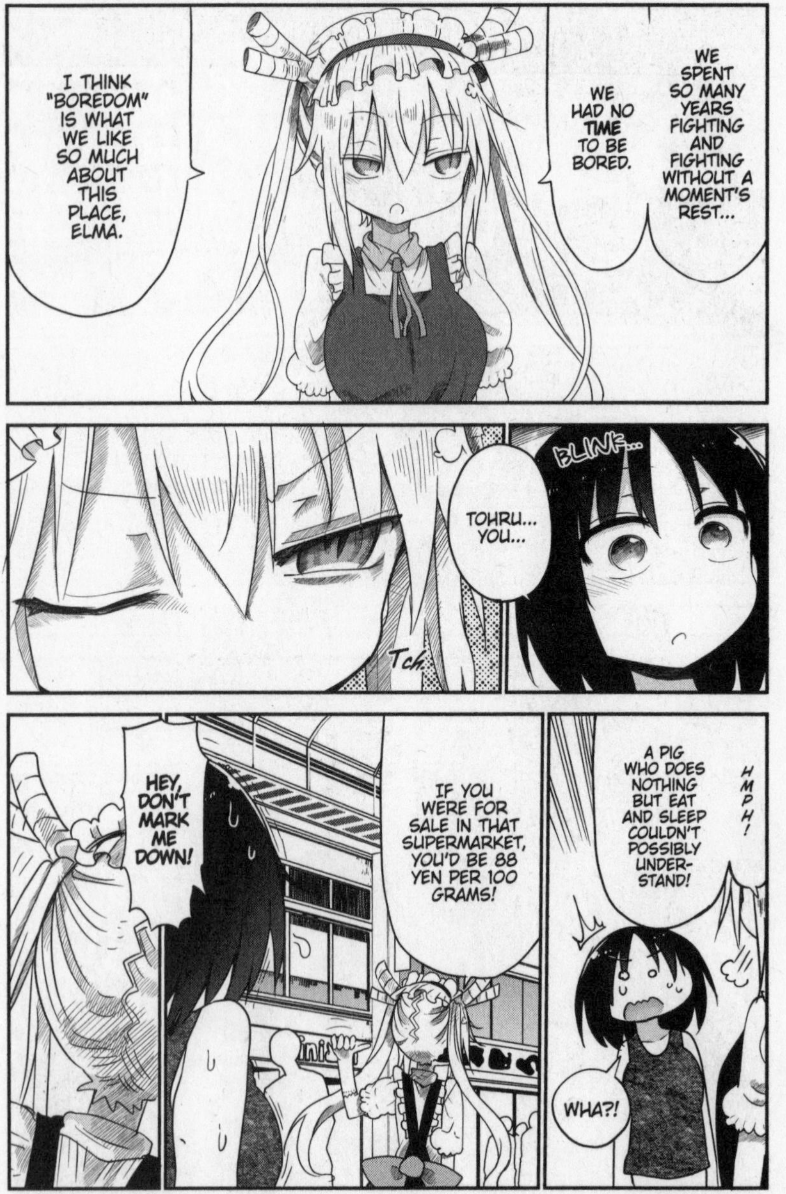
WE SPENT SO MANY YEARS FIGHTING AND FIGHTING WITHOUT A MOMENT'S REST...
WE HAD NO TIME TO BE BORED.
I THINK "BOREDOM" IS WHAT WE LIKE SO MUCH ABOUT THIS PLACE, ELMA.
BLINK...
TOHRU... YOU...
Tch
HMPH!
A PIG WHO DOES NOTHING BUT EAT AND SLEEP COULDN'T POSSIBLY UNDER-STAND!
WHA?!
IF YOU WERE FOR SALE IN THAT SUPERMARKET, YOU'D BE 88 YEN PER 100 GRAMS!
HEY, DON'T MARK ME DOWN!

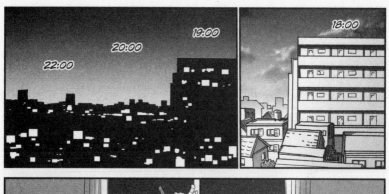

18:00
19:00
20:00
22:00
24:00
THE TIME WHEN HUMANS SLEEP...
I CAN FEEL THE EXHAUSTION OF EVERYONE NEARBY.
SLEEPING HUMANS IN THEIR HOMES AS FAR AS THE EYE CAN SEE.

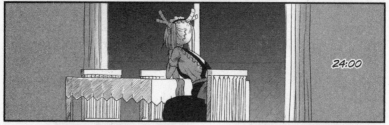

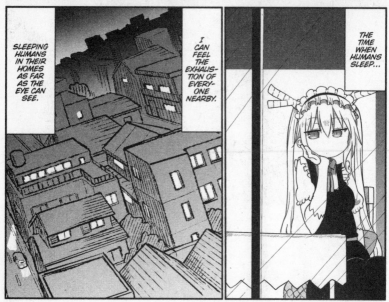

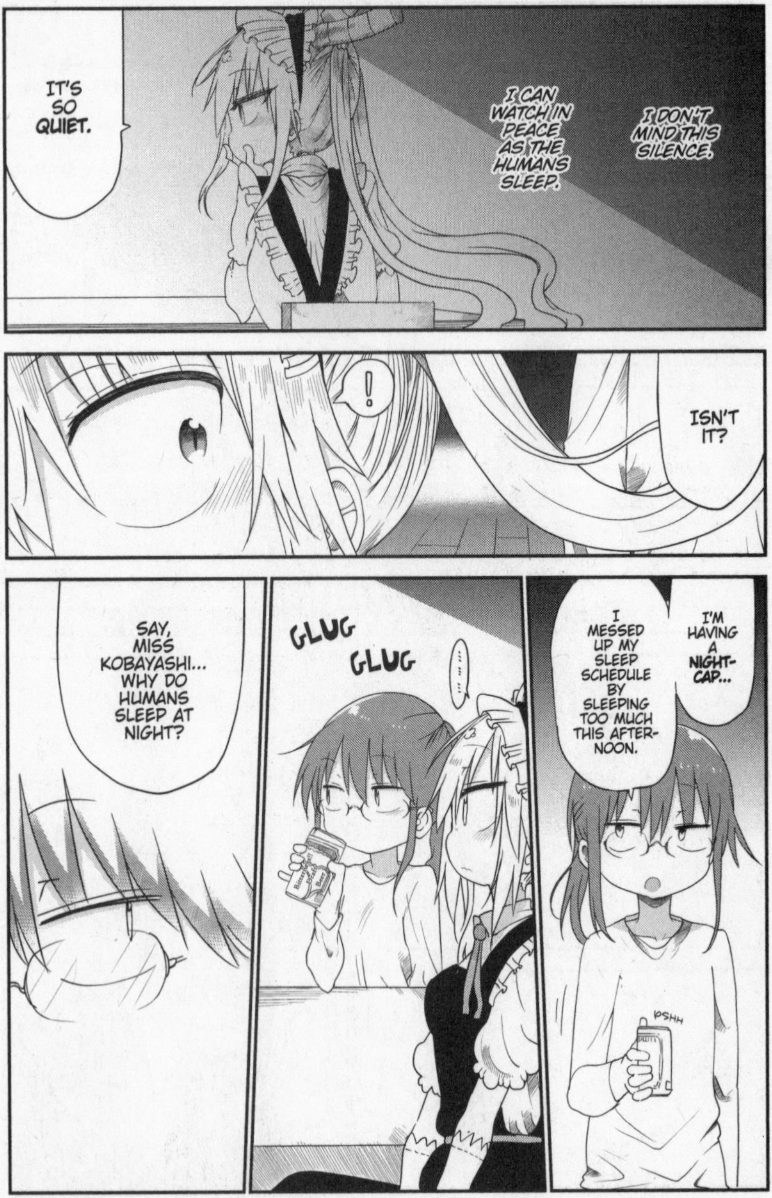
I DON'T MIND THIS SILENCE.
I CAN WATCH IN PEACE AS THE HUMANS SLEEP.
IT'S SO QUIET.
ISN'T IT?
!
I'M HAVING A NIGHT-CAP...
I MESSED UP MY SLEEP SCHEDULE BY SLEEPING TOO MUCH THIS AFTER-NOON.
GLUG
GLUG
......
SAY, MISS KOBAYASHI... WHY DO HUMANS SLEEP AT NIGHT?

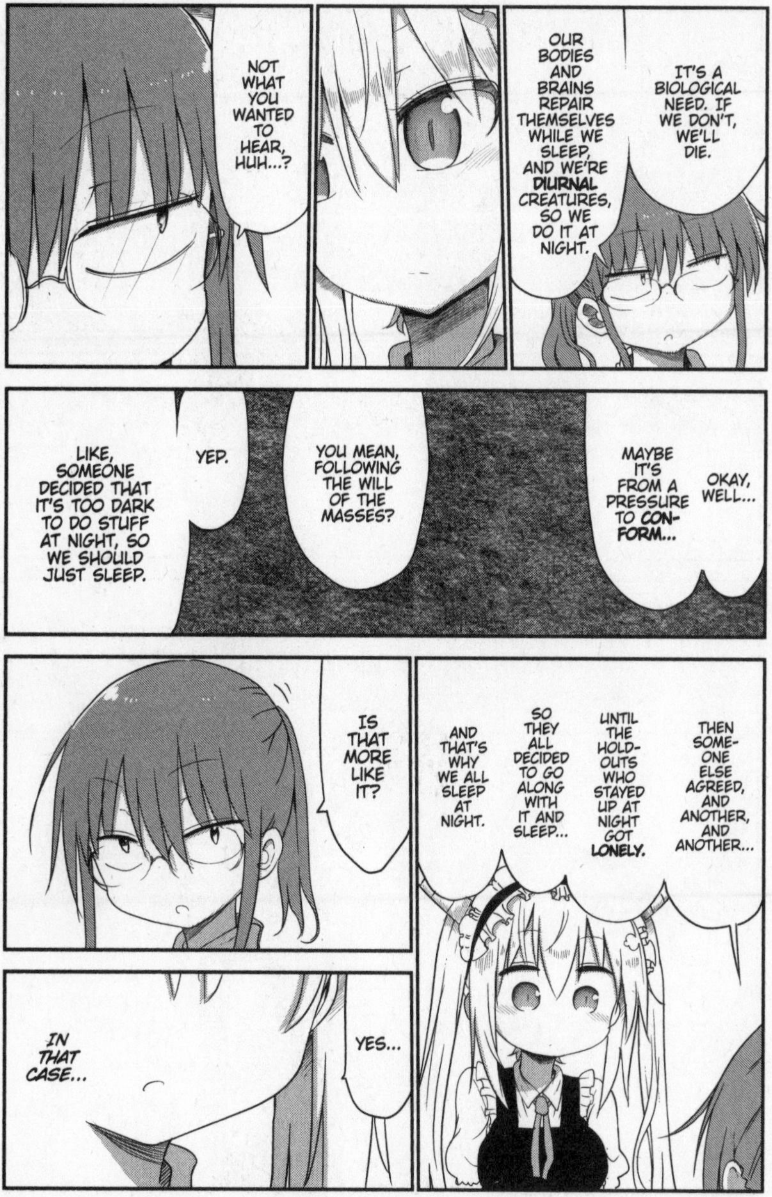
IT'S A BIOLOGICAL NEED. IF WE DON'T, WE'LL DIE.
OUR BODIES AND BRAINS REPAIR THEMSELVES WHILE WE SLEEP, AND WE'RE DIURNAL CREATURES, SO WE DO IT AT NIGHT.
NOT WHAT YOU WANTED TO HEAR, HUH...?
OKAY, WELL...
MAYBE IT'S FROM A PRESSURE TO CON-FORM...
YOU MEAN, FOLLOWING THE WILL OF THE MASSES?
YEP.
LIKE, SOMEONE DECIDED THAT IT'S TOO DARK TO DO STUFF AT NIGHT, SO WE SHOULD JUST SLEEP.
THEN SOMEONE ELSE AGREED, AND ANOTHER, AND ANOTHER...
UNTIL THE HOLD-OUTS WHO STAYED UP AT NIGHT GOT LONELY.
SO THEY ALL DECIDED TO GO ALONG WITH IT AND SLEEP...
AND THAT'S WHY WE ALL SLEEP AT NIGHT.
IS THAT MORE LIKE IT?
YES...
IN THAT CASE...

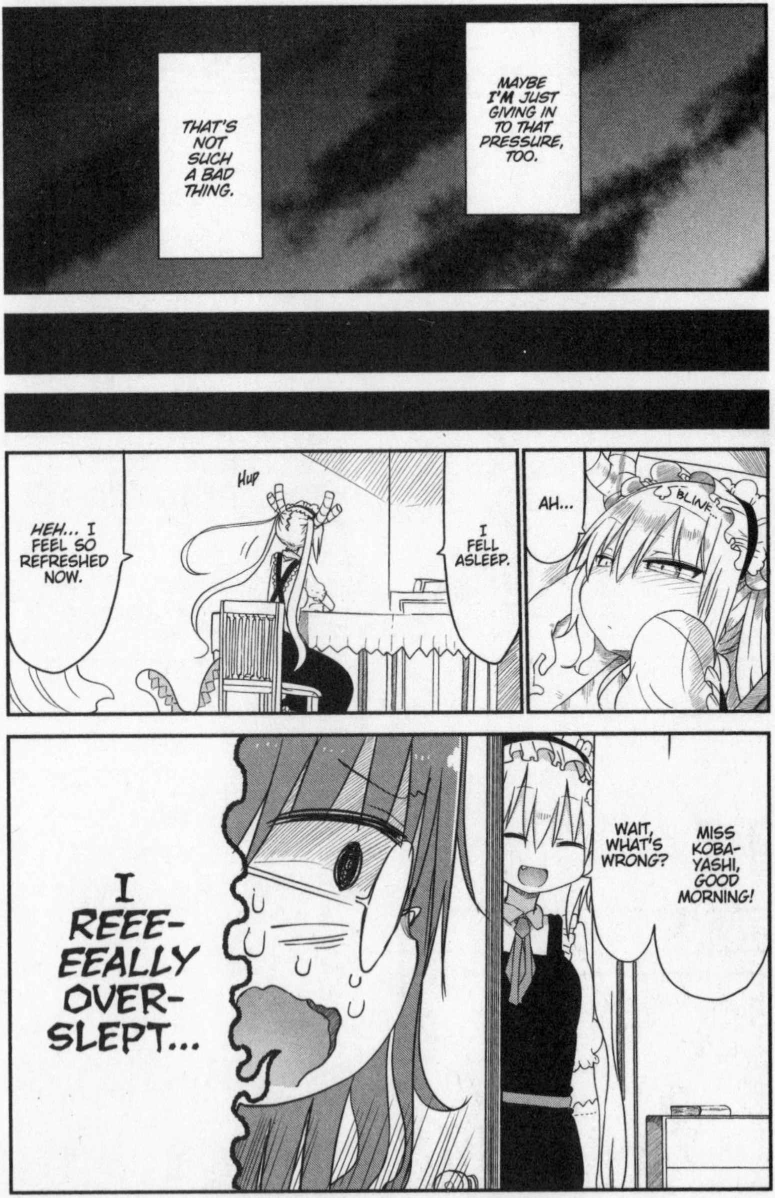
MAYBE I'M JUST GIVING IN TO THAT PRESSURE, TOO.
THAT'S NOT SUCH A BAD THING.
AH...
BLINK...
I FELL ASLEEP.
HUP
HEH... I FEEL SO REFRESHED NOW.
MISS KOBA-YASHI, GOOD MORNING!
WAIT, WHAT'S WRONG?
I REEEE-EEALLY OVER-SLEPT...

CHAPTER 41/END

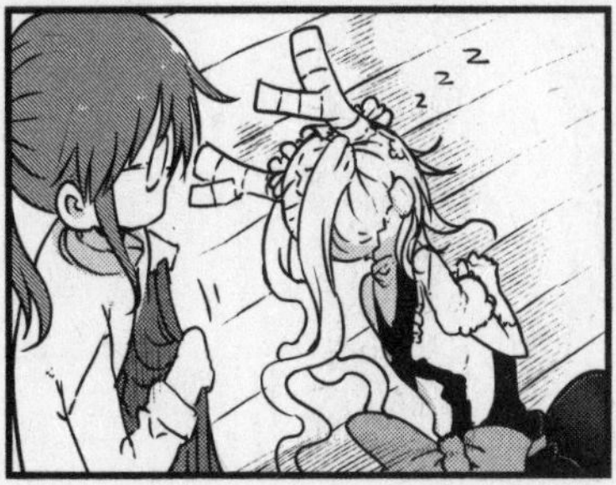
z z z

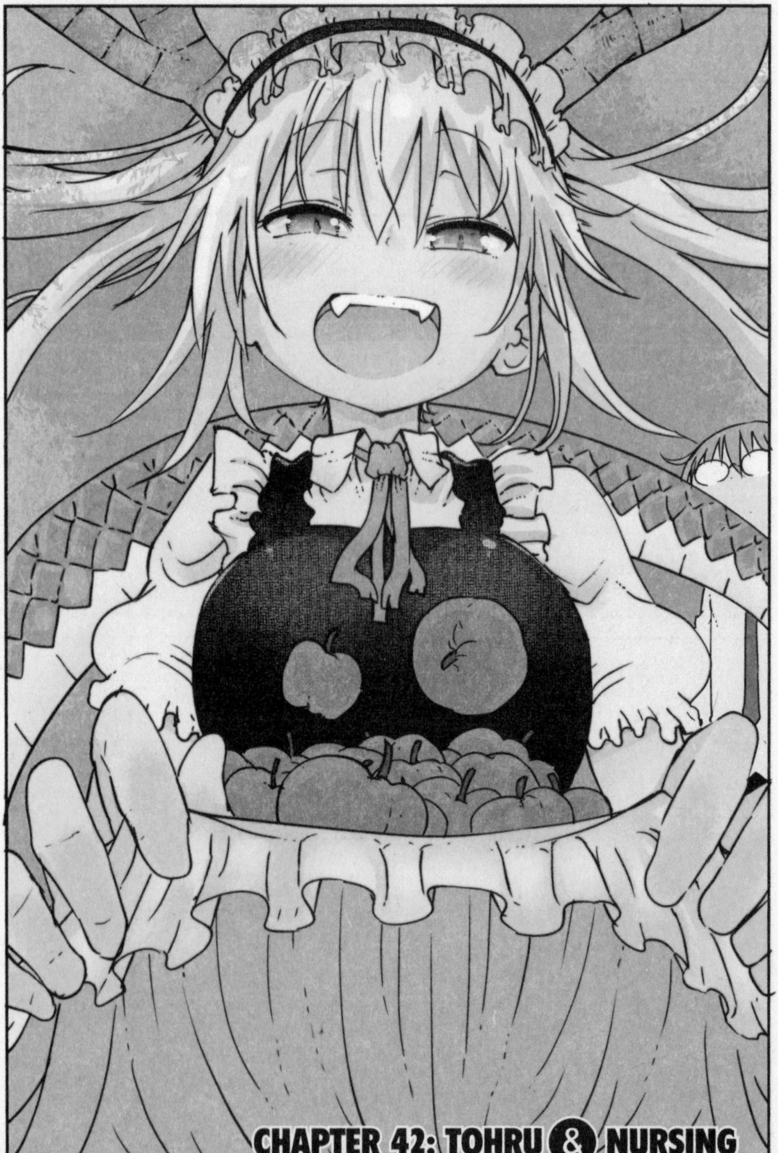
CHAPTER 42: TOHRU & NURSING

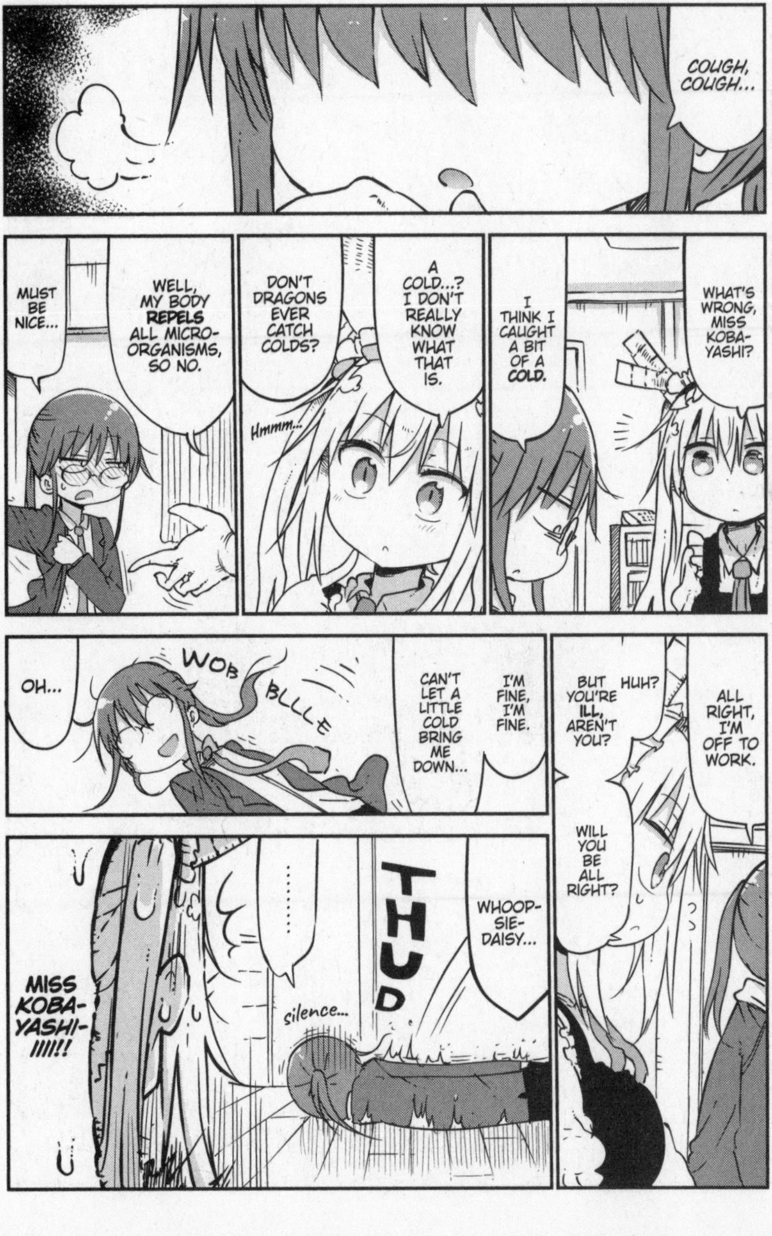
COUGH, COUGH...
WHAT'S WRONG, MISS KOBAYASHI?
I THINK I CAUGHT A BIT OF A COLD.
A COLD...? I DON'T REALLY KNOW WHAT THAT IS.
DON'T DRAGONS EVER CATCH COLDS?
Hmmm...
WELL, MY BODY REPELS ALL MICRO-ORGANISMS, SO NO.
MUST BE NICE...
ALL RIGHT, I'M OFF TO WORK.
HUH?
BUT YOU'RE ILL, AREN'T YOU?
WILL YOU BE ALL RIGHT?
I'M FINE, I'M FINE.
CAN'T LET A LITTLE COLD BRING ME DOWN...
WOBBLLLE
OH...
WHOOPSIE-DAISY...
THUD
......
silence...
MISS KOBAYASHI-IIIII!!

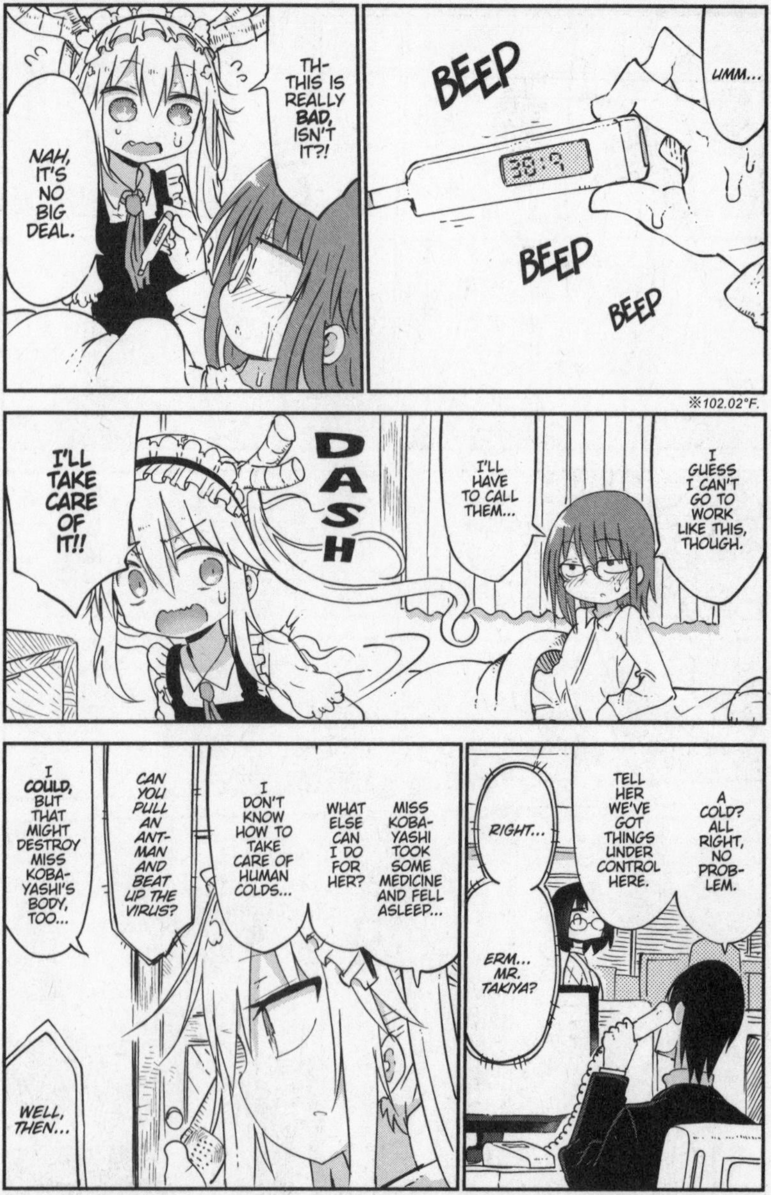
UMM...
BEEP
BEEP
BEEP
TH-THIS IS REALLY BAD, ISN'T IT?!
NAH, IT'S NO BIG DEAL.
I GUESS I CAN'T GO TO WORK LIKE THIS, THOUGH.
I'LL HAVE TO CALL THEM...
DASH
I'LL TAKE CARE OF IT!!
A COLD? ALL RIGHT, NO PROB-LEM.
TELL HER WE'VE GOT THINGS UNDER CONTROL HERE.
RIGHT...
ERM... MR. TAKIYA?
MISS KOBA-YASHI TOOK SOME MEDICINE AND FELL ASLEEP...
WHAT ELSE CAN I DO FOR HER?
I DON'T KNOW HOW TO TAKE CARE OF HUMAN COLDS...
CAN YOU PULL AN ANT-MAN AND BEAT UP THE VIRUS?
I COULD, BUT THAT MIGHT DESTROY MISS KOBA-YASHI'S BODY, TOO...
WELL, THEN...
※102.02°F.

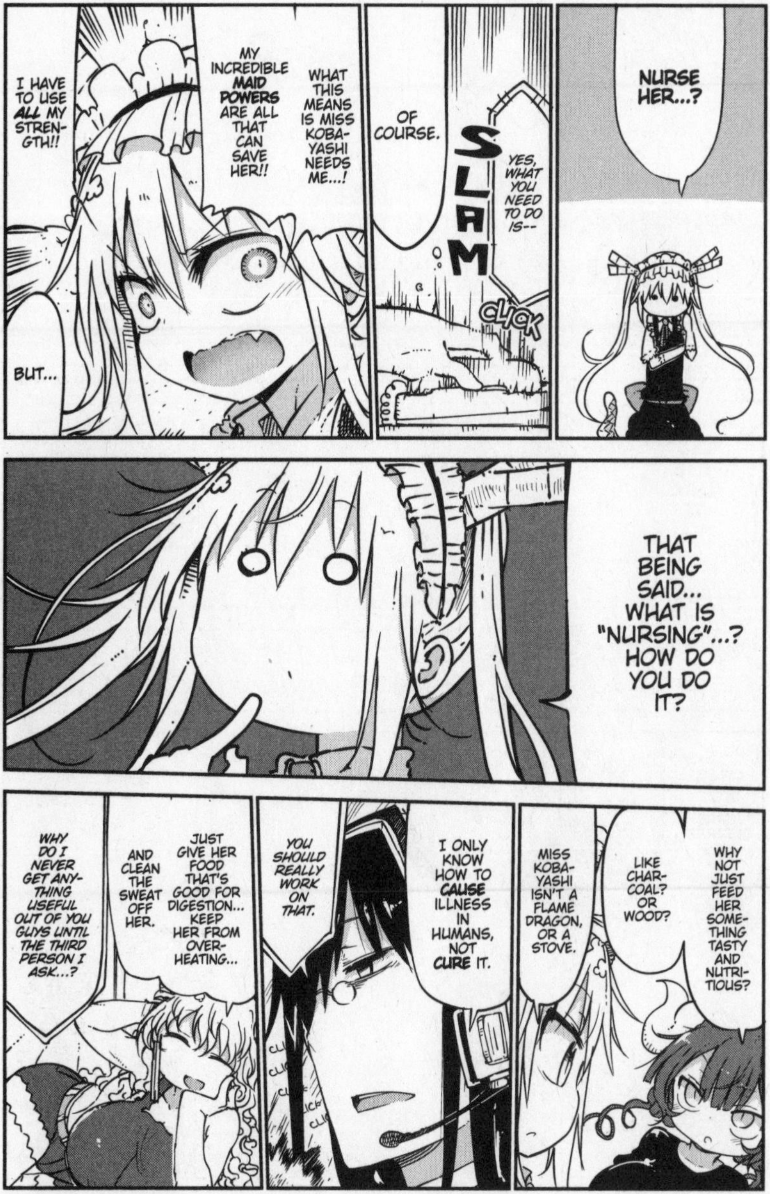
NURSE HER...?
YES, WHAT YOU NEED TO DO IS--
OF COURSE.
SLAM
CLICK
WHAT THIS MEANS IS MISS KOBAYASHI NEEDS ME...!
MY INCREDIBLE MAID POWERS ARE ALL THAT CAN SAVE HER!!
I HAVE TO USE ALL MY STRENGTH!!
BUT...
THAT BEING SAID... WHAT IS "NURSING"...? HOW DO YOU DO IT?
....
WHY NOT JUST FEED HER SOMETHING TASTY AND NUTRITIOUS?
LIKE CHARCOAL? OR WOOD?
MISS KOBAYASHI ISN'T A FLAME DRAGON, OR A STOVE.
I ONLY KNOW HOW TO CAUSE ILLNESS IN HUMANS, NOT CURE IT.
YOU SHOULD REALLY WORK ON THAT.
CLICK
JUST GIVE HER FOOD THAT'S GOOD FOR DIGESTION... KEEP HER FROM OVER-HEATING...
AND CLEAN THE SWEAT OFF HER.
WHY DO I NEVER GET ANYTHING USEFUL OUT OF YOU GUYS UNTIL THE THIRD PERSON I ASK...?

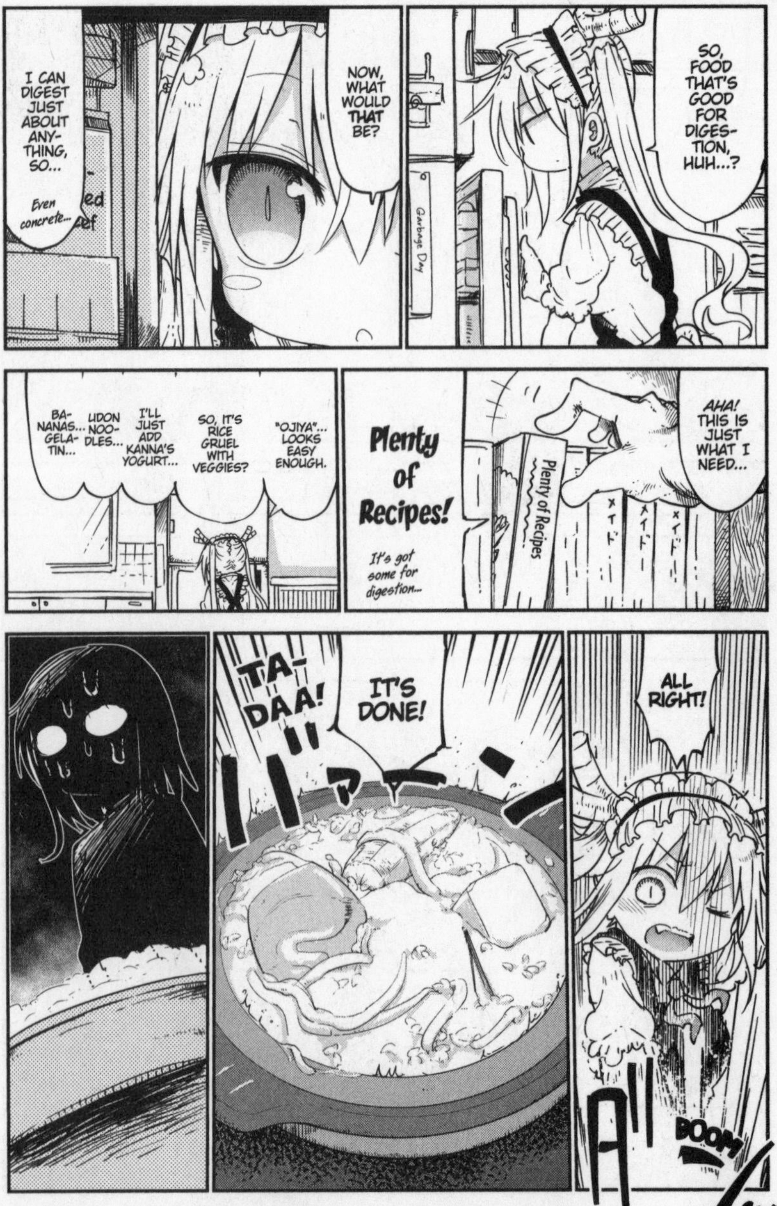
SO, FOOD THAT'S GOOD FOR DIGES-TION, HUH...?
Garbage Day
NOW, WHAT WOULD THAT BE?
I CAN DIGEST JUST ABOUT ANY-THING, SO...
Even concrete...
AHA! THIS IS JUST WHAT I NEED...
Plenty of Recipes
Plenty of Recipes!
It's got some for digestion...
"OJIYA"... LOOKS EASY ENOUGH.
SO, IT'S RICE GRUEL WITH VEGGIES?
I'LL JUST ADD KANNA'S YOGURT...
UDON NOO-DLES...
BA-NANAS... GELA-TIN...
ALL RIGHT!
BOOM
TA-DAA!!
IT'S DONE!

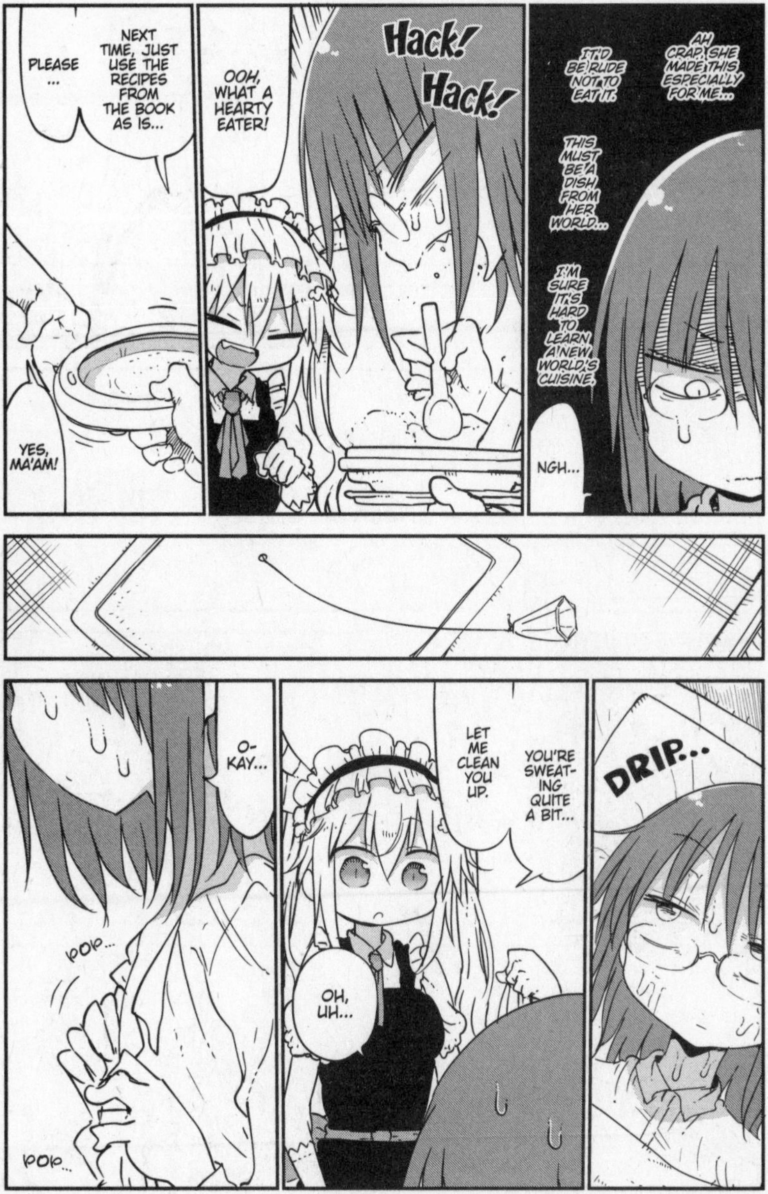
AH CRAP, SHE MADE THIS ESPECIALLY FOR ME...
IT'D BE RUDE NOT TO EAT IT.
THIS MUST BE A DISH FROM HER WORLD...
I'M SURE IT'S HARD TO LEARN A NEW WORLD'S CUISINE.
NGH...
Hack!
Hack!
OOH, WHAT A HEARTY EATER!
NEXT TIME, JUST USE THE RECIPES FROM THE BOOK AS IS...
PLEASE ...
YES, MA'AM!
DRIP...
YOU'RE SWEATING QUITE A BIT...
LET ME CLEAN YOU UP.
OH, UH...
O-KAY...
POP...
POP...

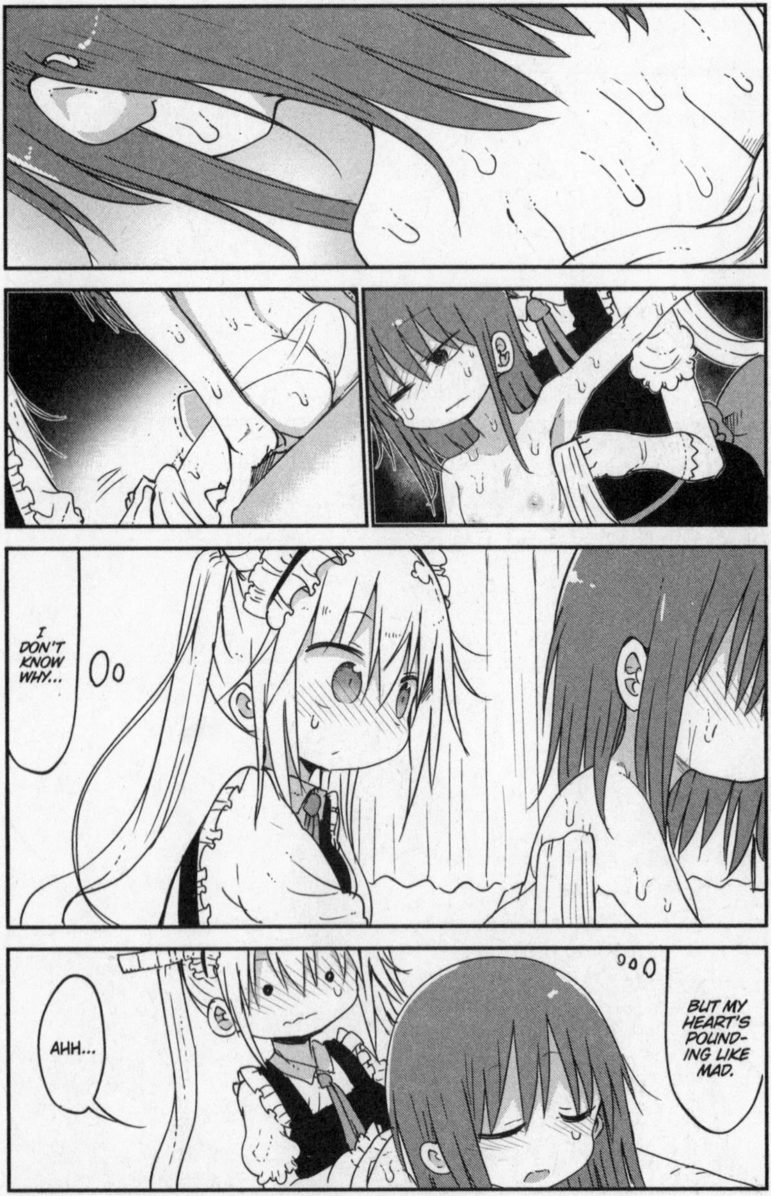
I DON'T KNOW WHY...
BUT MY HEART'S POUNDING LIKE MAD.
AHH...

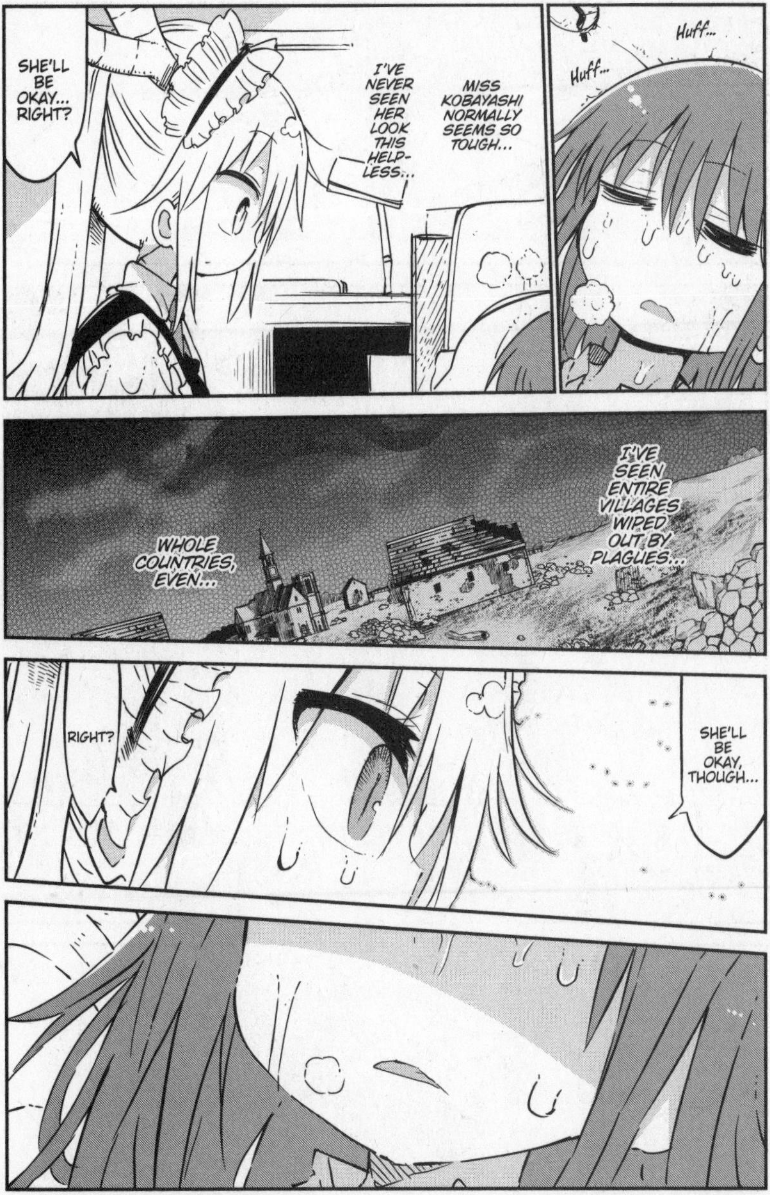
Huff...
Huff...
MISS KOBAYASHI NORMALLY SEEMS SO TOUGH...
I'VE NEVER SEEN HER LOOK THIS HELP-LESS...
SHE'LL BE OKAY... RIGHT?
I'VE SEEN ENTIRE VILLAGES WIPED OUT BY PLAGUES...
WHOLE COUNTRIES, EVEN...
SHE'LL BE OKAY, THOUGH...
RIGHT?

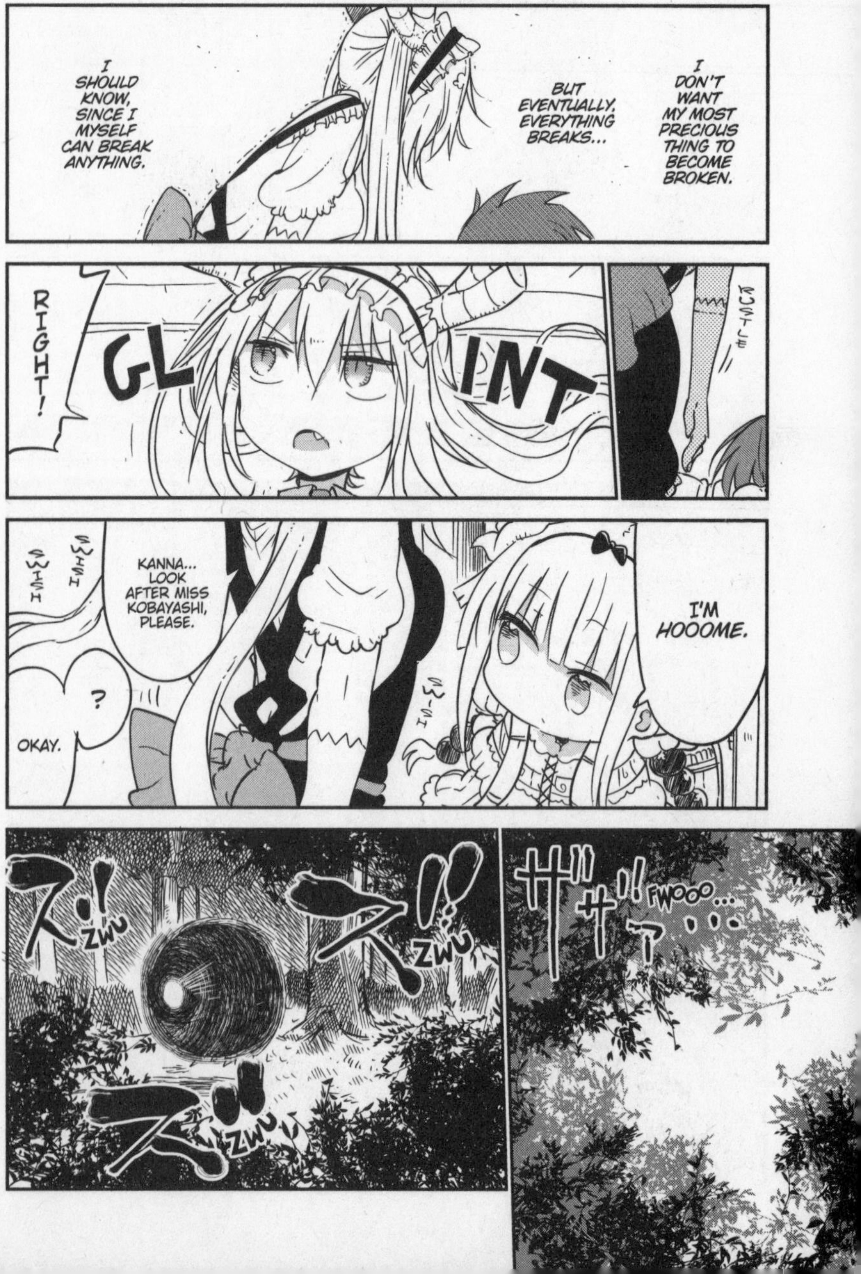
I DON'T WANT MY MOST PRECIOUS THING TO BECOME BROKEN.
BUT EVENTUALLY, EVERYTHING BREAKS...
I SHOULD KNOW, SINCE I MYSELF CAN BREAK ANYTHING.
RUSTLE
GLINT
...
RIGHT!
I'M HOOOME.
SWISH
KANNA... LOOK AFTER MISS KOBAYASHI, PLEASE.
SWISH SWISH
?
OKAY.
ザザァ...
FWOOO...
ズ!
ZWU
ズ!!
ZWU
ズ
ZWU

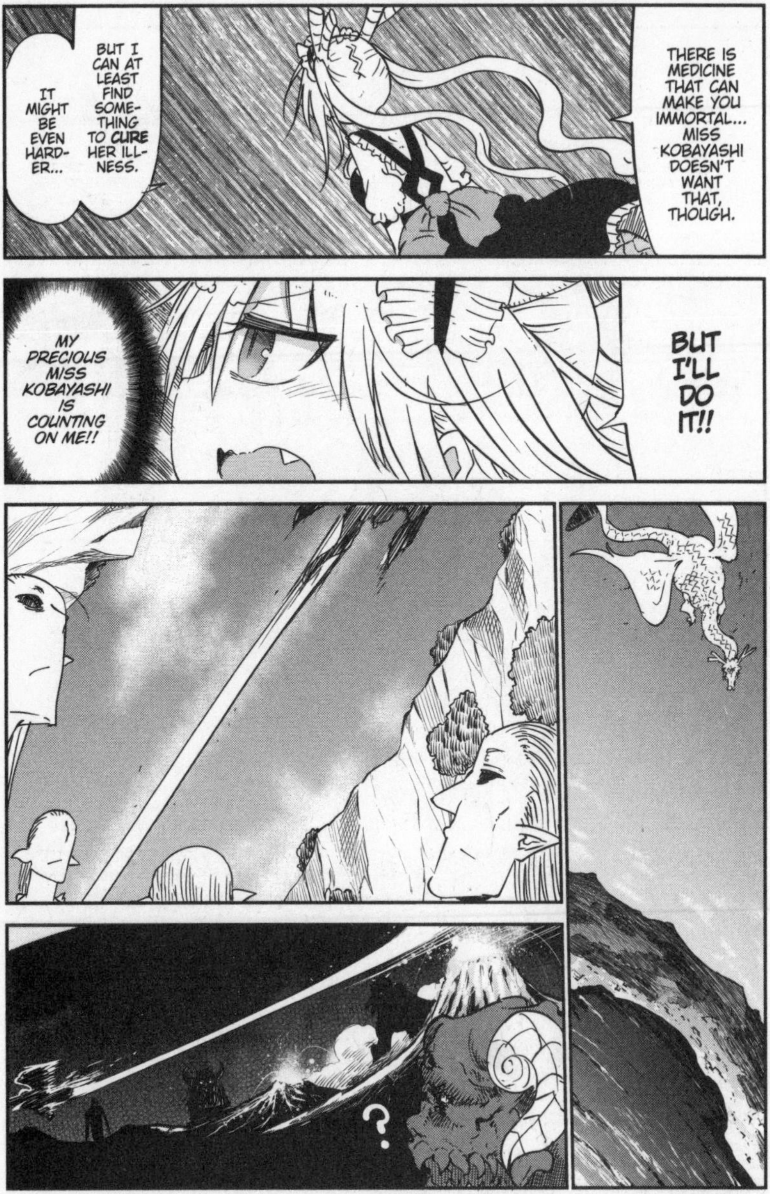
THERE IS MEDICINE THAT CAN MAKE YOU IMMORTAL... MISS KOBAYASHI DOESN'T WANT THAT, THOUGH.
BUT I CAN AT LEAST FIND SOME-THING TO CURE HER ILL-NESS.
IT MIGHT BE EVEN HARD-ER...
BUT I'LL DO IT!!
MY PRECIOUS MISS KOBAYASHI IS COUNTING ON ME!!
?

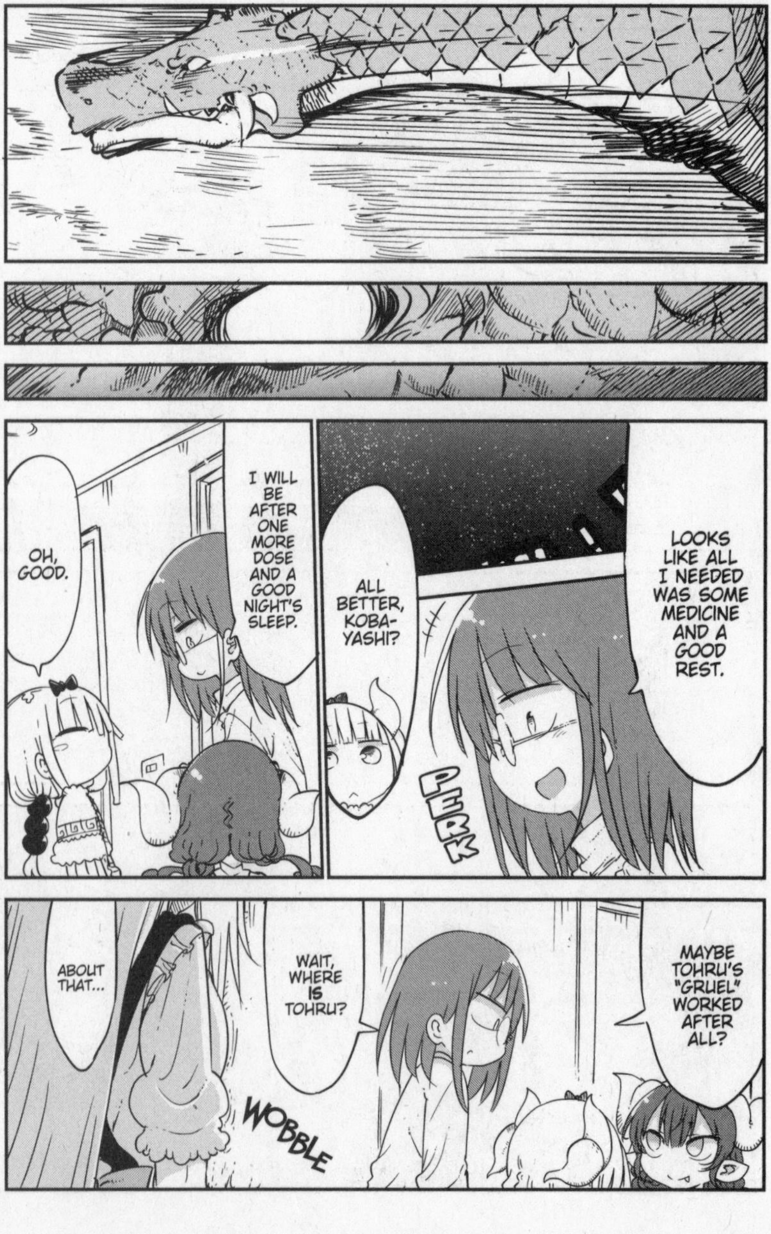
LOOKS LIKE ALL I NEEDED WAS SOME MEDICINE AND A GOOD REST.
ALL BETTER, KOBA-YASHI?
PERK
I WILL BE AFTER ONE MORE DOSE AND A GOOD NIGHT'S SLEEP.
OH, GOOD.
MAYBE TOHRU'S "GRUEL" WORKED AFTER ALL?
WAIT, WHERE IS TOHRU?
WOBBLE
ABOUT THAT...

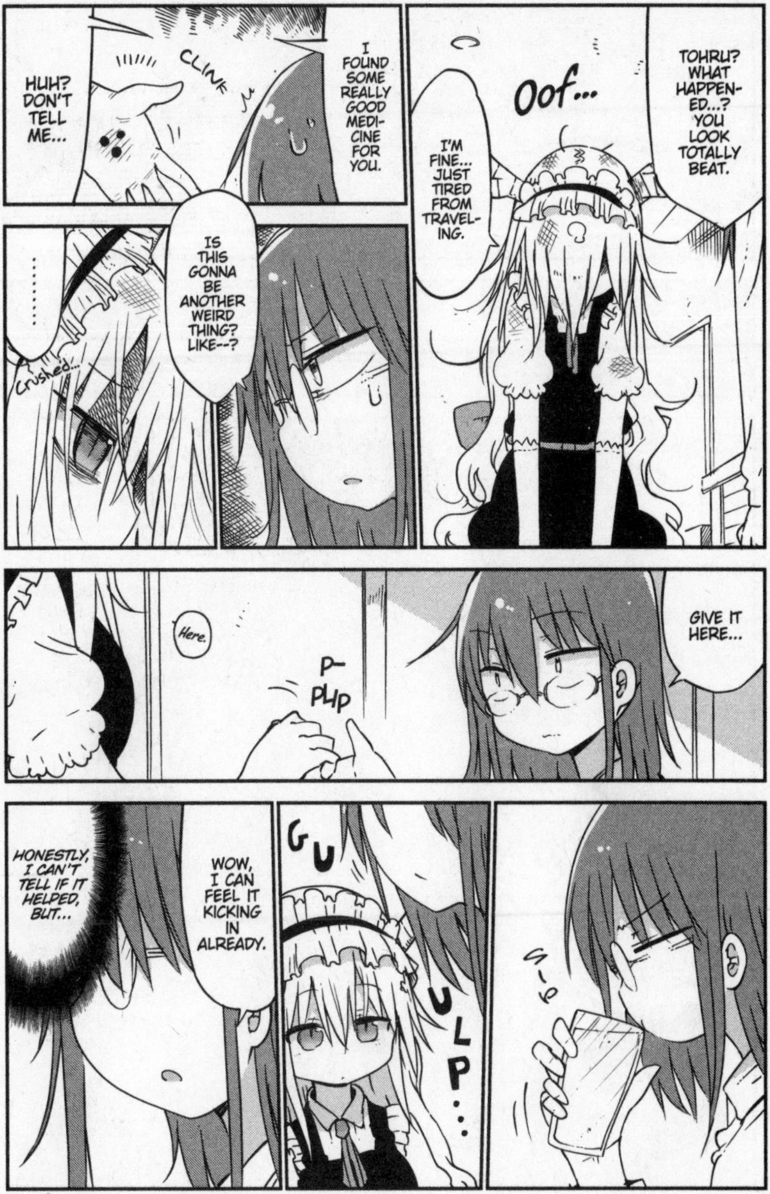
TOHRU? WHAT HAPPEN-ED...? YOU LOOK TOTALLY BEAT.
Oof...
I'M FINE... JUST TIRED FROM TRAVEL-ING.
I FOUND SOME REALLY GOOD MEDI-CINE FOR YOU.
CLINK
HUH? DON'T TELL ME...
IS THIS GONNA BE ANOTHER WEIRD THING? LIKE--?
......
Crushed...
GIVE IT HERE...
P-PLIP
Here.
GULP...
WOW, I CAN FEEL IT KICKING IN ALREADY.
HONESTLY, I CAN'T TELL IF IT HELPED, BUT...

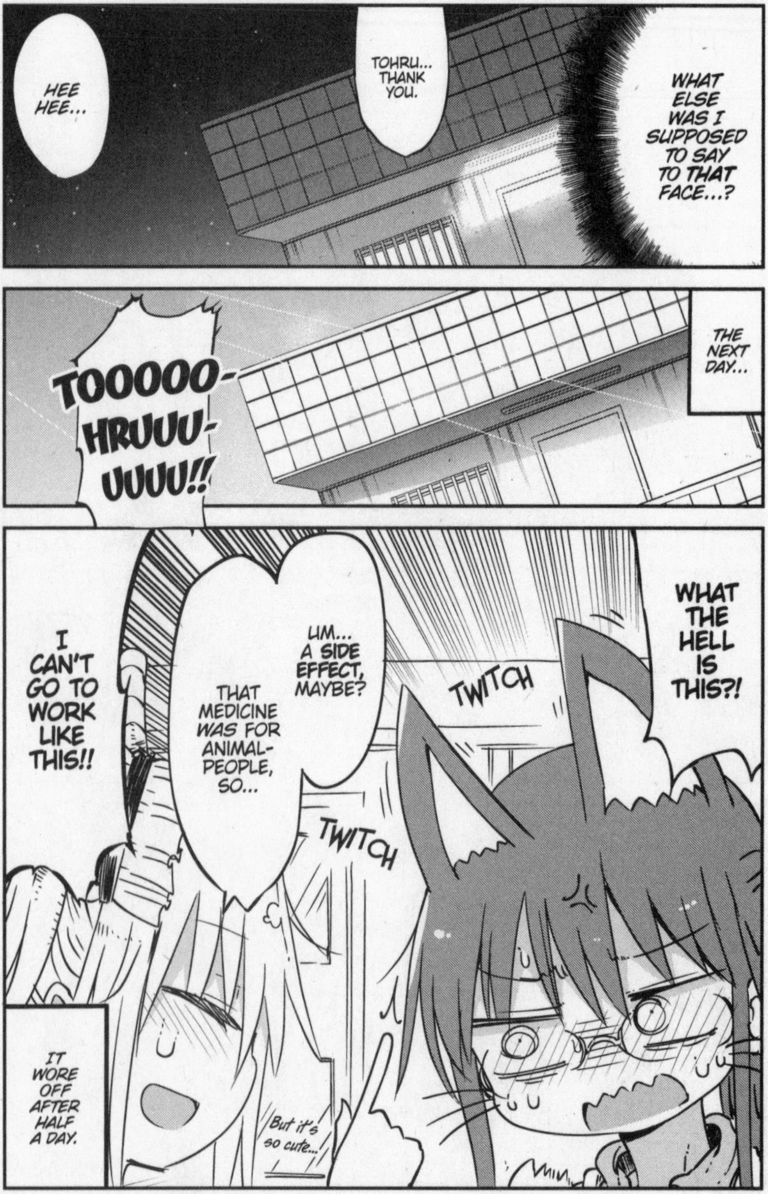
WHAT ELSE WAS I SUPPOSED TO SAY TO THAT FACE...?
TOHRU... THANK YOU.
HEE HEE...
THE NEXT DAY...
TOOOOO-HRUUU-UUUU!!
WHAT THE HELL IS THIS?!
TWITCH
UM... A SIDE EFFECT, MAYBE?
THAT MEDICINE WAS FOR ANIMAL-PEOPLE, SO...
I CAN'T GO TO WORK LIKE THIS!!
TWITCH
But it's so cute...
IT WORE OFF AFTER HALF A DAY.

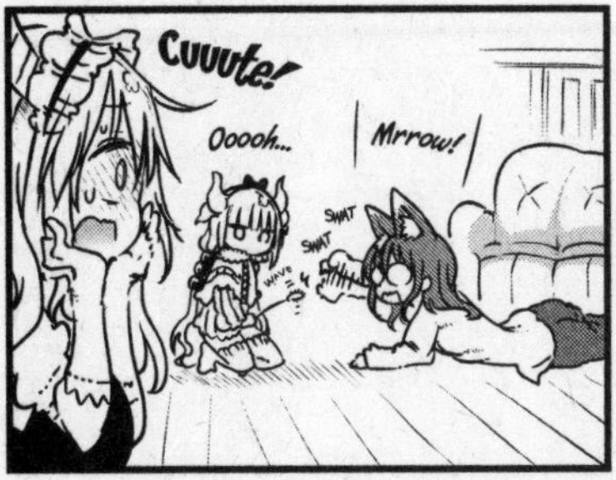
Mrrow!
Cuuute!
Ooooh...
SWAT
SWAT
WAVE

Miss Kobayashi's Dragon Maid

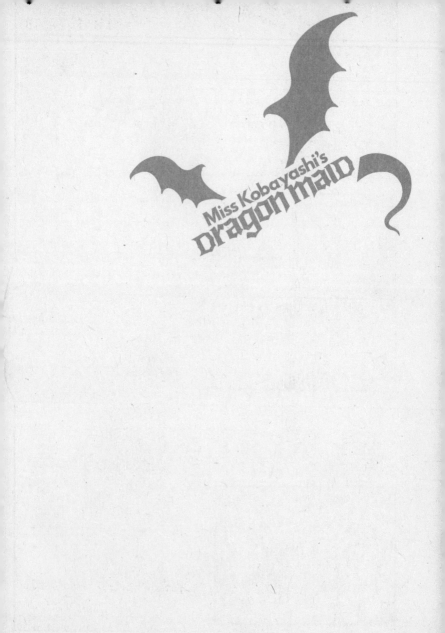

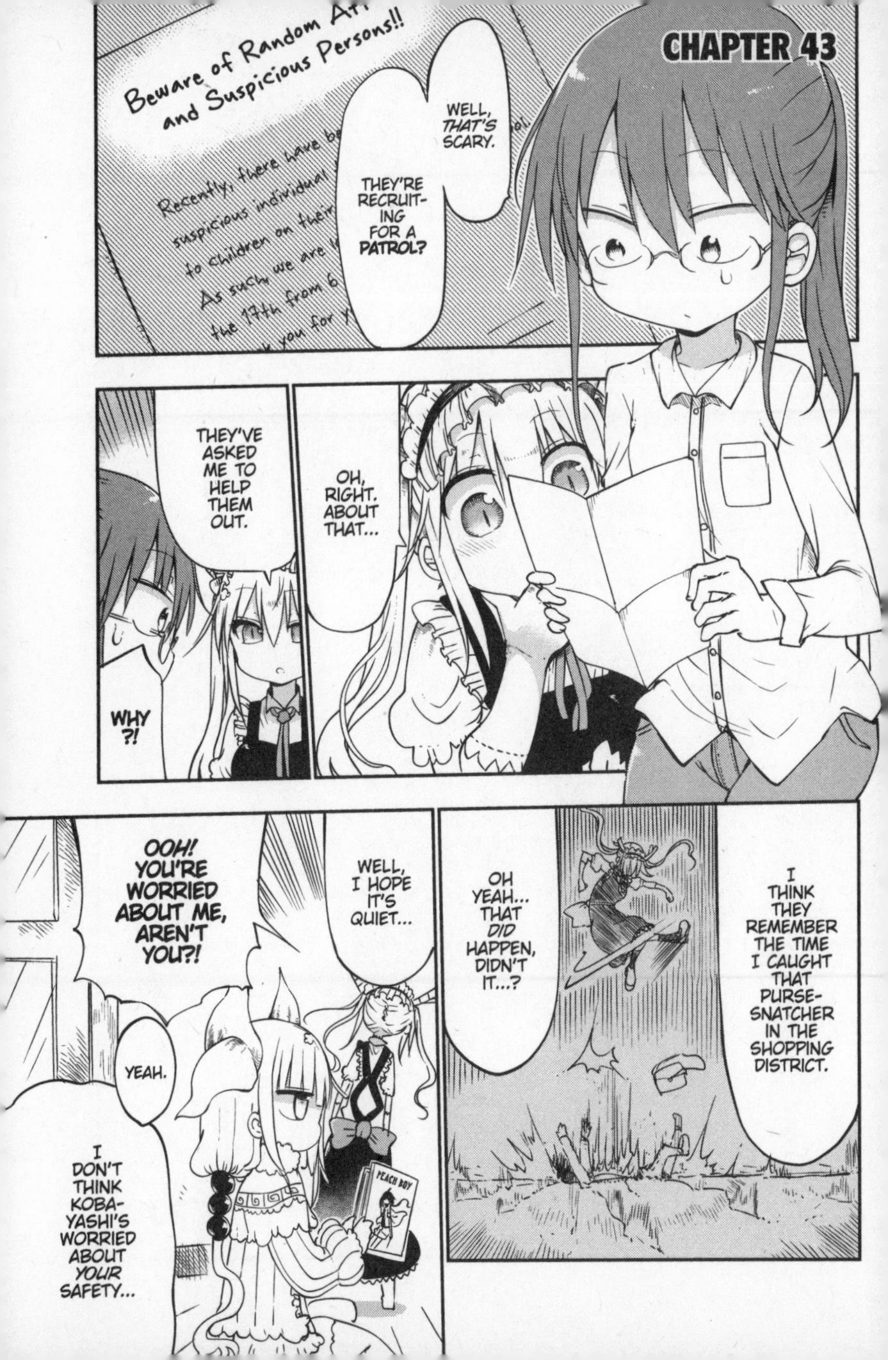
CHAPTER 43
Beware of Random
and Suspicious Persons!!
WELL, *THAT'S* SCARY.
THEY'RE RECRUIT-ING FOR A **PATROL**?
OH, RIGHT. ABOUT THAT...
THEY'VE ASKED ME TO HELP THEM OUT.
WHY?!
I THINK THEY REMEMBER THE TIME I CAUGHT THAT PURSE-SNATCHER IN THE SHOPPING DISTRICT.
OH YEAH... THAT *DID* HAPPEN, DIDN'T IT...?
WELL, I HOPE IT'S QUIET...
OOH! YOU'RE WORRIED ABOUT ME, AREN'T YOU?!
YEAH.
I DON'T THINK KOBA-YASHI'S WORRIED ABOUT *YOUR* SAFETY...
PEACH BOY

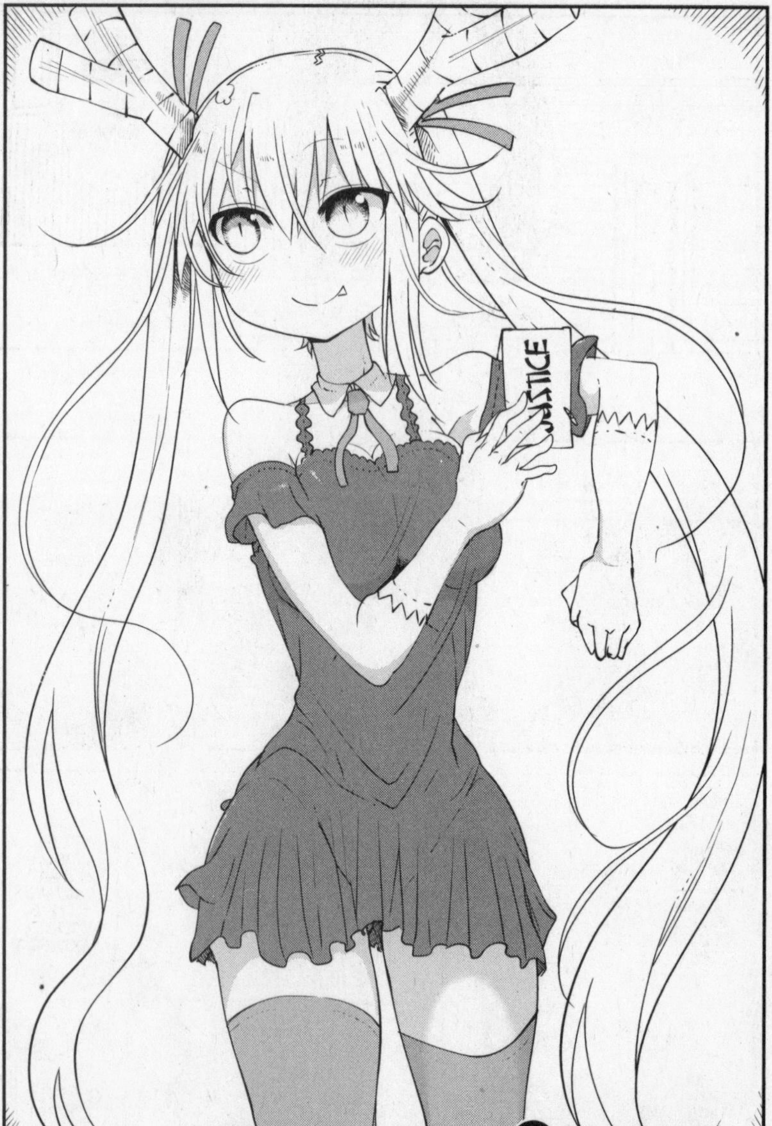
JUSTICE
CHAPTER 43: TOHRU & THE PATROL

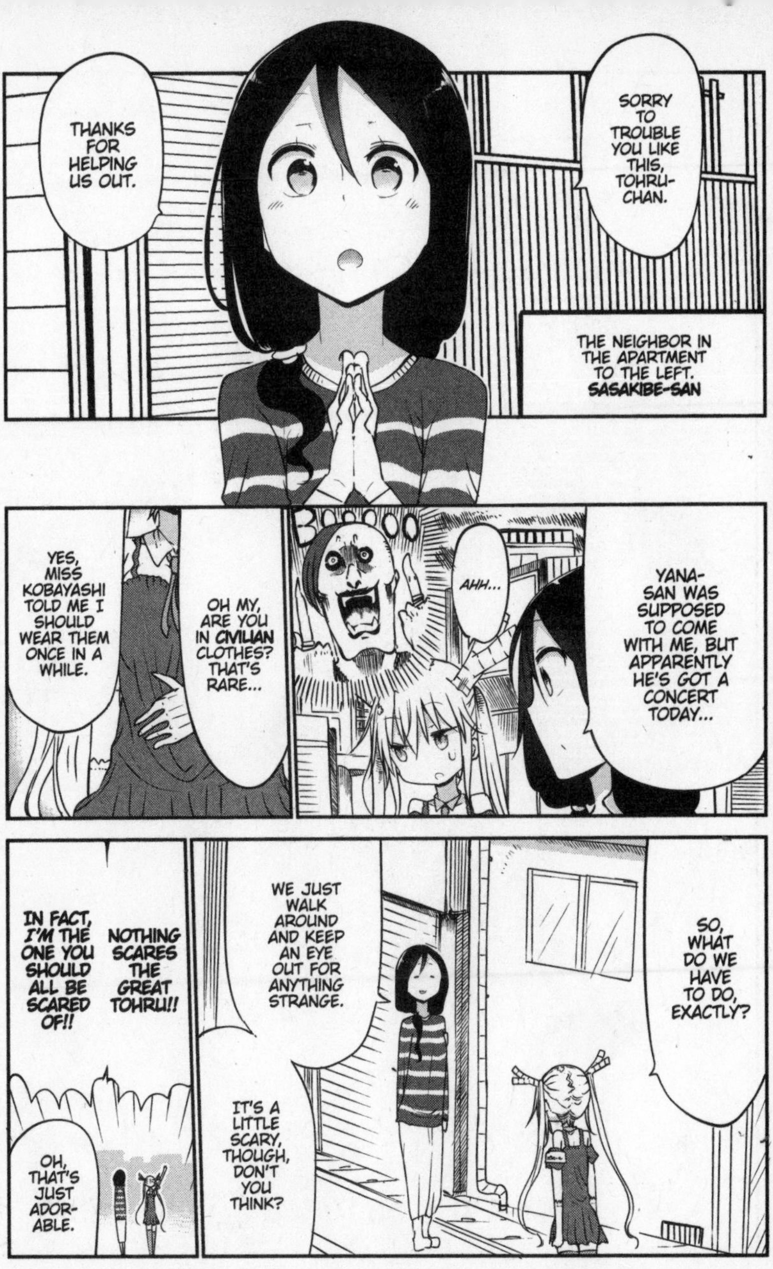
SORRY TO TROUBLE YOU LIKE THIS, TOHRU-CHAN.
THANKS FOR HELPING US OUT.
THE NEIGHBOR IN THE APARTMENT TO THE LEFT. SASAKIBE-SAN
YANA-SAN WAS SUPPOSED TO COME WITH ME, BUT APPARENTLY HE'S GOT A CONCERT TODAY...
AHH...
OH MY, ARE YOU IN CIVILIAN CLOTHES? THAT'S RARE...
YES, MISS KOBAYASHI TOLD ME I SHOULD WEAR THEM ONCE IN A WHILE.
SO, WHAT DO WE HAVE TO DO, EXACTLY?
WE JUST WALK AROUND AND KEEP AN EYE OUT FOR ANYTHING STRANGE.
IT'S A LITTLE SCARY, THOUGH, DON'T YOU THINK?
NOTHING SCARES THE GREAT TOHRU!!
IN FACT, I'M THE ONE YOU SHOULD ALL BE SCARED OF!!
OH, THAT'S JUST ADORABLE.

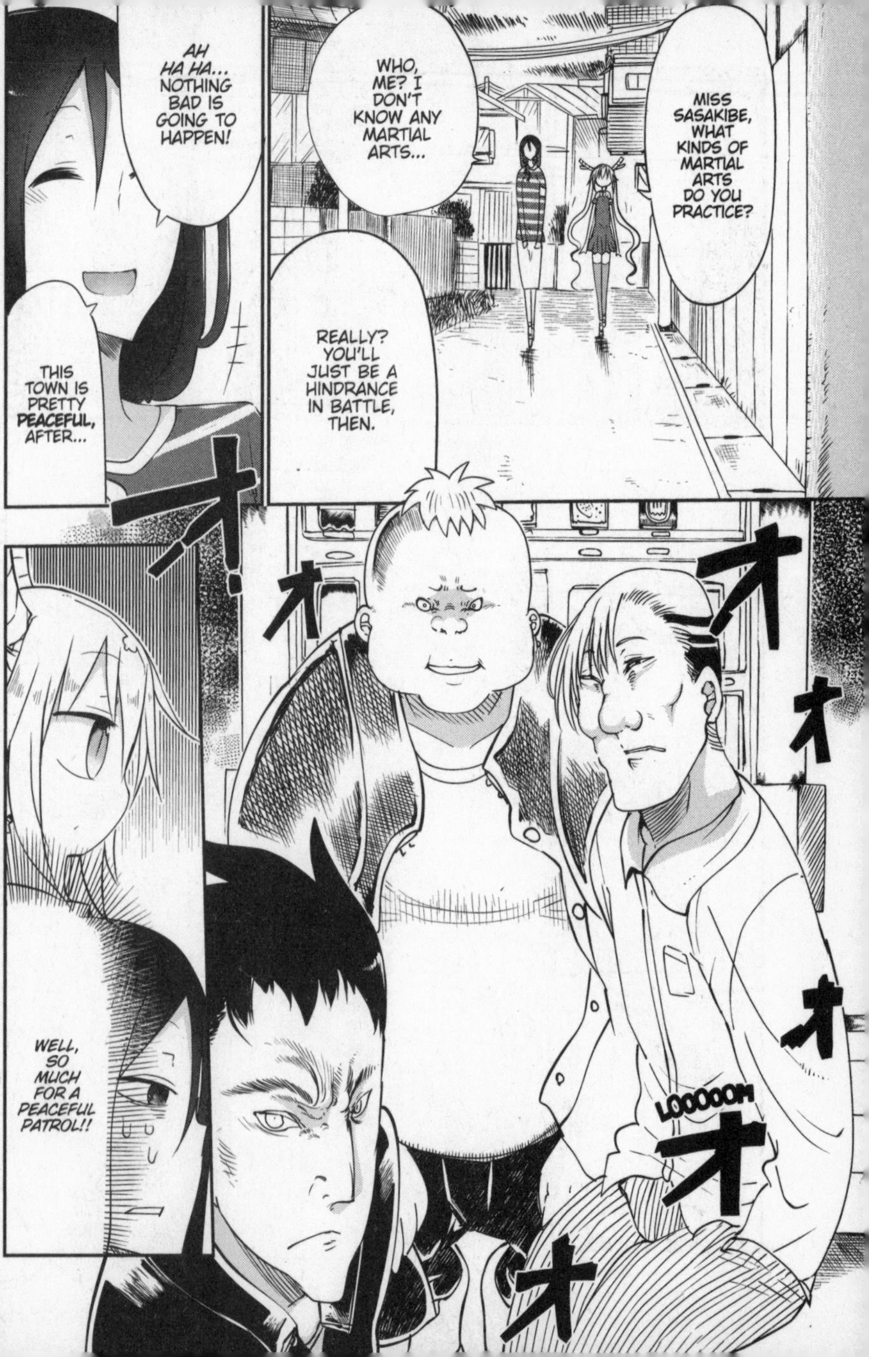
MISS SASAKIBE, WHAT KINDS OF MARTIAL ARTS DO YOU PRACTICE?
WHO, ME? I DON'T KNOW ANY MARTIAL ARTS...
REALLY? YOU'LL JUST BE A HINDRANCE IN BATTLE, THEN.
AH HA HA... NOTHING BAD IS GOING TO HAPPEN!
THIS TOWN IS PRETTY PEACEFUL, AFTER...
LOOOOOM
WELL, SO MUCH FOR A PEACEFUL PATROL!!

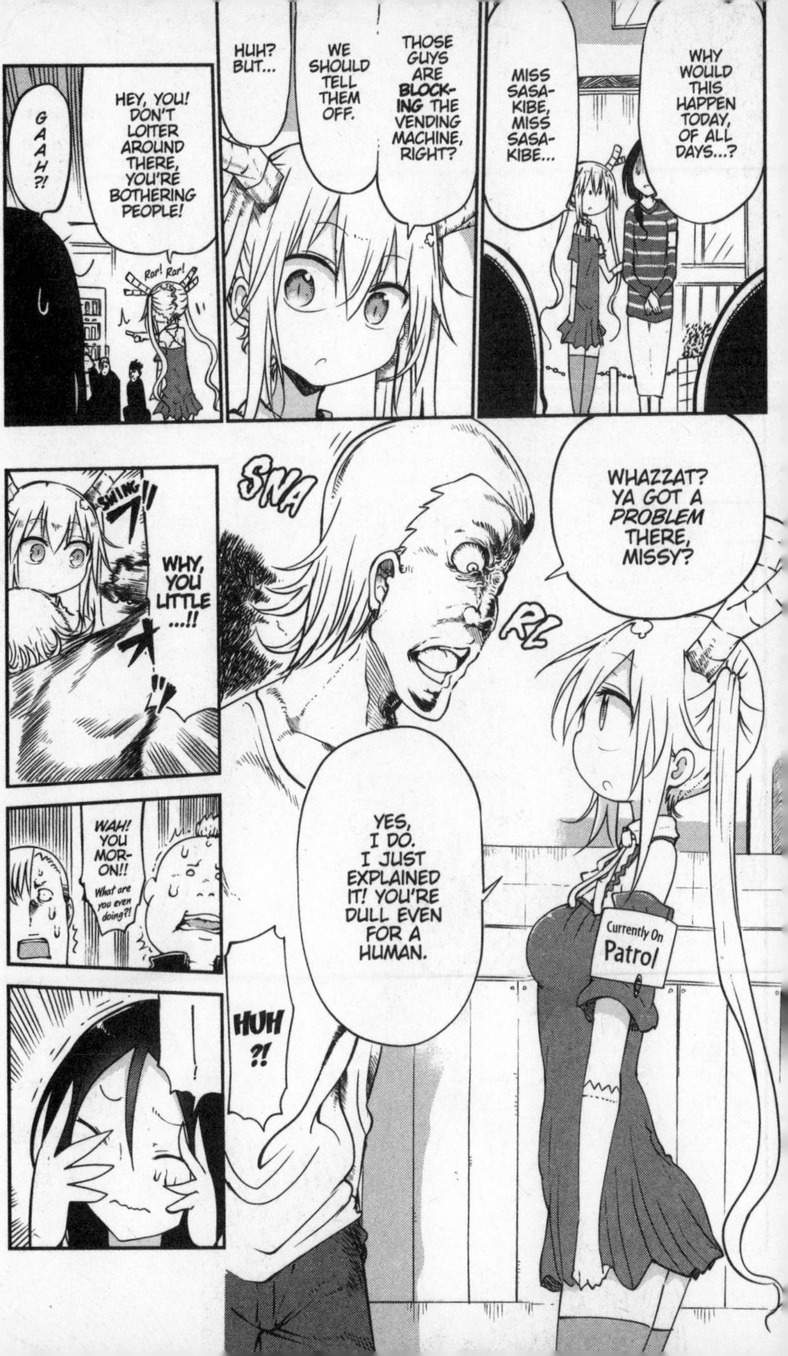
WHY WOULD THIS HAPPEN TODAY, OF ALL DAYS...?
MISS SASAKIBE, MISS SASAKIBE...
THOSE GUYS ARE BLOCKING THE VENDING MACHINE, RIGHT?
WE SHOULD TELL THEM OFF.
HUH? BUT...
HEY, YOU! DON'T LOITER AROUND THERE, YOU'RE BOTHERING PEOPLE!
Rar! Rar!
GAAAH?!
WHAZZAT? YA GOT A PROBLEM THERE, MISSY?
SNA
RL
YES, I DO. I JUST EXPLAINED IT! YOU'RE DULL EVEN FOR A HUMAN.
HUH ?!
SWING
WHY, YOU LITTLE ...!!
WAH! YOU MORON!!
What are you even doing?!

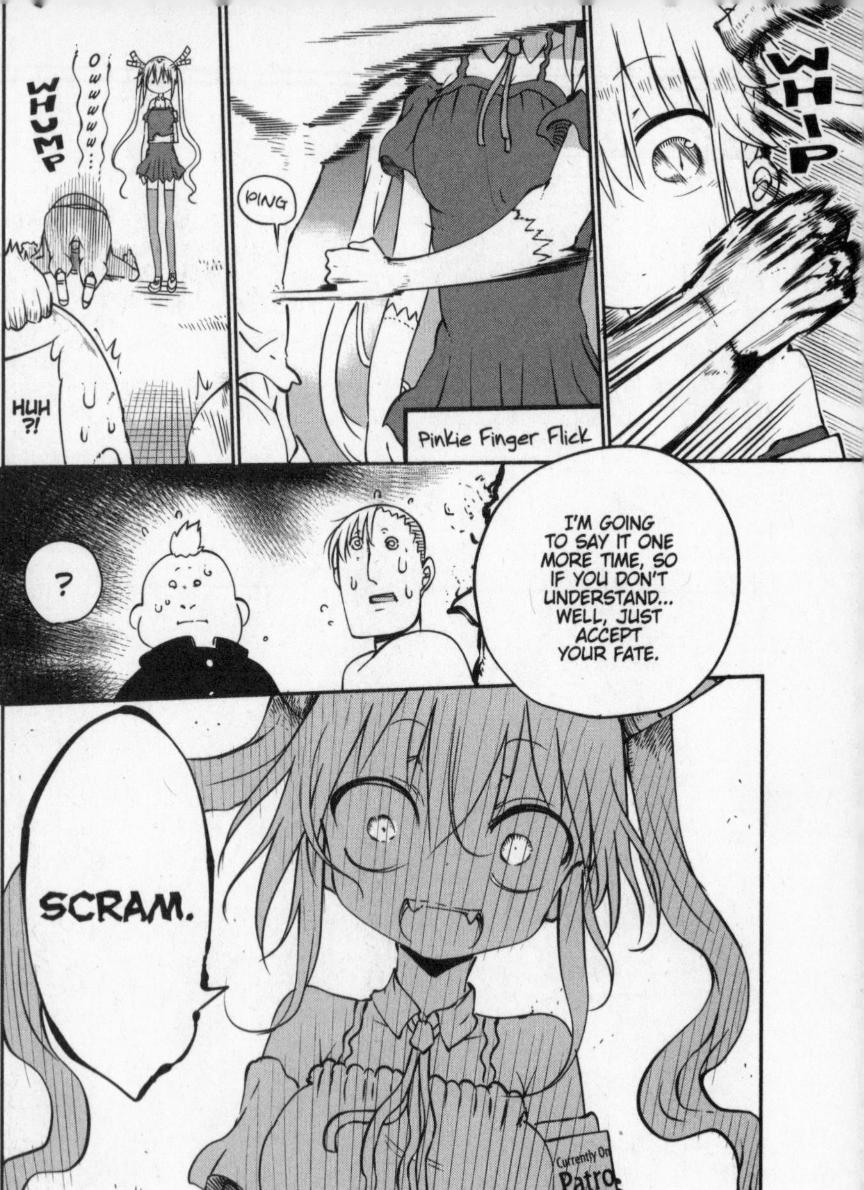
WHIP
PING
Pinkie Finger Flick
WHUMP
OWWWWW...
HUH ?!
I'M GOING TO SAY IT ONE MORE TIME, SO IF YOU DON'T UNDERSTAND... WELL, JUST ACCEPT YOUR FATE.
?
SCRAM.

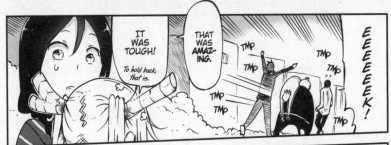

EEEEEEEK!
TMP
TMP
TMP
TMP
TMP
TMP
TMP
THAT WAS AMAZING.
IT WAS TOUGH!
To hold back, that is.
J-JUST YOU WAIT!! YOU JUST PICKED A FIGHT WITH THE DRAGON BUSTERS, THE BADDEST GANG IN TOWN!!
WE'RE GONNA ROUND UP OUR BUDDIES AND GET YOU FOR THIS!!
WOW, YOU COULDN'T POSSIBLY HAVE PICKED A MORE INFURIATING NAME.
WELL, THAT'S THAT. LET'S CONTINUE OUR PATROL, SHALL WE?
THEY SAID THEY'D BE BACK...
SHOULDN'T WE CALL THE POLICE?
TRUE, WE WILL NEED SOMEONE TO DISPOSE OF THEM AFTER.
"DISPOSE OF"? AFTER WHAT...?
WELL, OBVIOUSLY I MEAN...
!

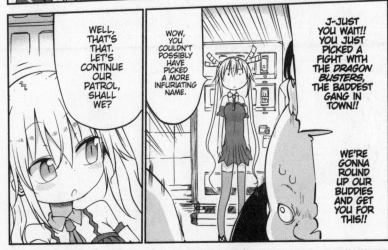

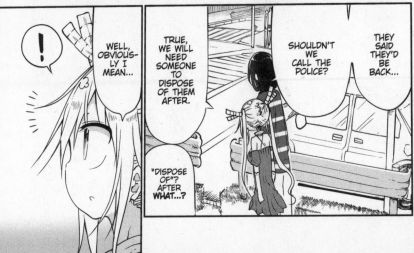

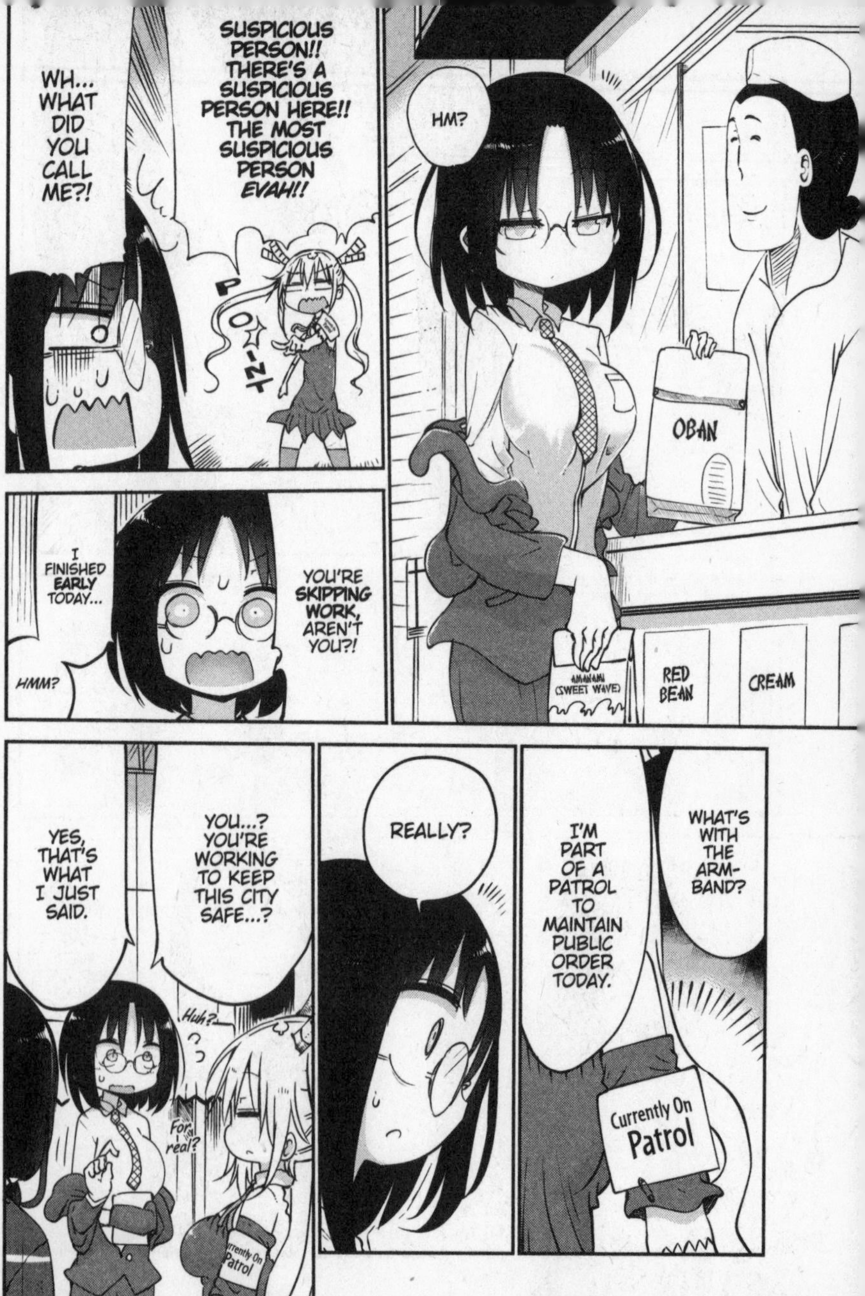
HM?
OBAN
AMANAMI (SWEET WAVE)
RED BEAN
CREAM
SUSPICIOUS PERSON!! THERE'S A SUSPICIOUS PERSON HERE!! THE MOST SUSPICIOUS PERSON EVAH!!
POINT
WH... WHAT DID YOU CALL ME?!
YOU'RE SKIPPING WORK, AREN'T YOU?!
I FINISHED EARLY TODAY...
HMM?
WHAT'S WITH THE ARM-BAND?
I'M PART OF A PATROL TO MAINTAIN PUBLIC ORDER TODAY.
Currently On Patrol
REALLY?
YOU...? YOU'RE WORKING TO KEEP THIS CITY SAFE...?
YES, THAT'S WHAT I JUST SAID.
Huh?
For real?
Currently On Patrol

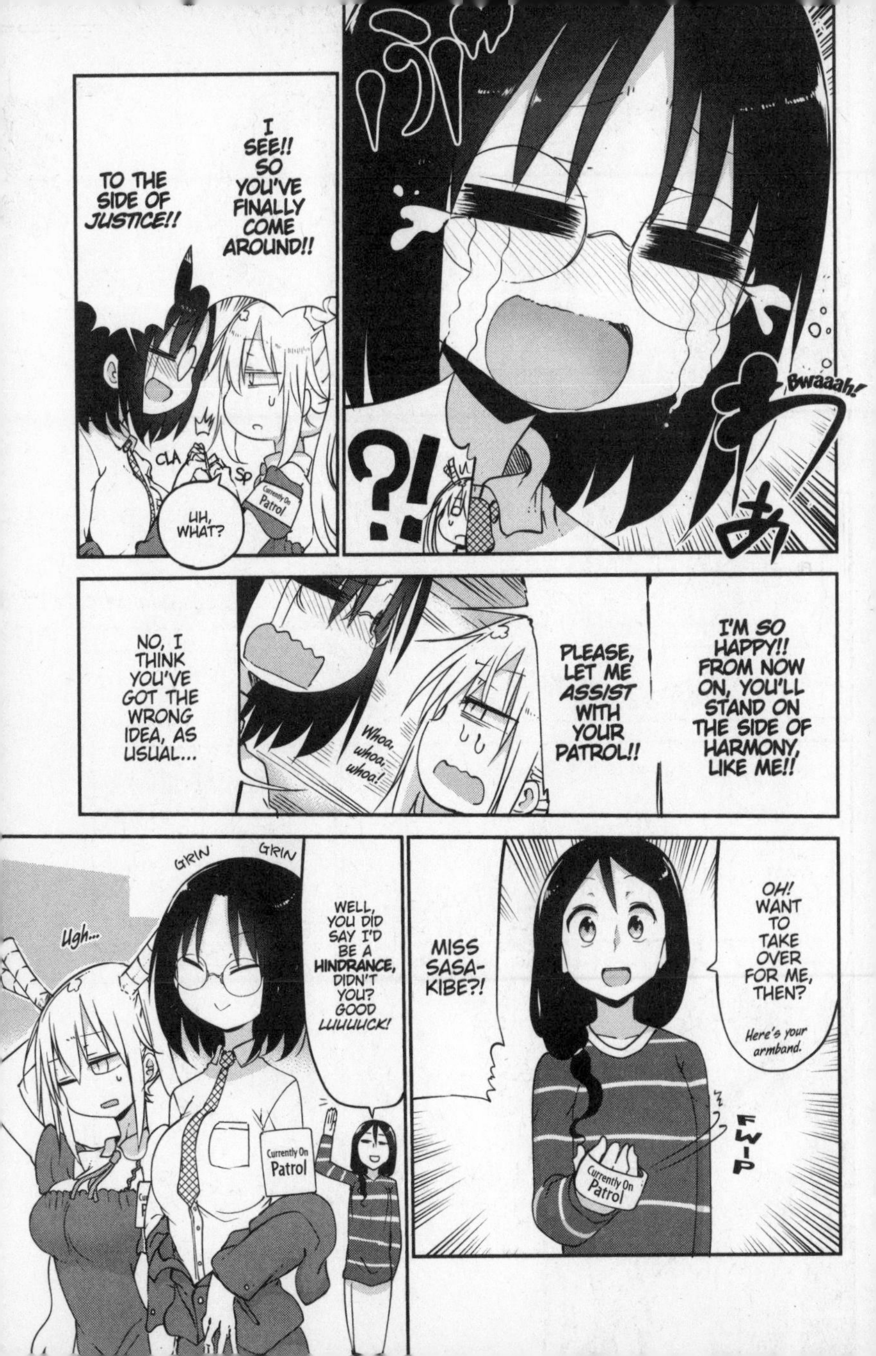
Bwaaah!
あ
?!
I SEE!! SO YOU'VE FINALLY COME AROUND!!
TO THE SIDE OF JUSTICE!!
CLA
SP
Currently On Patrol
UH, WHAT?
I'M SO HAPPY!! FROM NOW ON, YOU'LL STAND ON THE SIDE OF HARMONY, LIKE ME!!
PLEASE, LET ME ASSIST WITH YOUR PATROL!!
Whoa, whoa, whoa!
NO, I THINK YOU'VE GOT THE WRONG IDEA, AS USUAL...
OH! WANT TO TAKE OVER FOR ME, THEN?
Here's your armband.
FWIP
Currently On Patrol
MISS SASA-KIBE?!
GRIN GRIN
WELL, YOU DID SAY I'D BE A HINDRANCE, DIDN'T YOU? GOOD LUUUUCK!
Ugh...
Currently On Patrol

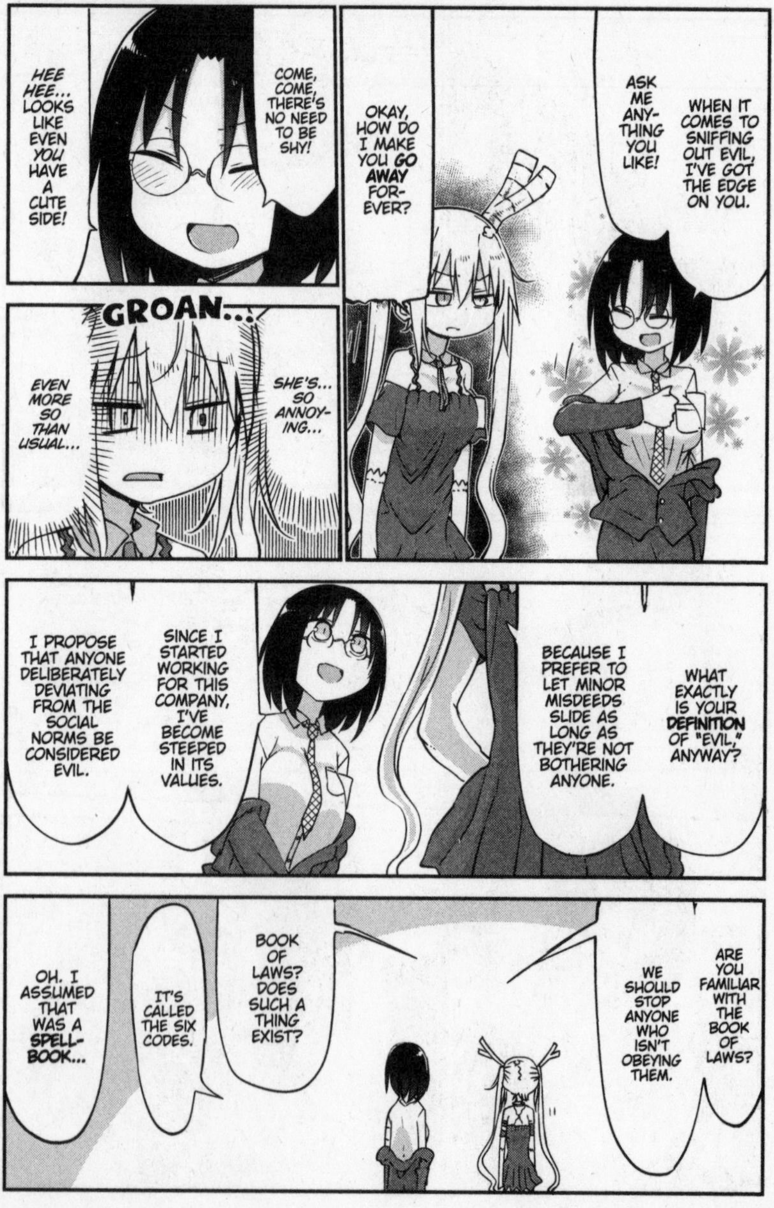
WHEN IT COMES TO SNIFFING OUT EVIL, I'VE GOT THE EDGE ON YOU.
ASK ME ANYTHING YOU LIKE!
OKAY, HOW DO I MAKE YOU GO AWAY FOREVER?
COME, COME, THERE'S NO NEED TO BE SHY!
HEE HEE... LOOKS LIKE EVEN YOU HAVE A CUTE SIDE!
GROAN...
SHE'S... SO ANNOYING...
EVEN MORE SO THAN USUAL...
WHAT EXACTLY IS YOUR DEFINITION OF "EVIL," ANYWAY?
BECAUSE I PREFER TO LET MINOR MISDEEDS SLIDE AS LONG AS THEY'RE NOT BOTHERING ANYONE.
SINCE I STARTED WORKING FOR THIS COMPANY, I'VE BECOME STEEPED IN ITS VALUES.
I PROPOSE THAT ANYONE DELIBERATELY DEVIATING FROM THE SOCIAL NORMS BE CONSIDERED EVIL.
ARE YOU FAMILIAR WITH THE BOOK OF LAWS?
WE SHOULD STOP ANYONE WHO ISN'T OBEYING THEM.
BOOK OF LAWS? DOES SUCH A THING EXIST?
IT'S CALLED THE SIX CODES.
OH. I ASSUMED THAT WAS A SPELLBOOK...

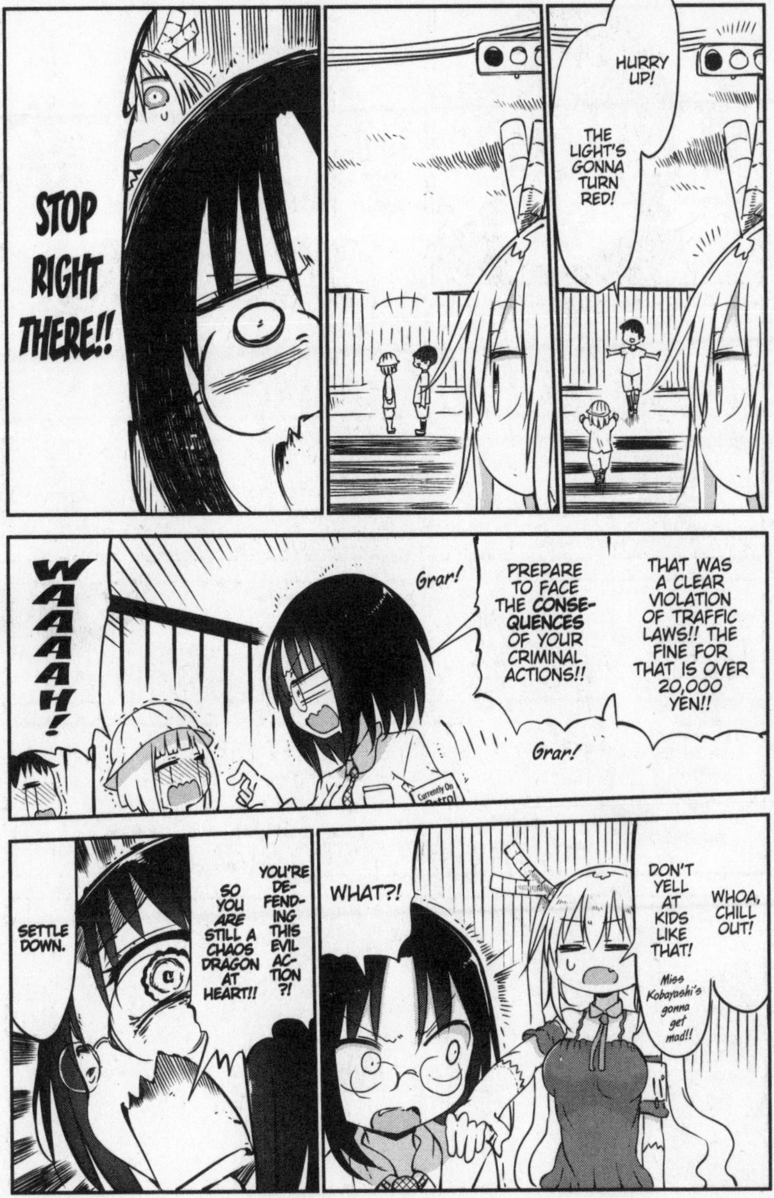
HURRY UP!
THE LIGHT'S GONNA TURN RED!
STOP RIGHT THERE!!
THAT WAS A CLEAR VIOLATION OF TRAFFIC LAWS!! THE FINE FOR THAT IS OVER 20,000 YEN!!
PREPARE TO FACE THE CONSEQUENCES OF YOUR CRIMINAL ACTIONS!!
Grar!
Grar!
WAAAAAH!
Currently On
WHOA, CHILL OUT!
DON'T YELL AT KIDS LIKE THAT!
Miss Kobayashi's gonna get mad!!
WHAT?!
YOU'RE DEFENDING THIS EVIL ACTION?!
SO YOU ARE STILL A CHAOS DRAGON AT HEART!!
SETTLE DOWN.

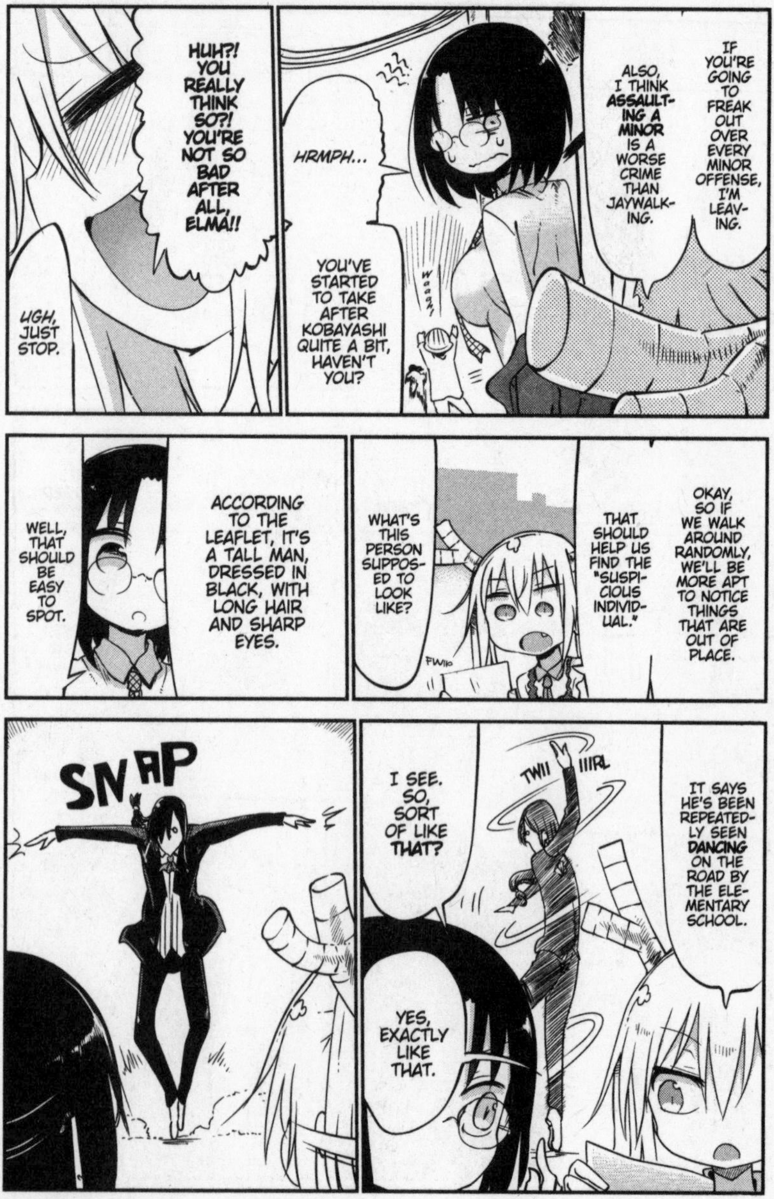
IF YOU'RE GOING TO FREAK OUT OVER EVERY MINOR OFFENSE, I'M LEAVING.
ALSO, I THINK **ASSAULTING A MINOR** IS A WORSE CRIME THAN JAYWALKING.
HRMPH...
YOU'VE STARTED TO TAKE AFTER KOBAYASHI QUITE A BIT, HAVEN'T YOU?
HUH?! YOU REALLY THINK SO?! YOU'RE NOT SO BAD AFTER ALL, ELMA!!
UGH, JUST STOP.
OKAY, SO IF WE WALK AROUND RANDOMLY, WE'LL BE MORE APT TO NOTICE THINGS THAT ARE OUT OF PLACE.
THAT SHOULD HELP US FIND THE "SUSPICIOUS INDIVIDUAL."
WHAT'S THIS PERSON SUPPOSED TO LOOK LIKE?
FWIP
ACCORDING TO THE LEAFLET, IT'S A TALL MAN, DRESSED IN BLACK, WITH LONG HAIR AND SHARP EYES.
WELL, THAT SHOULD BE EASY TO SPOT.
IT SAYS HE'S BEEN REPEATEDLY SEEN **DANCING** ON THE ROAD BY THE ELEMENTARY SCHOOL.
TWIIIIRL
I SEE. SO, SORT OF LIKE **THAT**?
YES, EXACTLY LIKE THAT.
SNAP

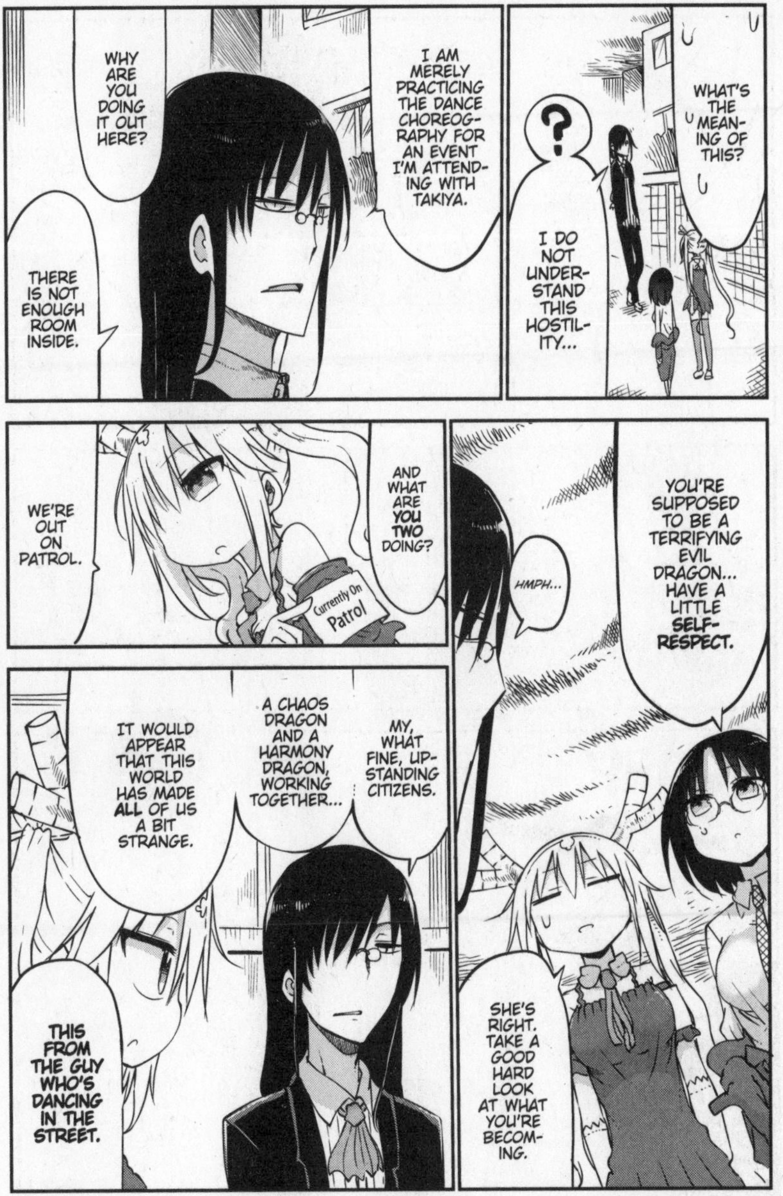
WHAT'S THE MEANING OF THIS?
?
I DO NOT UNDERSTAND THIS HOSTILITY...
I AM MERELY PRACTICING THE DANCE CHOREOG-RAPHY FOR AN EVENT I'M ATTEND-ING WITH TAKIYA.
WHY ARE YOU DOING IT OUT HERE?
THERE IS NOT ENOUGH ROOM INSIDE.
YOU'RE SUPPOSED TO BE A TERRIFYING EVIL DRAGON... HAVE A LITTLE **SELF-RESPECT.**
HMPH...
SHE'S RIGHT. TAKE A GOOD HARD LOOK AT WHAT YOU'RE BECOM-ING.
AND WHAT ARE **YOU TWO** DOING?
WE'RE OUT ON PATROL.
Currently On Patrol
MY, WHAT FINE, UP-STANDING CITIZENS.
A CHAOS DRAGON AND A HARMONY DRAGON, WORKING TOGETHER...
IT WOULD APPEAR THAT THIS WORLD HAS MADE **ALL** OF US A BIT STRANGE.
THIS FROM THE GUY WHO'S DANCING IN THE STREET.

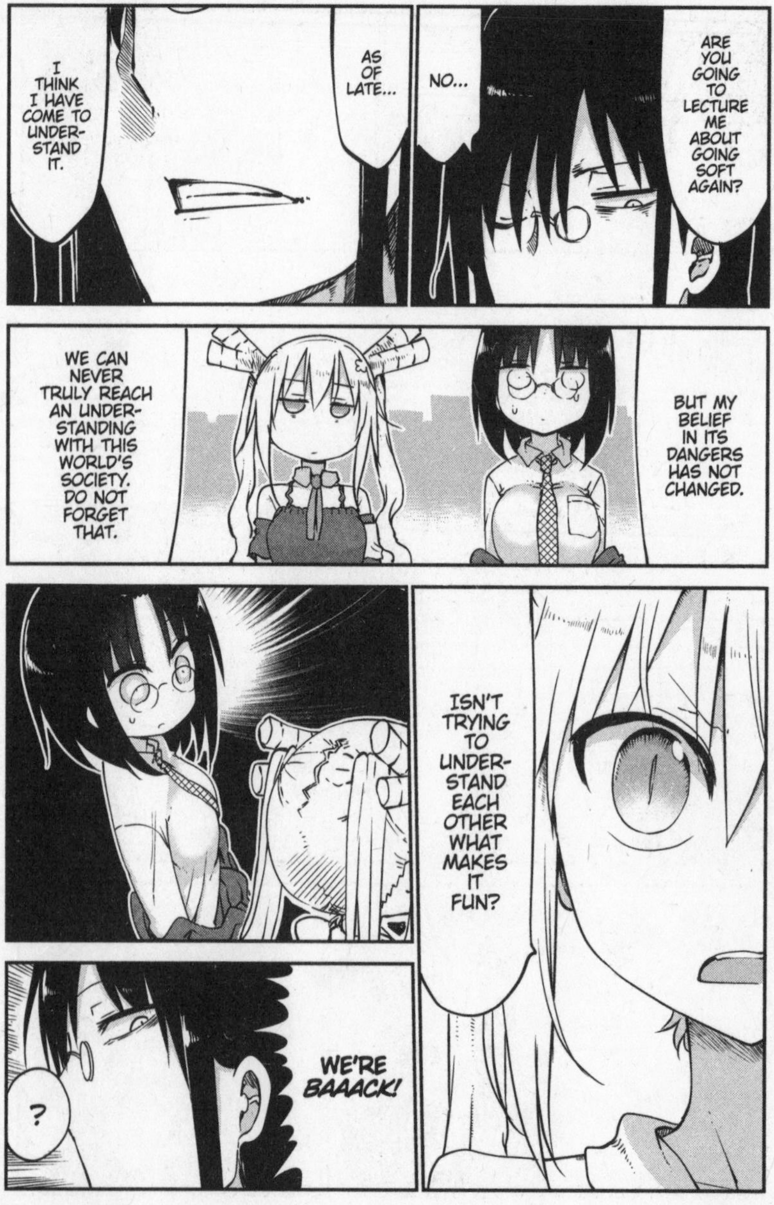
ARE YOU GOING TO LECTURE ME ABOUT GOING SOFT AGAIN?
NO...
AS OF LATE...
I THINK I HAVE COME TO UNDER-STAND IT.
BUT MY BELIEF IN ITS DANGERS HAS NOT CHANGED.
WE CAN NEVER TRULY REACH AN UNDER-STANDING WITH THIS WORLD'S SOCIETY. DO NOT FORGET THAT.
ISN'T TRYING TO UNDER-STAND EACH OTHER WHAT MAKES IT FUN?
WE'RE BAAACK!
?

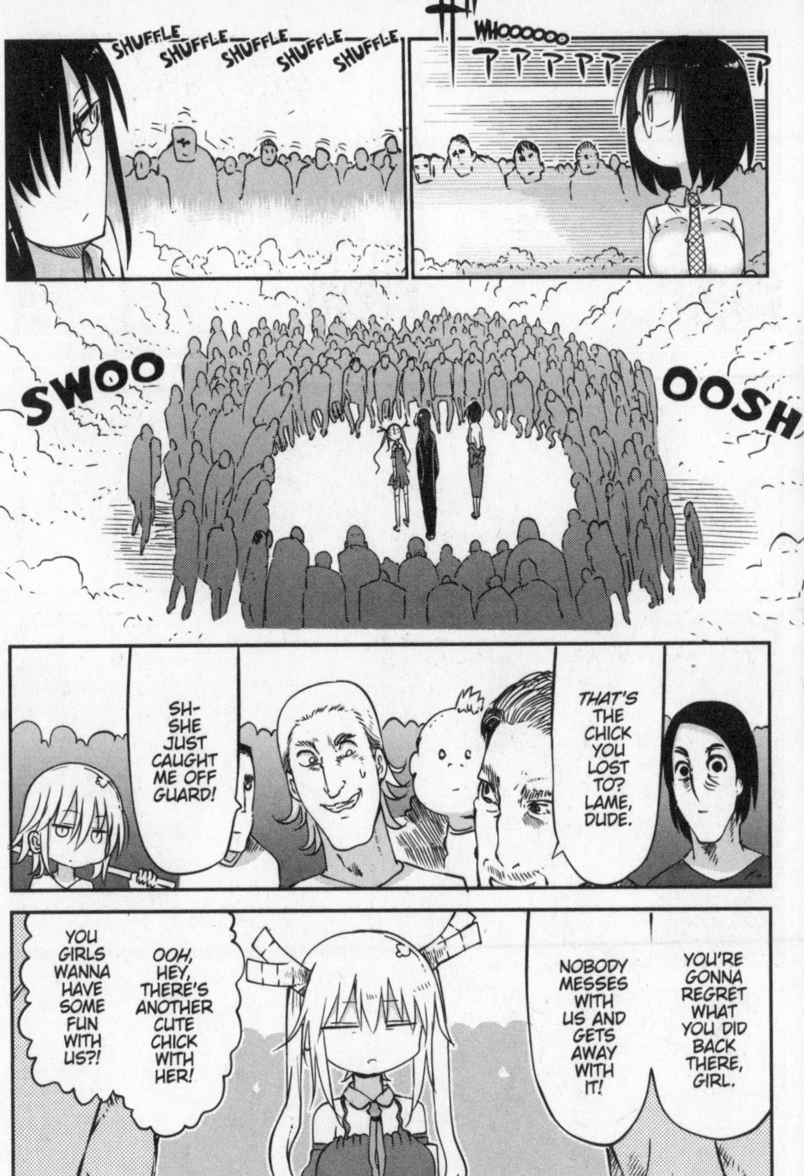
WHOOOOOOO
SHUFFLE
SHUFFLE
SHUFFLE
SHUFFLE
SHUFFLE
SWOO
OOSH
THAT'S THE CHICK YOU LOST TO? LAME, DUDE.
SH-SHE JUST CAUGHT ME OFF GUARD!
YOU'RE GONNA REGRET WHAT YOU DID BACK THERE, GIRL.
NOBODY MESSES WITH US AND GETS AWAY WITH IT!
OOH, HEY, THERE'S ANOTHER CUTE CHICK WITH HER!
YOU GIRLS WANNA HAVE SOME FUN WITH US?!

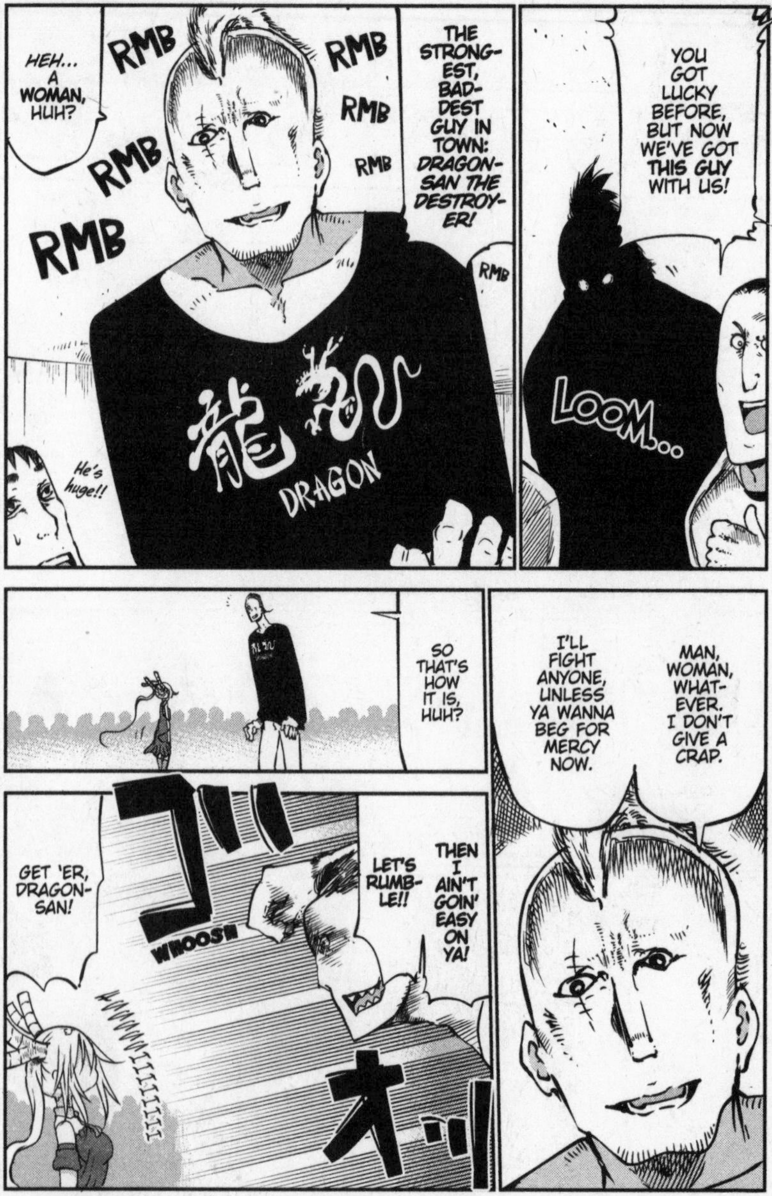
YOU GOT LUCKY BEFORE, BUT NOW WE'VE GOT THIS GUY WITH US!
LOOM...
THE STRONGEST, BADDEST GUY IN TOWN: DRAGON-SAN THE DESTROYER!
RMB
RMB
RMB
RMB
RMB
HEH... A WOMAN, HUH?
RMB
RMB
龍
DRAGON
He's huge!!
MAN, WOMAN, WHATEVER. I DON'T GIVE A CRAP.
I'LL FIGHT ANYONE, UNLESS YA WANNA BEG FOR MERCY NOW.
SO THAT'S HOW IT IS, HUH?
THEN I AIN'T GOIN' EASY ON YA!
LET'S RUMBLE!!
ゴッ
WHOOSH
GET 'ER, DRAGON-SAN!
オッ!

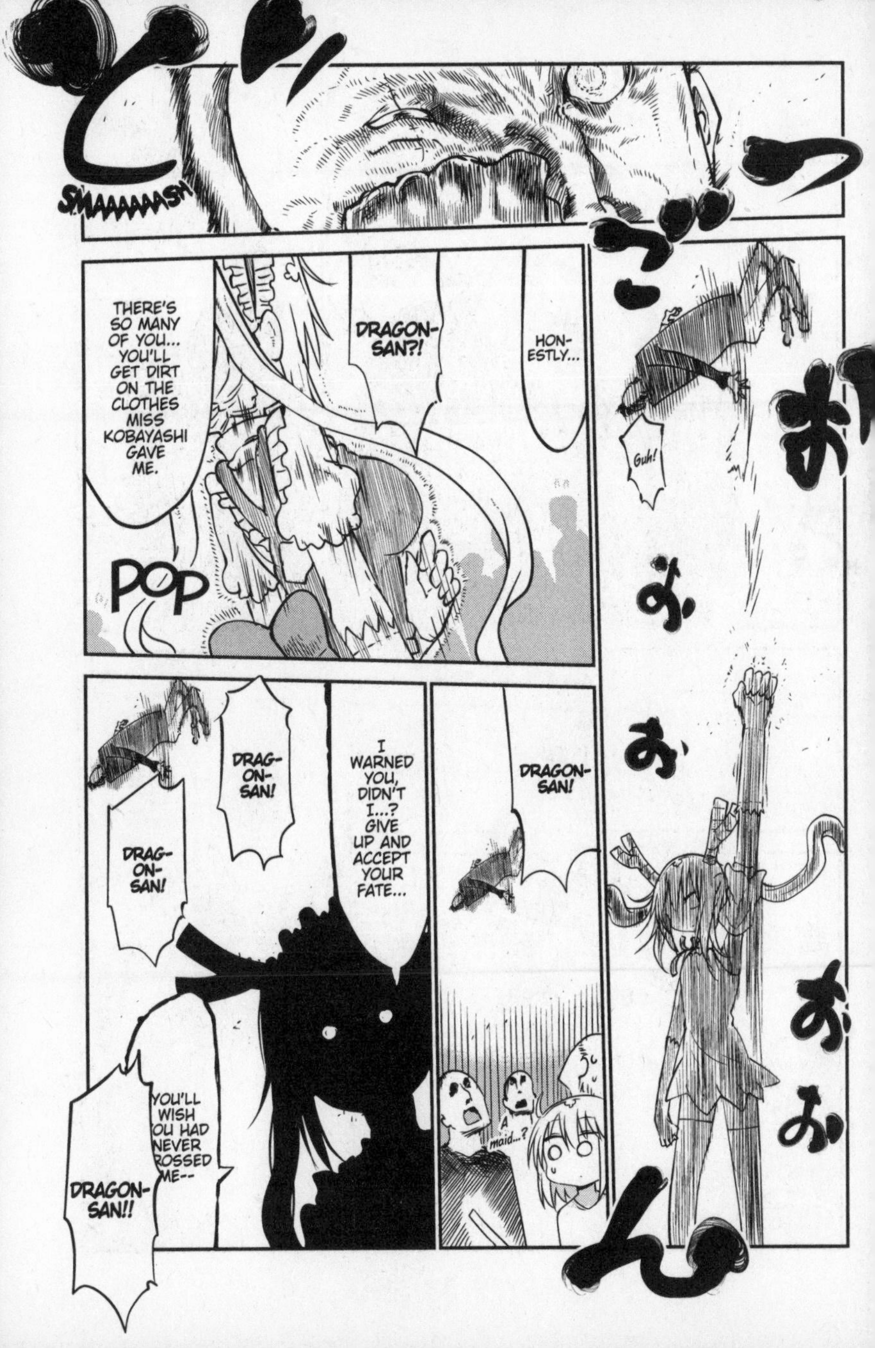

SMAAAAAASH
Guh!
HON-ESTLY...
DRAGON-SAN?!
THERE'S SO MANY OF YOU... YOU'LL GET DIRT ON THE CLOTHES MISS KOBAYASHI GAVE ME.
POP
DRAGON-SAN!
A maid...?
I WARNED YOU, DIDN'T I...? GIVE UP AND ACCEPT YOUR FATE...
DRAG-ON-SAN!
DRAG-ON-SAN!
YOU'LL WISH OU HAD NEVER ROSSED ME--
DRAGON-SAN!!

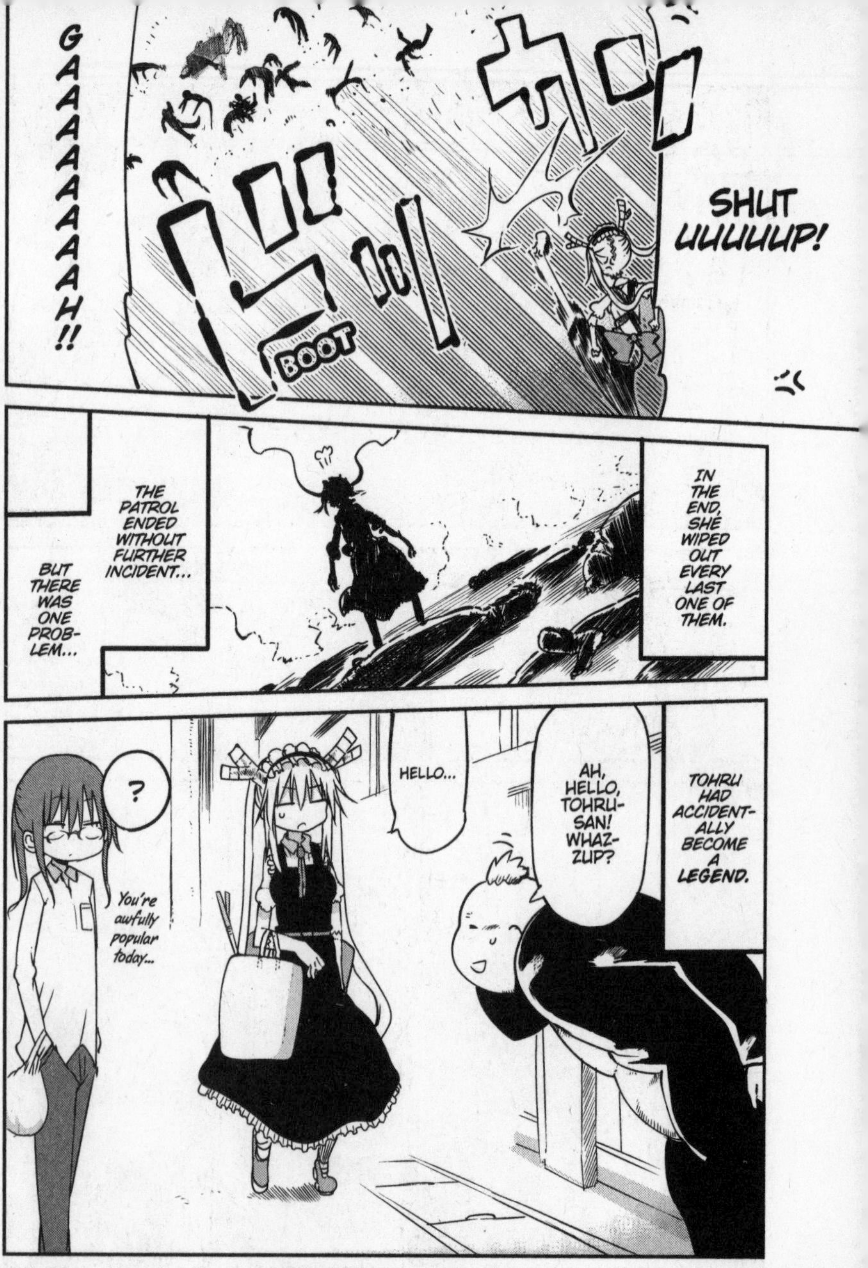
SHUT UUUUUP!
BOOT
GAAAAAAAAAAH!!
IN THE END, SHE WIPED OUT EVERY LAST ONE OF THEM.
THE PATROL ENDED WITHOUT FURTHER INCIDENT...
BUT THERE WAS ONE PROB-LEM...
TOHRU HAD ACCIDENT-ALLY BECOME A LEGEND.
AH, HELLO, TOHRU-SAN! WHAZ-ZUP?
HELLO...
?
You're awfully popular today...

CHAPTER 43/END

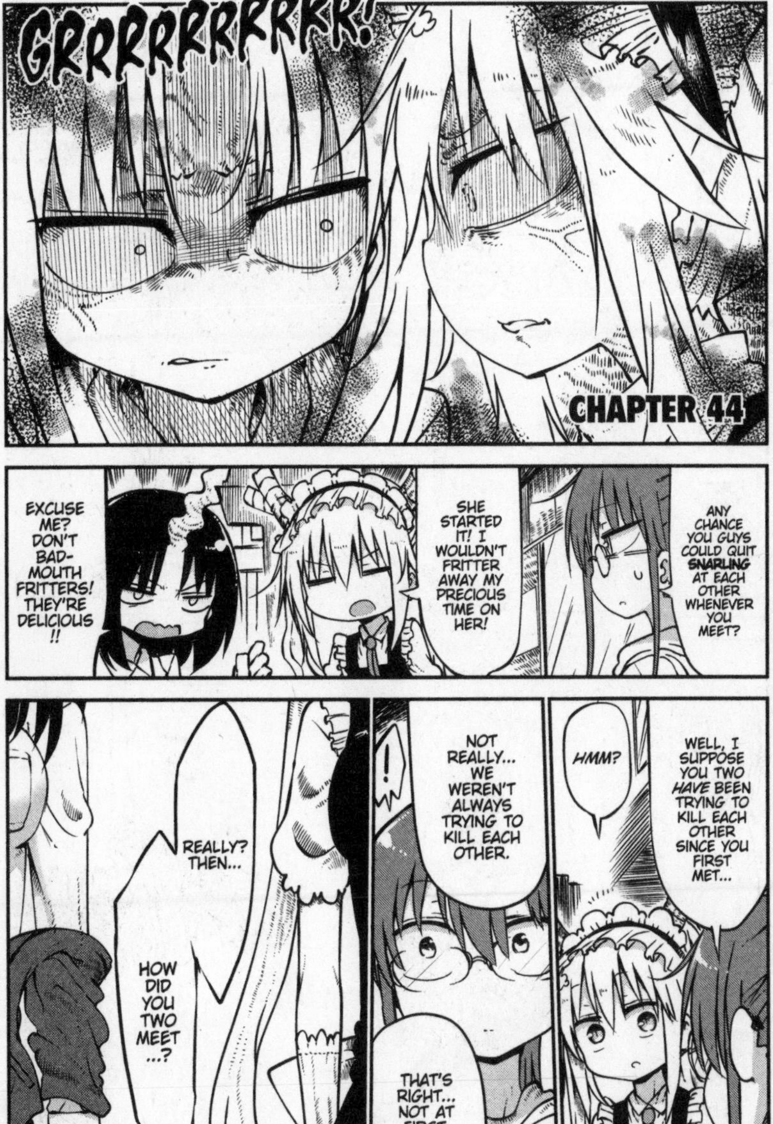
GRRRRRRRRRR!
CHAPTER 44
ANY CHANCE YOU GUYS COULD QUIT SNARLING AT EACH OTHER WHENEVER YOU MEET?
SHE STARTED IT! I WOULDN'T FRITTER AWAY MY PRECIOUS TIME ON HER!
EXCUSE ME? DON'T BAD-MOUTH FRITTERS! THEY'RE DELICIOUS!!
WELL, I SUPPOSE YOU TWO HAVE BEEN TRYING TO KILL EACH OTHER SINCE YOU FIRST MET...
HMM?
!
NOT REALLY... WE WEREN'T ALWAYS TRYING TO KILL EACH OTHER.
THAT'S RIGHT... NOT AT FIRST, ANYWAY.
REALLY? THEN...
HOW DID YOU TWO MEET...?

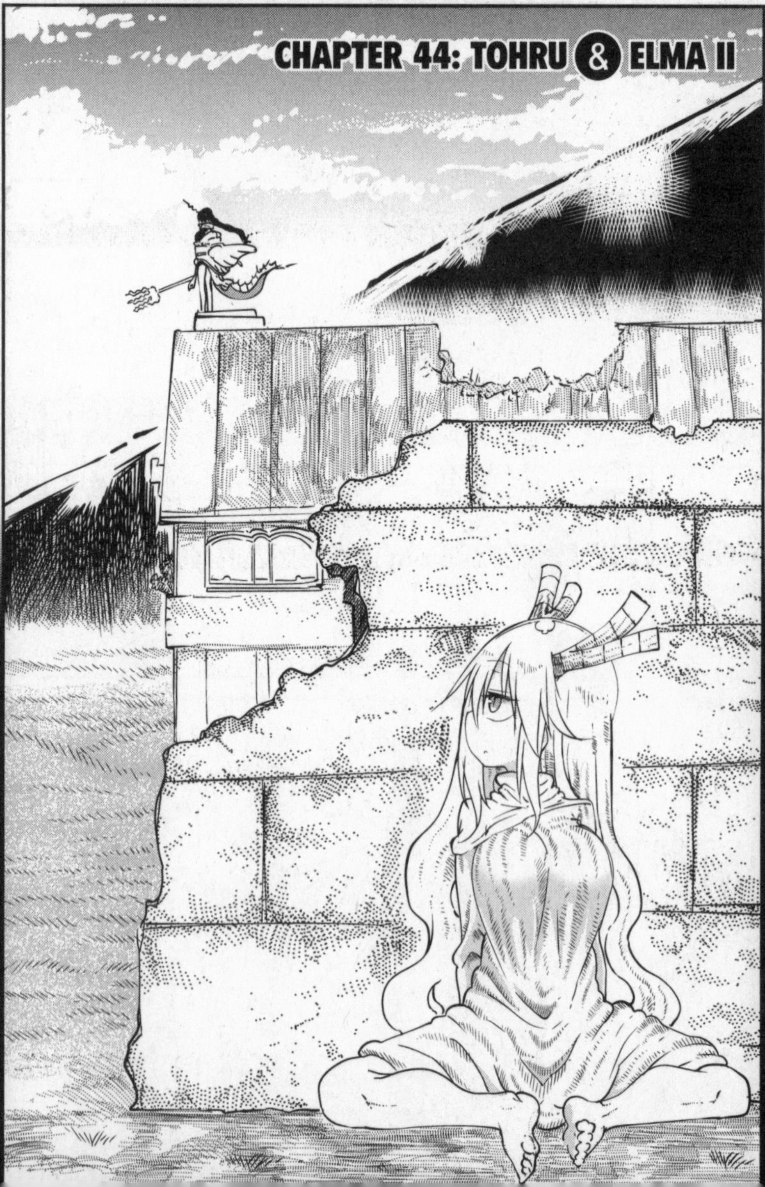
CHAPTER 44: TOHRU & ELMA II

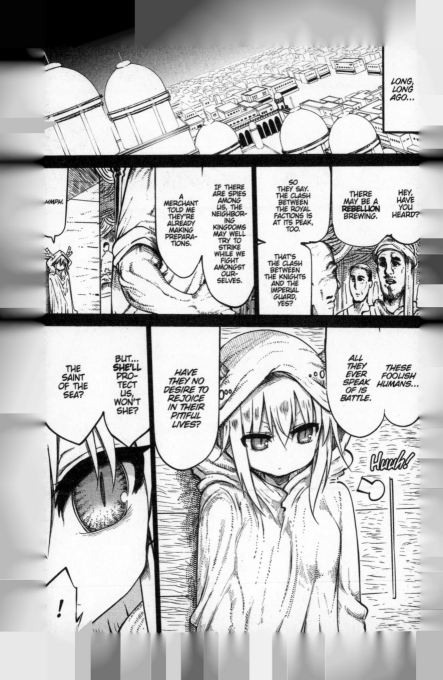

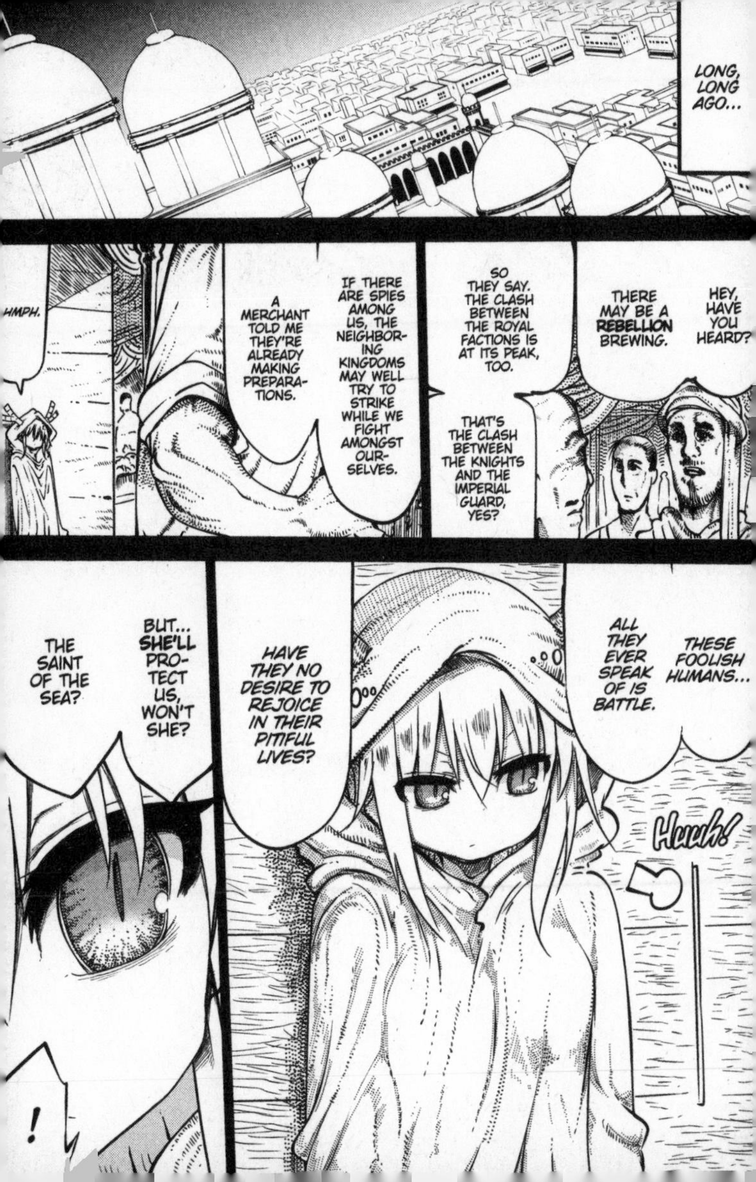
LONG, LONG AGO...
HEY, HAVE YOU HEARD?
THERE MAY BE A REBELLION BREWING.
SO THEY SAY. THE CLASH BETWEEN THE ROYAL FACTIONS IS AT ITS PEAK, TOO.
THAT'S THE CLASH BETWEEN THE KNIGHTS AND THE IMPERIAL GUARD, YES?
IF THERE ARE SPIES AMONG US, THE NEIGHBORING KINGDOMS MAY WELL TRY TO STRIKE WHILE WE FIGHT AMONGST OURSELVES.
A MERCHANT TOLD ME THEY'RE ALREADY MAKING PREPARATIONS.
HMPH.
THESE FOOLISH HUMANS...
ALL THEY EVER SPEAK OF IS BATTLE.
HAVE THEY NO DESIRE TO REJOICE IN THEIR PITIFUL LIVES?
BUT... SHE'LL PROTECT US, WON'T SHE?
THE SAINT OF THE SEA?
!

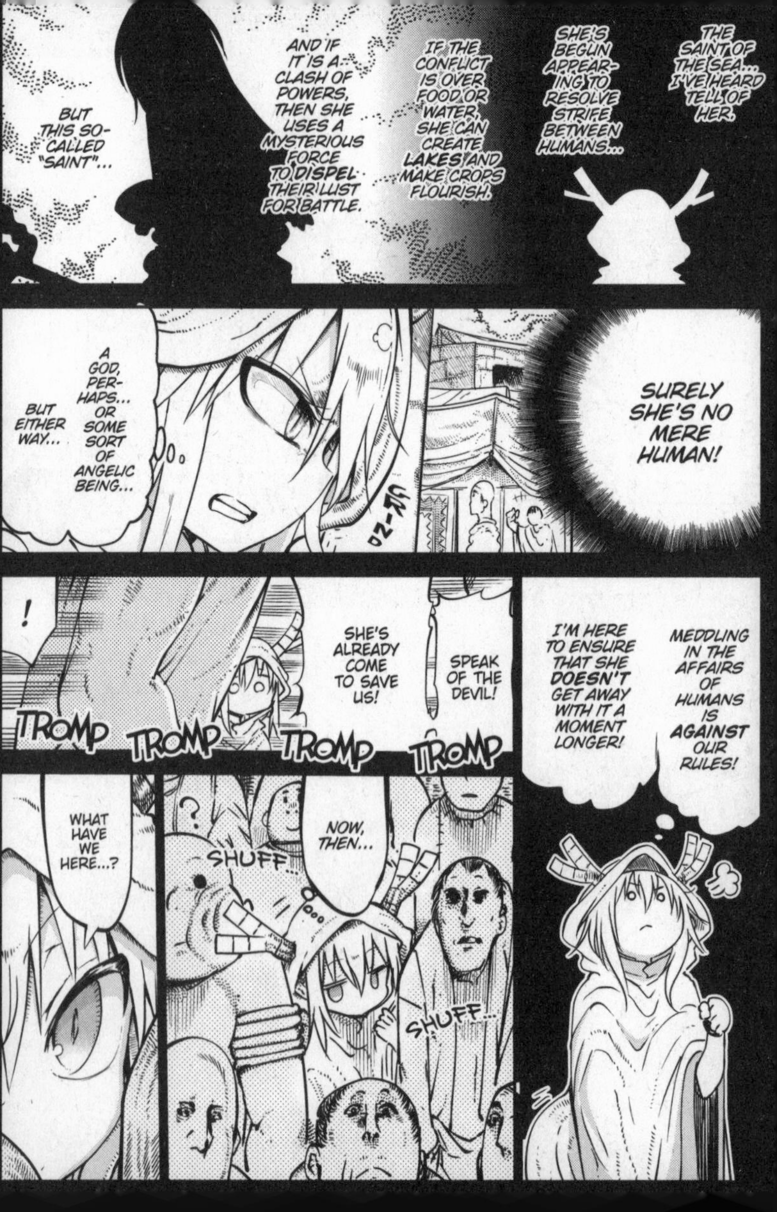
THE SAINT OF THE SEA... I'VE HEARD TELL OF HER.
SHE'S BEGUN APPEARING TO RESOLVE STRIFE BETWEEN HUMANS...
IF THE CONFLICT IS OVER FOOD OR WATER, SHE CAN CREATE LAKES AND MAKE CROPS FLOURISH.
AND IF IT IS A CLASH OF POWERS, THEN SHE USES A MYSTERIOUS FORCE TO DISPEL THEIR LUST FOR BATTLE.
BUT THIS SO-CALLED "SAINT"...
SURELY SHE'S NO MERE HUMAN!
A GOD, PERHAPS... OR SOME SORT OF ANGELIC BEING...
BUT EITHER WAY...
MEDDLING IN THE AFFAIRS OF HUMANS IS AGAINST OUR RULES!
I'M HERE TO ENSURE THAT SHE DOESN'T GET AWAY WITH IT A MOMENT LONGER!
SPEAK OF THE DEVIL!
SHE'S ALREADY COME TO SAVE US!
TROMP
TROMP
TROMP
TROMP
!
NOW, THEN...
SHUFF...
?
SHUFF...
WHAT HAVE WE HERE...?

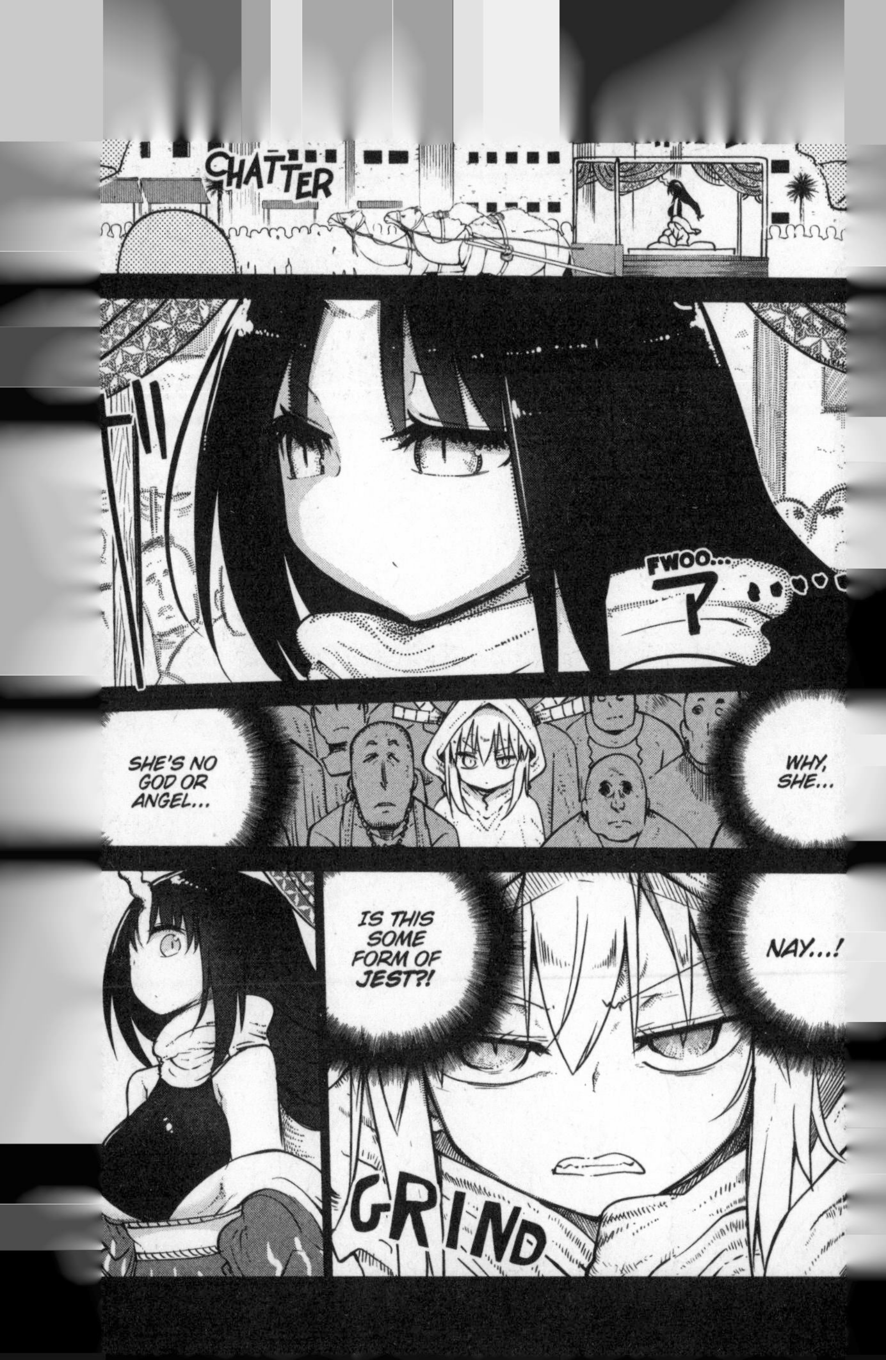
CHATTER
FWOO...
WHY, SHE...
SHE'S NO GOD OR ANGEL...
NAY...!
IS THIS SOME FORM OF JEST?!
GRIND

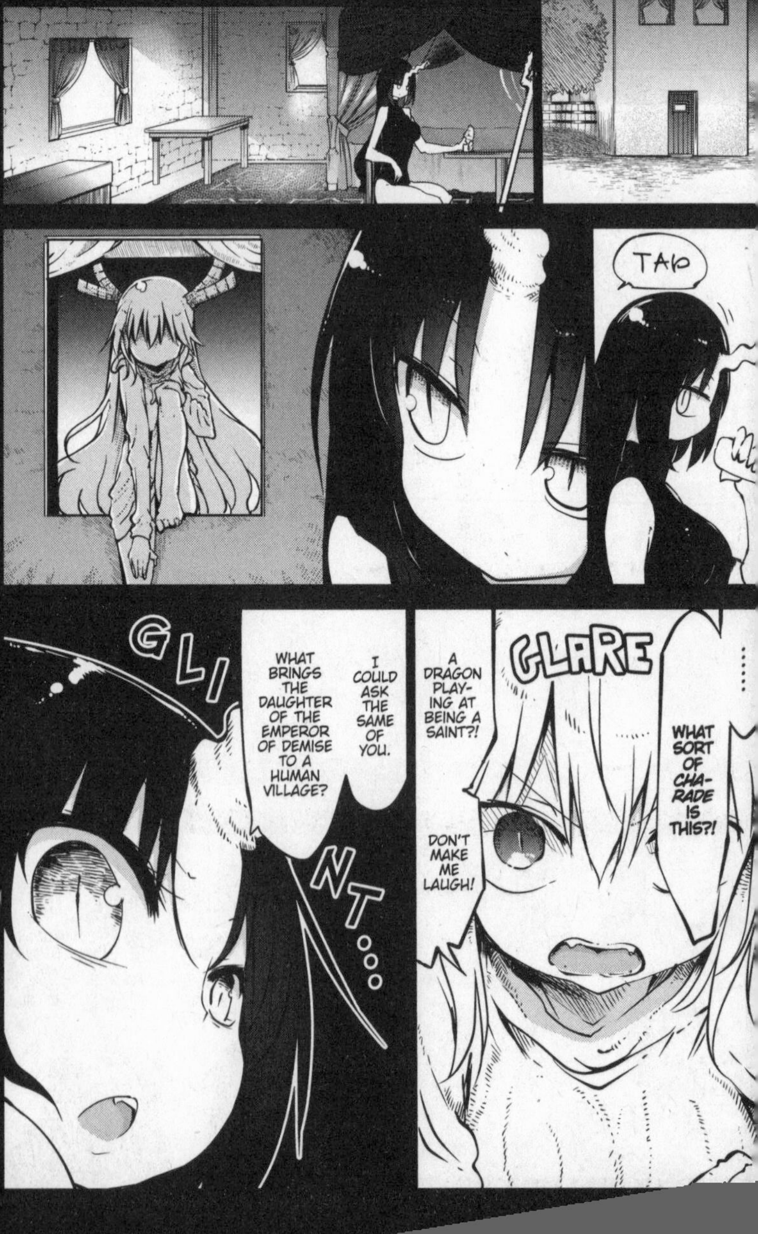
TAP
GLARE
WHAT SORT OF CHA-RADE IS THIS?!
A DRAGON PLAY-ING AT BEING A SAINT?!
DON'T MAKE ME LAUGH!
I COULD ASK THE SAME OF YOU.
WHAT BRINGS THE DAUGHTER OF THE EMPEROR OF DEMISE TO A HUMAN VILLAGE?
GLINT...

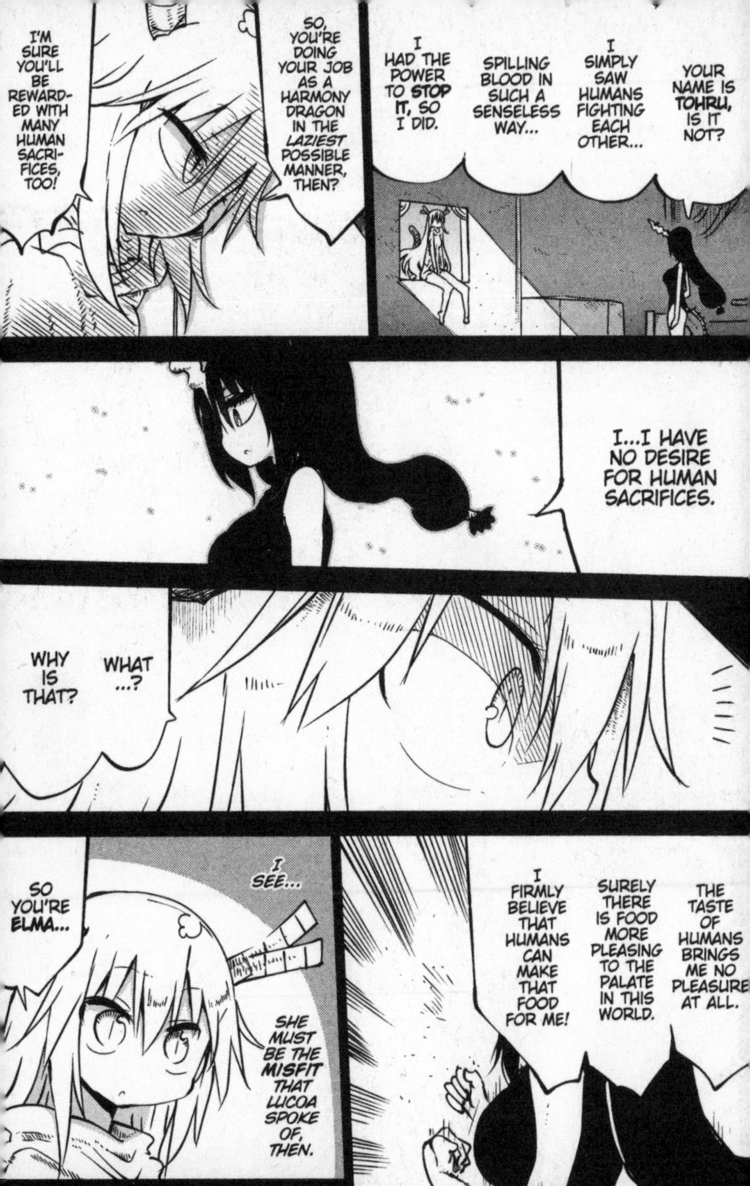
YOUR NAME IS **TOHRU,** IS IT NOT?
I SIMPLY SAW HUMANS FIGHTING EACH OTHER...
SPILLING BLOOD IN SUCH A SENSELESS WAY...
I HAD THE POWER TO **STOP IT,** SO I DID.
SO, YOU'RE DOING YOUR JOB AS A HARMONY DRAGON IN THE *LAZIEST* POSSIBLE MANNER, THEN?
I'M SURE YOU'LL BE REWARDED WITH MANY HUMAN SACRIFICES, TOO!
I...I HAVE NO DESIRE FOR HUMAN SACRIFICES.
WHAT ...?
WHY IS THAT?
THE TASTE OF HUMANS BRINGS ME NO PLEASURE AT ALL.
SURELY THERE IS FOOD MORE PLEASING TO THE PALATE IN THIS WORLD.
I FIRMLY BELIEVE THAT HUMANS CAN MAKE THAT FOOD FOR ME!
I SEE...
SO YOU'RE **ELMA...**
SHE MUST BE THE **MISFIT** THAT LUCOA SPOKE OF, THEN.

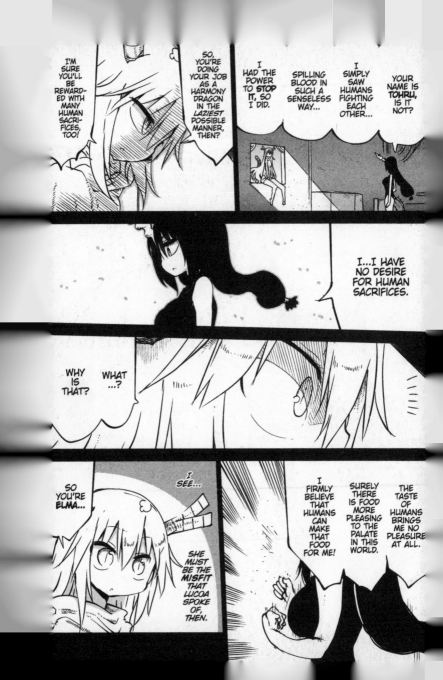

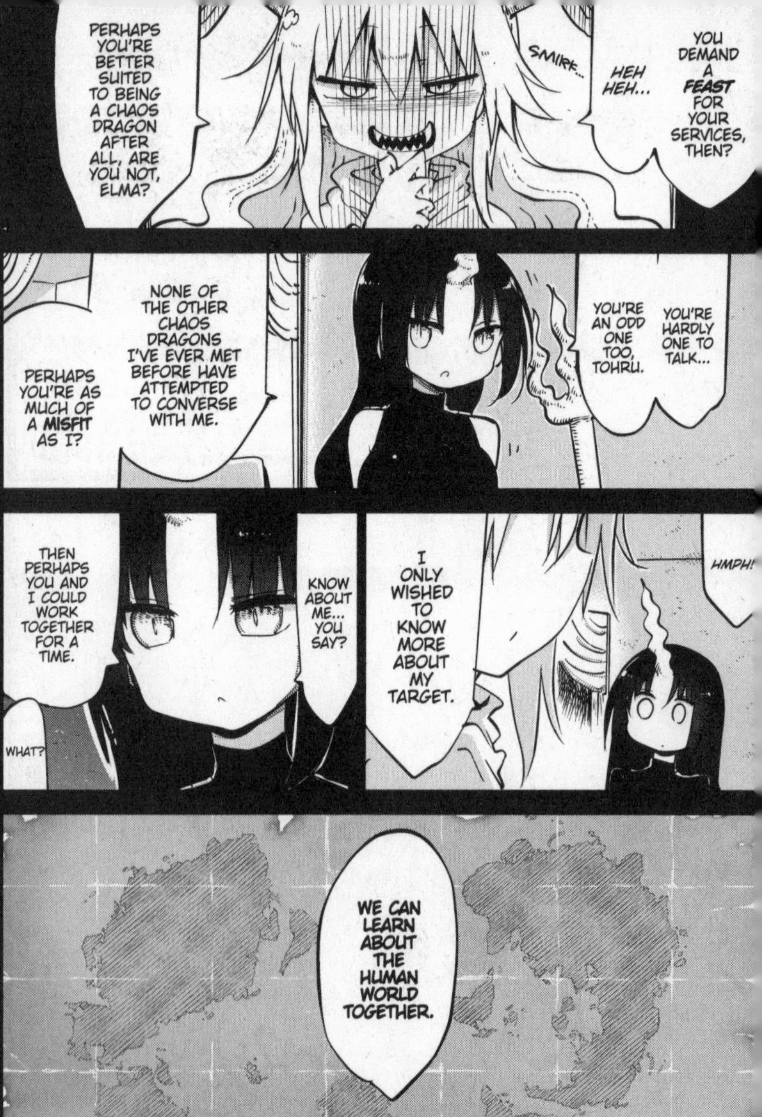
YOU DEMAND A FEAST FOR YOUR SERVICES, THEN?
HEH HEH...
SMIRK...
PERHAPS YOU'RE BETTER SUITED TO BEING A CHAOS DRAGON AFTER ALL, ARE YOU NOT, ELMA?
YOU'RE HARDLY ONE TO TALK...
YOU'RE AN ODD ONE TOO, TOHRU.
NONE OF THE OTHER CHAOS DRAGONS I'VE EVER MET BEFORE HAVE ATTEMPTED TO CONVERSE WITH ME.
PERHAPS YOU'RE AS MUCH OF A MISFIT AS I?
HMPH!
I ONLY WISHED TO KNOW MORE ABOUT MY TARGET.
KNOW ABOUT ME... YOU SAY?
THEN PERHAPS YOU AND I COULD WORK TOGETHER FOR A TIME.
WHAT?
WE CAN LEARN ABOUT THE HUMAN WORLD TOGETHER.

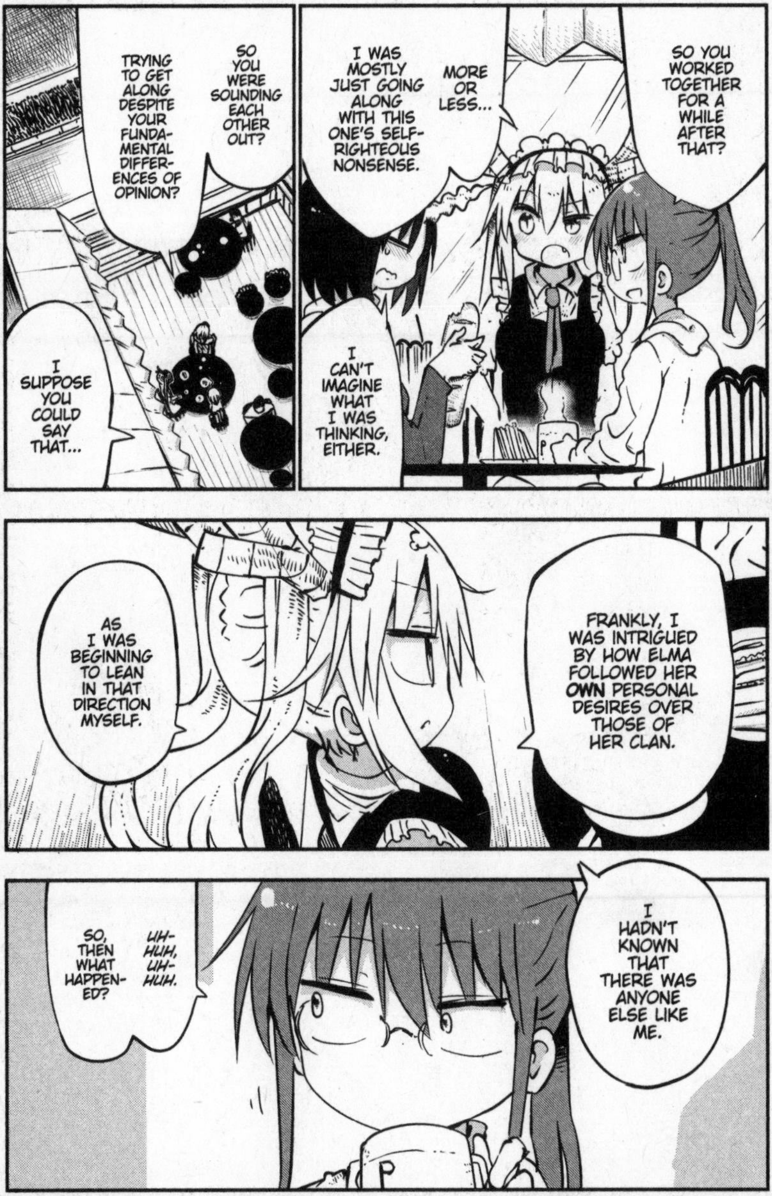
SO YOU WORKED TOGETHER FOR A WHILE AFTER THAT?
MORE OR LESS...
I WAS MOSTLY JUST GOING ALONG WITH THIS ONE'S SELF-RIGHTEOUS NONSENSE.
I CAN'T IMAGINE WHAT I WAS THINKING, EITHER.
SO YOU WERE SOUNDING EACH OTHER OUT?
TRYING TO GET ALONG DESPITE YOUR FUNDAMENTAL DIFFERENCES OF OPINION?
I SUPPOSE YOU COULD SAY THAT...
FRANKLY, I WAS INTRIGUED BY HOW ELMA FOLLOWED HER **OWN** PERSONAL DESIRES OVER THOSE OF HER CLAN.
AS I WAS BEGINNING TO LEAN IN THAT DIRECTION MYSELF.
I HADN'T KNOWN THAT THERE WAS ANYONE ELSE LIKE ME.
UH-HUH, UH-HUH.
SO, THEN WHAT HAPPENED?

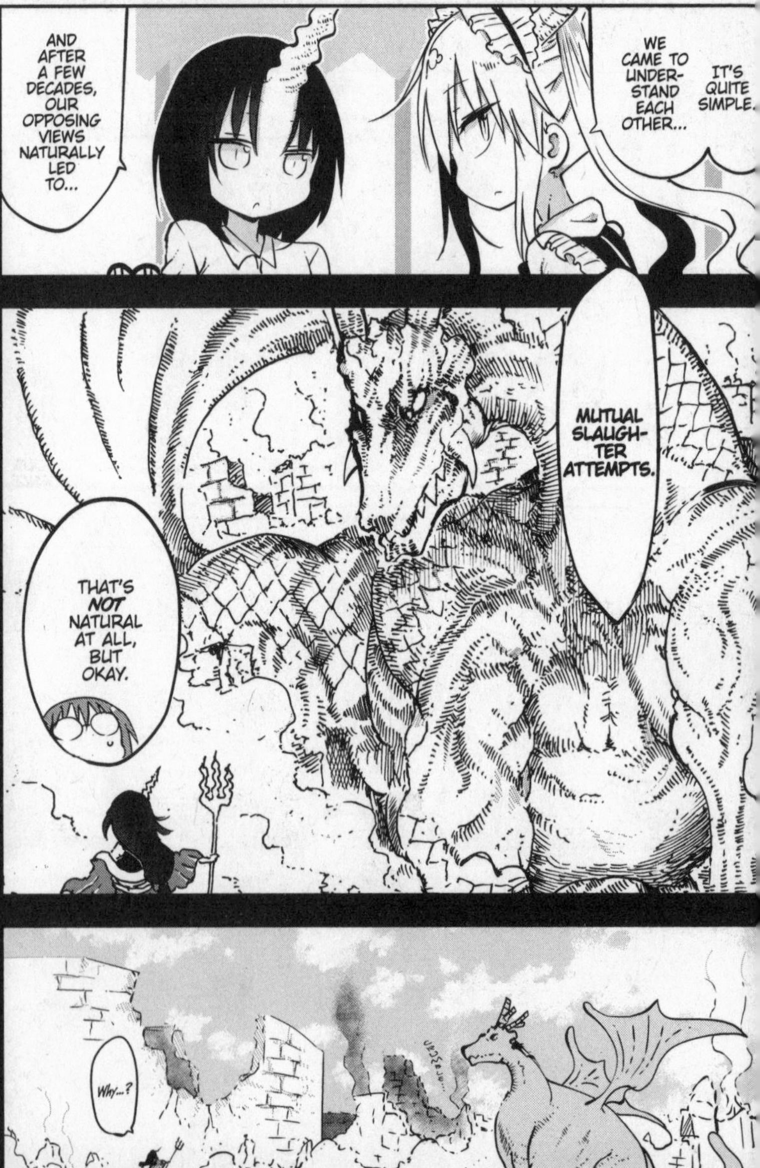
IT'S QUITE SIMPLE.
WE CAME TO UNDER-STAND EACH OTHER...
AND AFTER A FEW DECADES, OUR OPPOSING VIEWS NATURALLY LED TO...
MUTUAL SLAUGH-TER ATTEMPTS.
THAT'S *NOT* NATURAL AT ALL, BUT OKAY.
Why...?

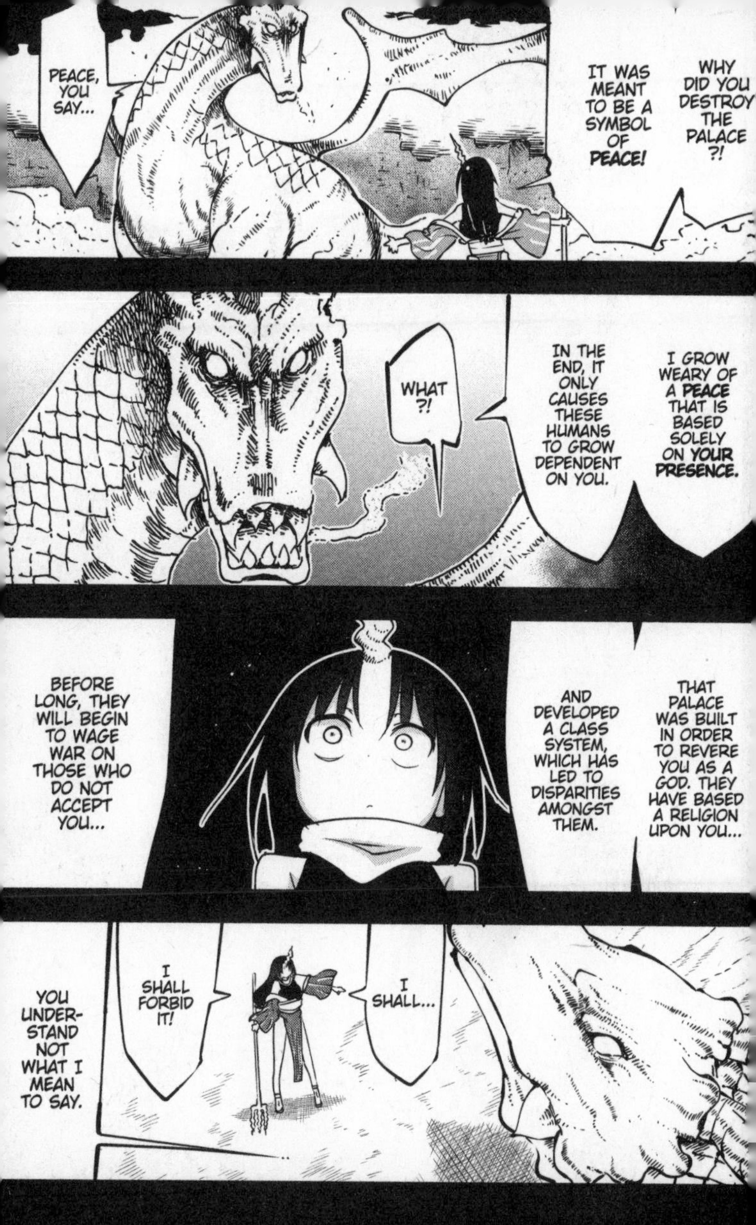
WHY DID YOU DESTROY THE PALACE ?!
IT WAS MEANT TO BE A SYMBOL OF PEACE!
PEACE, YOU SAY...
I GROW WEARY OF A PEACE THAT IS BASED SOLELY ON YOUR PRESENCE.
IN THE END, IT ONLY CAUSES THESE HUMANS TO GROW DEPENDENT ON YOU.
WHAT ?!
THAT PALACE WAS BUILT IN ORDER TO REVERE YOU AS A GOD. THEY HAVE BASED A RELIGION UPON YOU...
AND DEVELOPED A CLASS SYSTEM, WHICH HAS LED TO DISPARITIES AMONGST THEM.
BEFORE LONG, THEY WILL BEGIN TO WAGE WAR ON THOSE WHO DO NOT ACCEPT YOU...
I SHALL...
I SHALL FORBID IT!
YOU UNDER-STAND NOT WHAT I MEAN TO SAY.

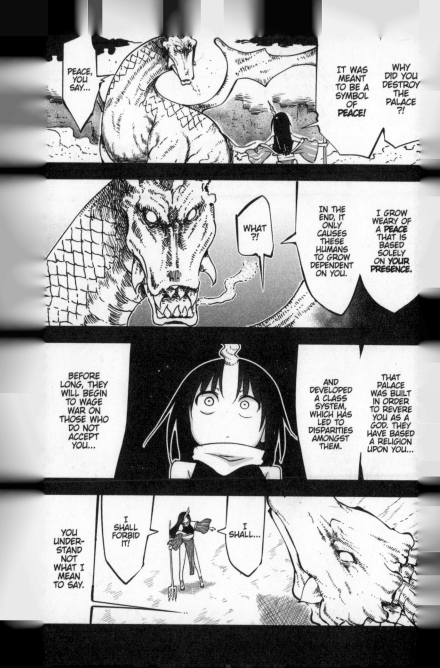

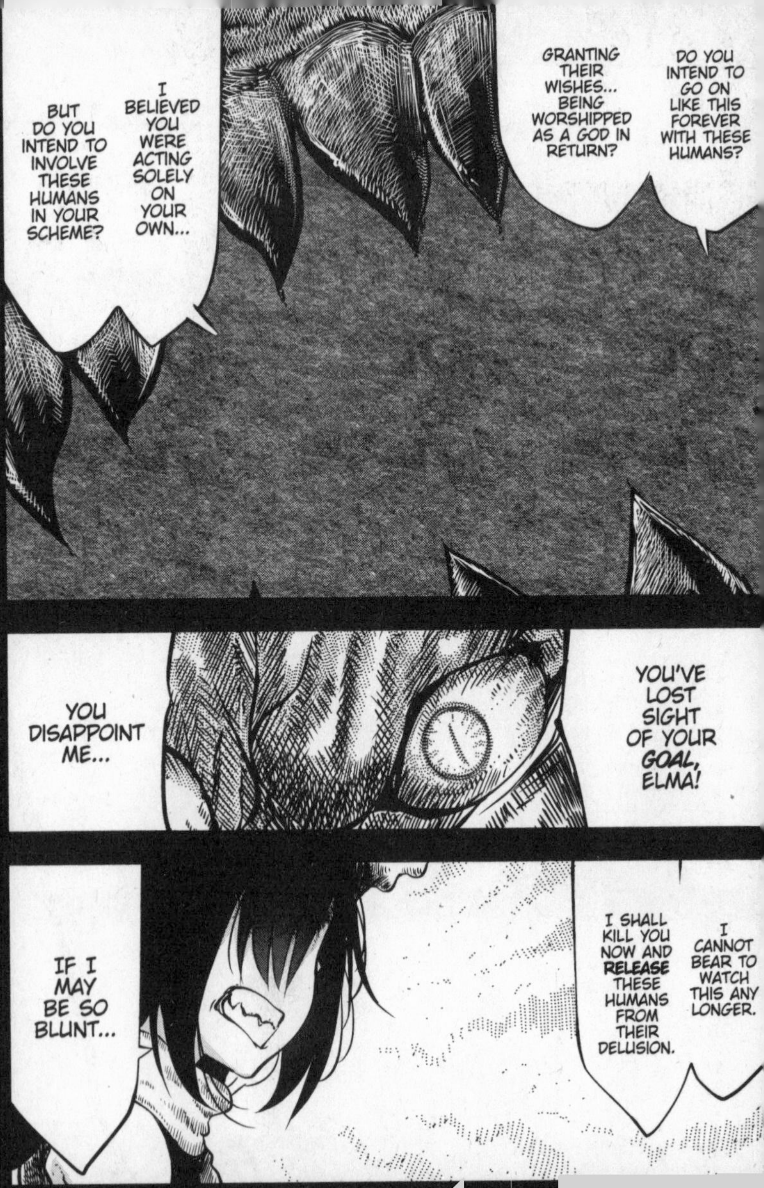
DO YOU INTEND TO GO ON LIKE THIS FOREVER WITH THESE HUMANS?
GRANTING THEIR WISHES... BEING WORSHIPPED AS A GOD IN RETURN?
I BELIEVED YOU WERE ACTING SOLELY ON YOUR OWN...
BUT DO YOU INTEND TO INVOLVE THESE HUMANS IN YOUR SCHEME?
YOU'VE LOST SIGHT OF YOUR **GOAL,** ELMA!
YOU DISAPPOINT ME...
I CANNOT BEAR TO WATCH THIS ANY LONGER.
I SHALL KILL YOU NOW AND **RELEASE** THESE HUMANS FROM THEIR DELUSION.
IF I MAY BE SO BLUNT...

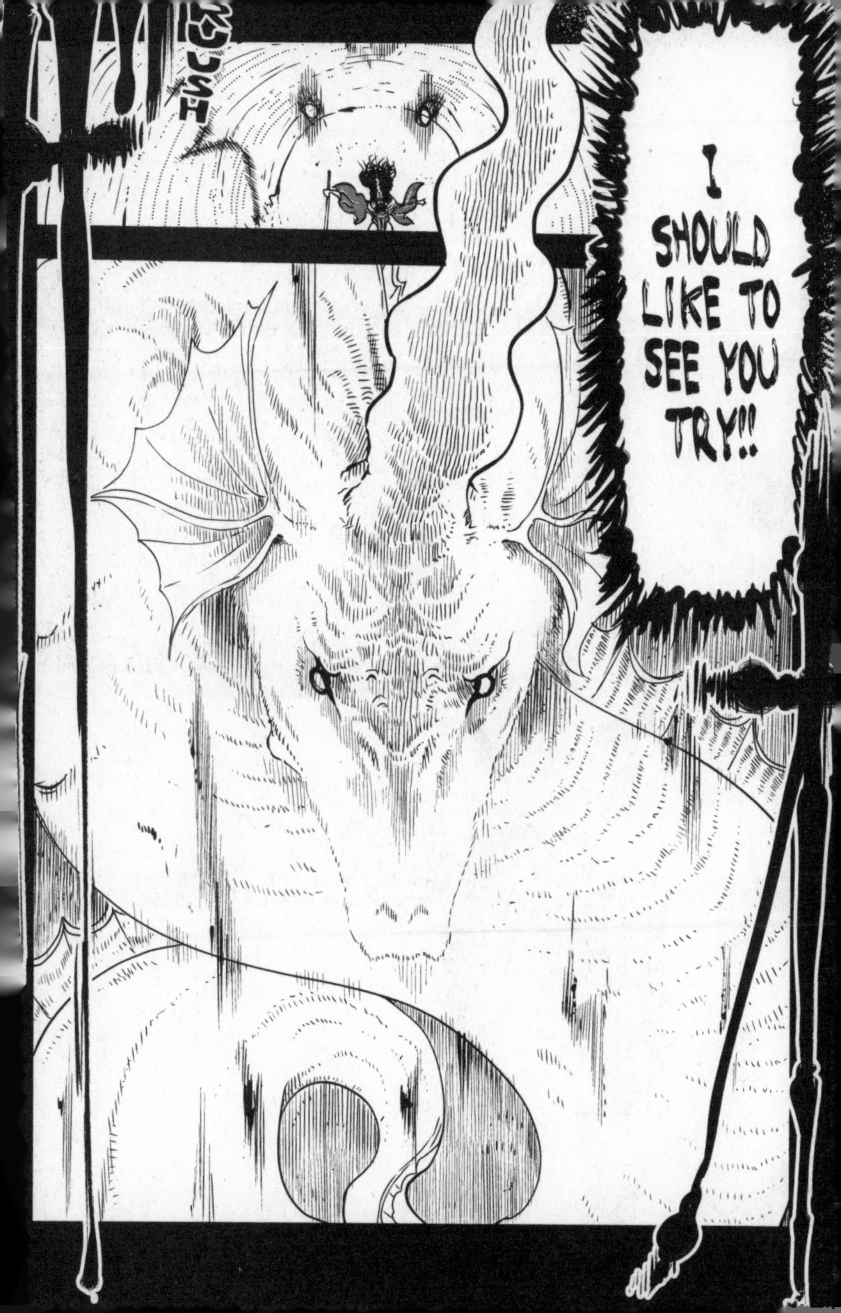
I SHOULD LIKE TO SEE YOU TRY!!

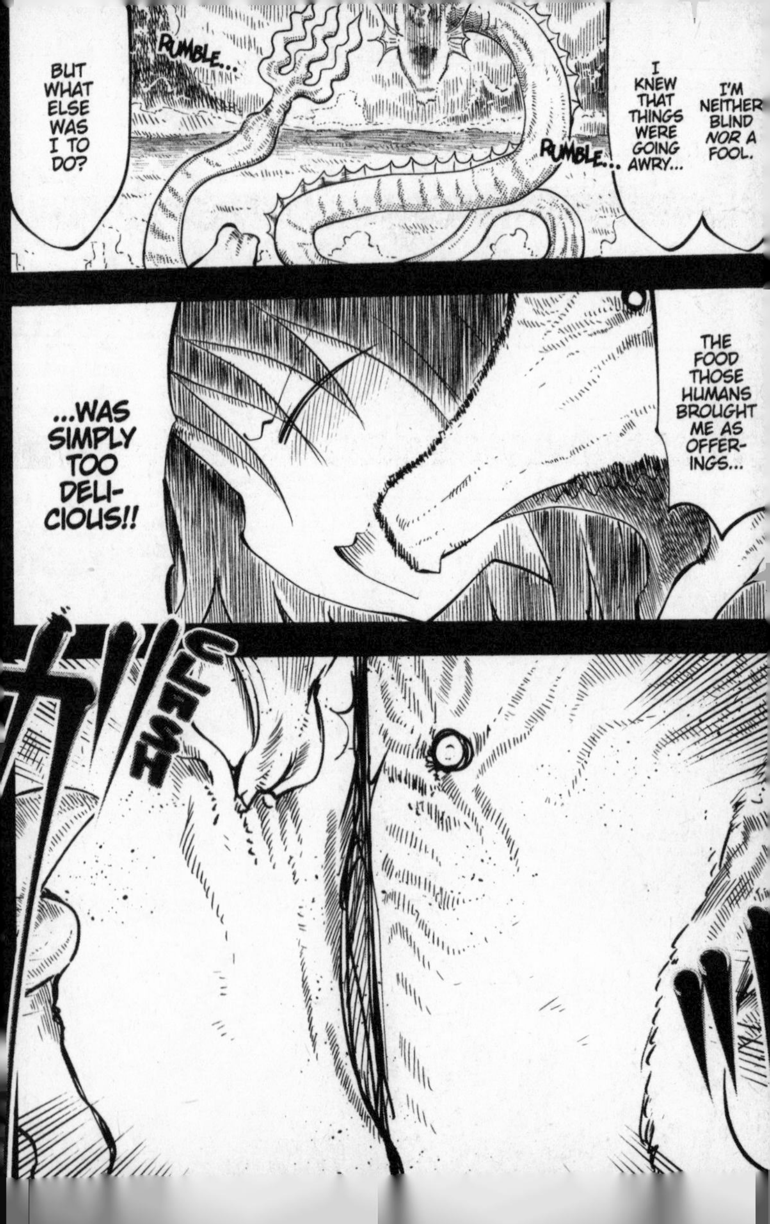
I'M NEITHER BLIND NOR A FOOL.
I KNEW THAT THINGS WERE GOING AWRY...
RUMBLE...
RUMBLE...
BUT WHAT ELSE WAS I TO DO?
THE FOOD THOSE HUMANS BROUGHT ME AS OFFER-INGS...
...WAS SIMPLY TOO DELI-CIOUS!!
CLASH

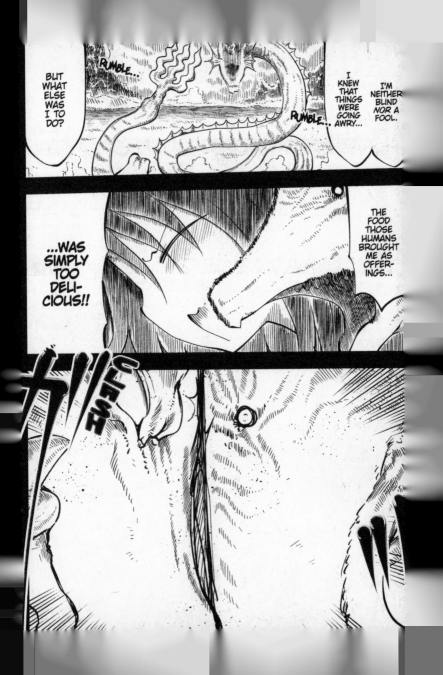

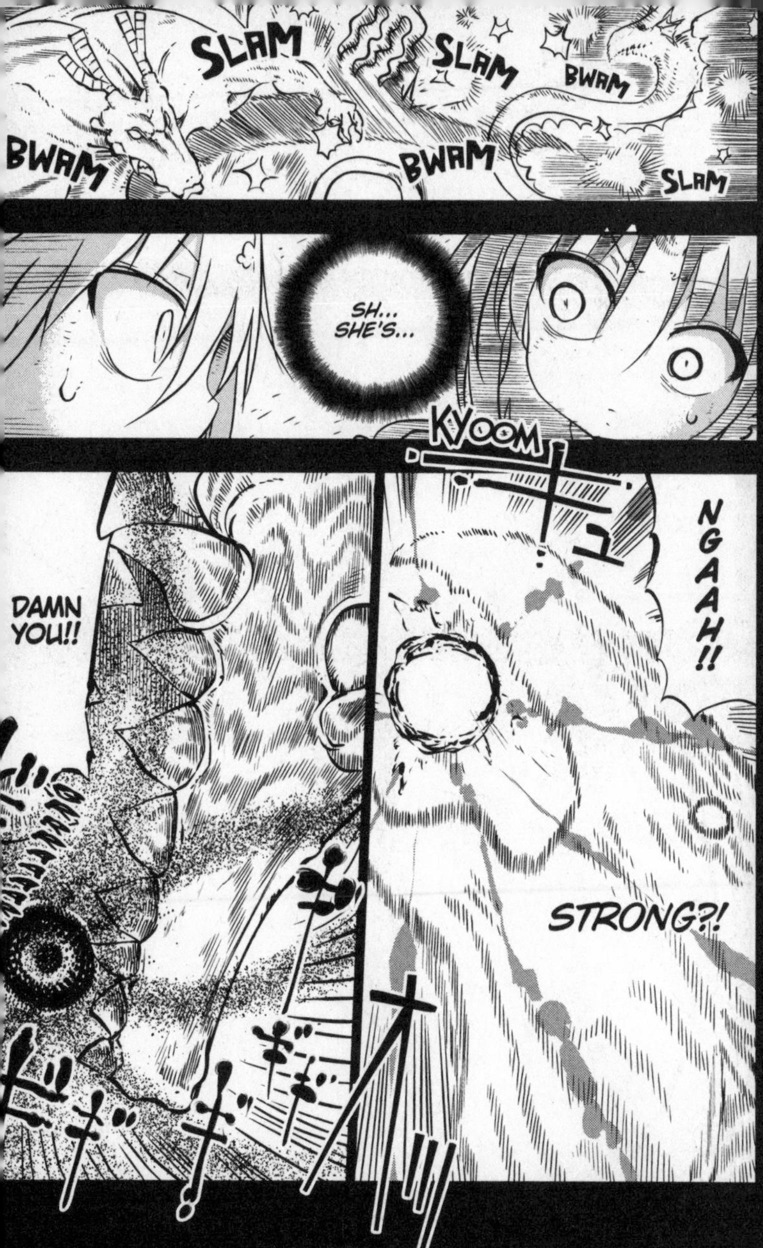
SLAM
BWAM
SLAM
BWAM
SLAM
BWAM
SH... SHE'S...
KYOOM
NGAAH!!
STRONG?!
DAMN YOU!!

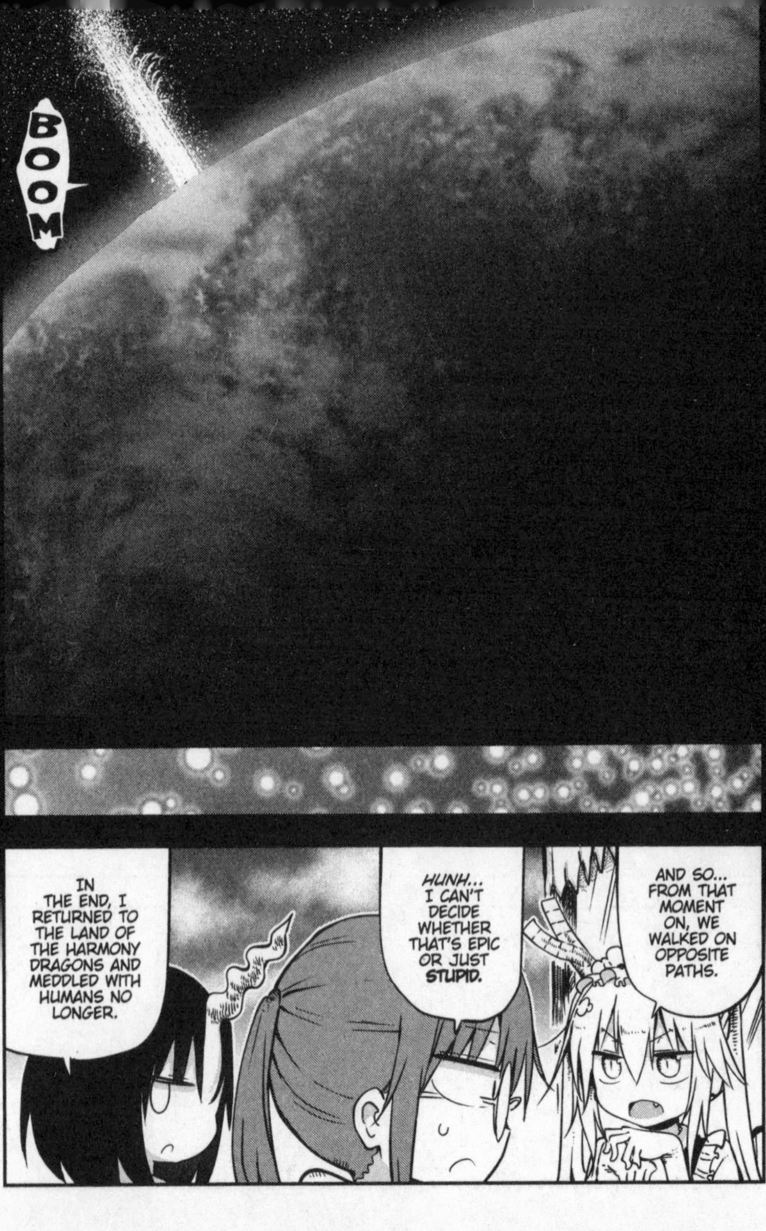
BOOM
AND SO... FROM THAT MOMENT ON, WE WALKED ON OPPOSITE PATHS.
HUNH... I CAN'T DECIDE WHETHER THAT'S EPIC OR JUST STUPID.
IN THE END, I RETURNED TO THE LAND OF THE HARMONY DRAGONS AND MEDDLED WITH HUMANS NO LONGER.

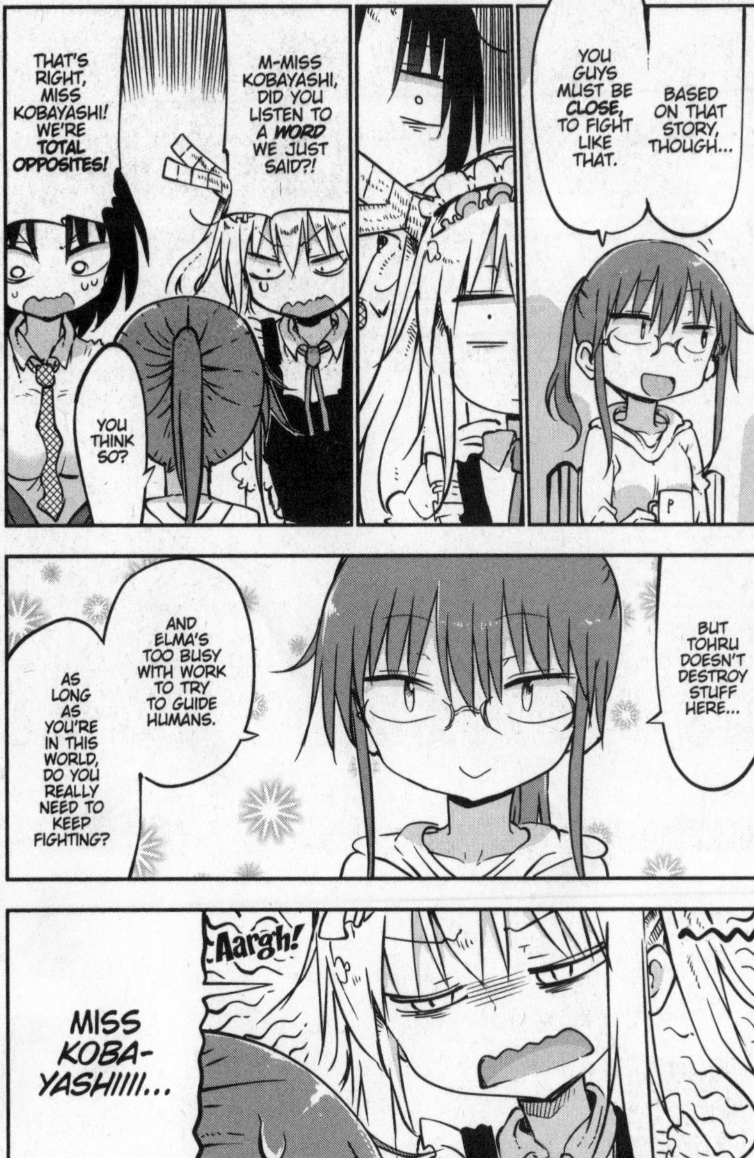
BASED ON THAT STORY, THOUGH...
YOU GUYS MUST BE **CLOSE**, TO FIGHT LIKE THAT.
M-MISS KOBAYASHI, DID YOU LISTEN TO A ***WORD*** WE JUST SAID?!
THAT'S RIGHT, MISS KOBAYASHI! WE'RE **TOTAL OPPOSITES!**
YOU THINK SO?
BUT TOHRU DOESN'T DESTROY STUFF HERE...
AND ELMA'S TOO BUSY WITH WORK TO TRY TO GUIDE HUMANS.
AS LONG AS YOU'RE IN THIS WORLD, DO YOU REALLY NEED TO KEEP FIGHTING?
Aargh!
MISS KOBA-YASHIIIII...

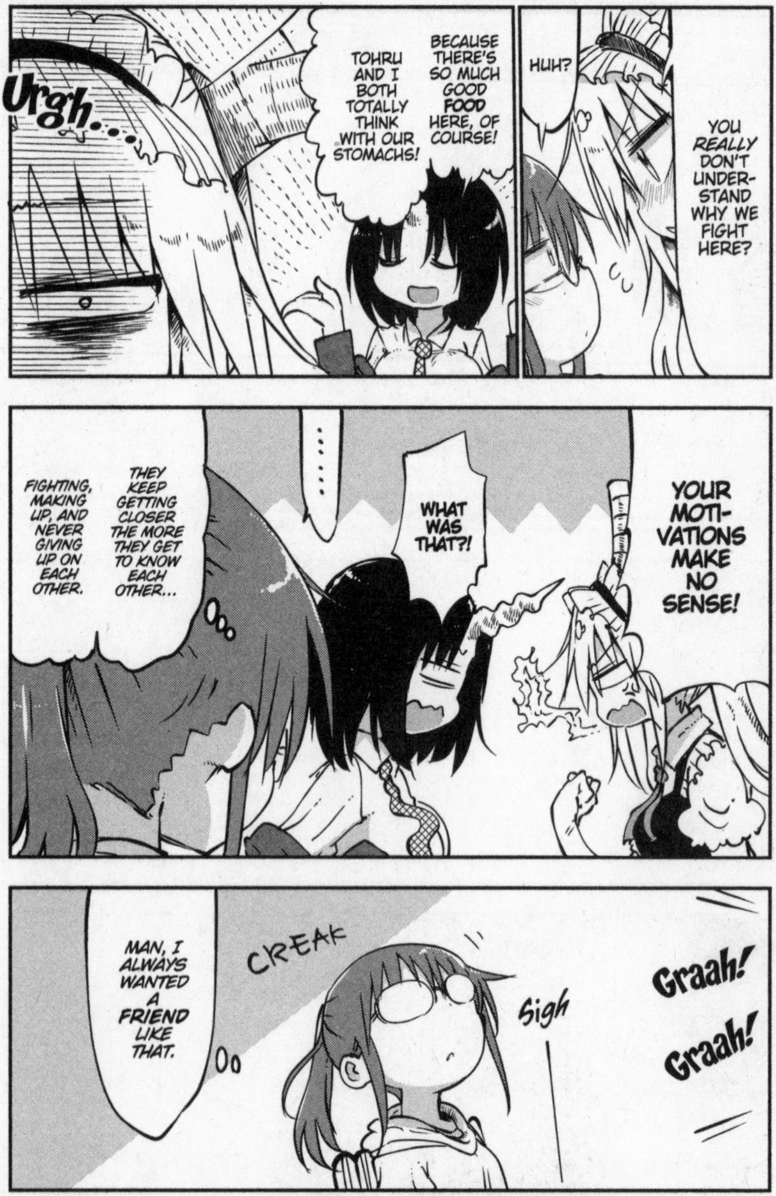
HUH?
YOU REALLY DON'T UNDER-STAND WHY WE FIGHT HERE?
BECAUSE THERE'S SO MUCH GOOD FOOD HERE, OF COURSE!
TOHRU AND I BOTH TOTALLY THINK WITH OUR STOMACHS!
Urgh...
YOUR MOTI-VATIONS MAKE NO SENSE!
WHAT WAS THAT?!
......
THEY KEEP GETTING CLOSER THE MORE THEY GET TO KNOW EACH OTHER...
FIGHTING, MAKING UP, AND NEVER GIVING UP ON EACH OTHER.
Graah!
Graah!
Sigh
CREAK
MAN, I ALWAYS WANTED A FRIEND LIKE THAT.

CHAPTER 44/END

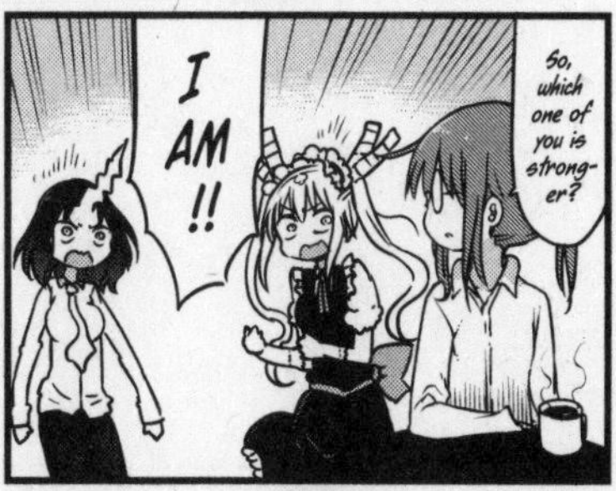
So, which one of you is stronger?
I AM !!

Miss Kobayashi's
Dragon Maid

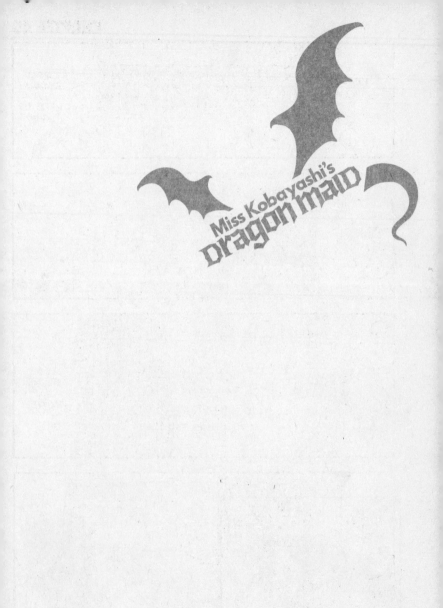

CHAPTER 45

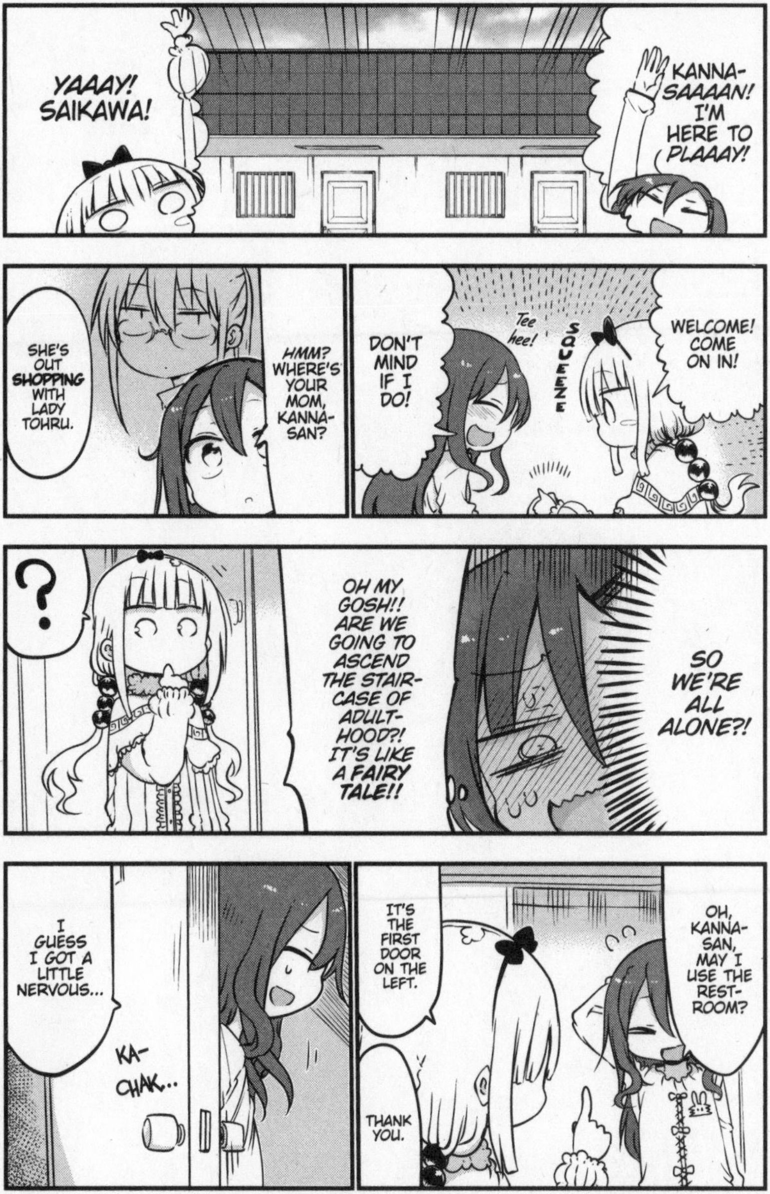

KANNA-SAAAAN! I'M HERE TO PLAAAY!
YAAAY! SAIKAWA!
WELCOME! COME ON IN!
SQUEEZE
Tee hee!
DON'T MIND IF I DO!
HMM? WHERE'S YOUR MOM, KANNA-SAN?
SHE'S OUT SHOPPING WITH LADY TOHRU.
SO WE'RE ALL ALONE?!
OH MY GOSH!! ARE WE GOING TO ASCEND THE STAIR-CASE OF ADULT-HOOD?! IT'S LIKE A FAIRY TALE!!
?
OH, KANNA-SAN, MAY I USE THE REST-ROOM?
IT'S THE FIRST DOOR ON THE LEFT.
THANK YOU.
I GUESS I GOT A LITTLE NERVOUS...
KA-CHAK...

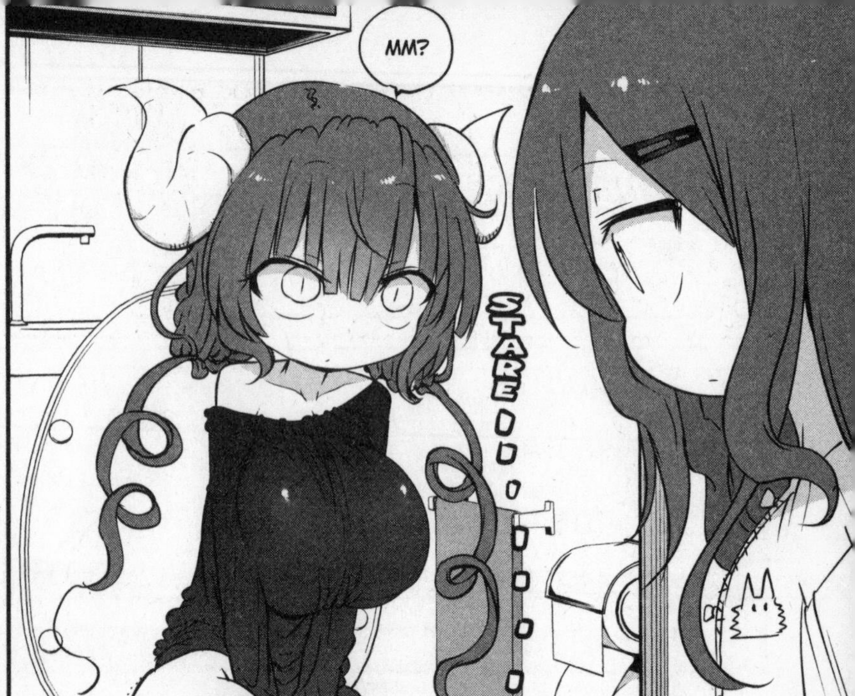
MM?
STARE
CHAPTER 45: ILULU & SAIKAWA

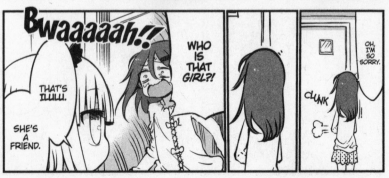

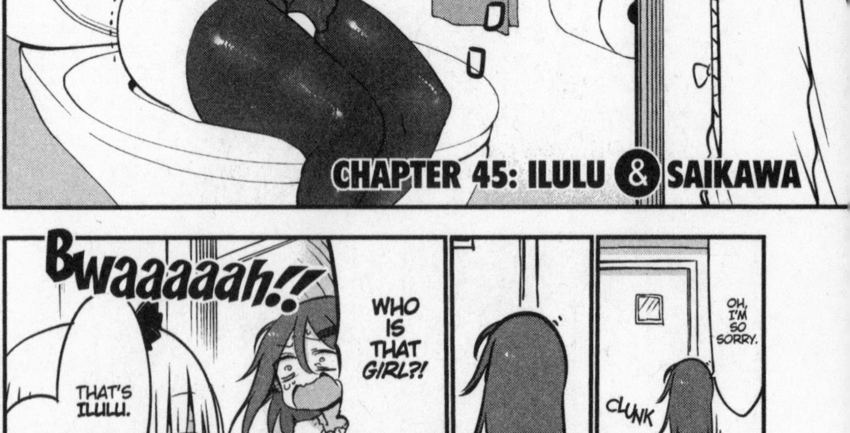
OH, I'M SO SORRY.
CLUNK
Bwaaaaaah!!
WHO IS THAT GIRL?!
THAT'S ILULU.
SHE'S A FRIEND.

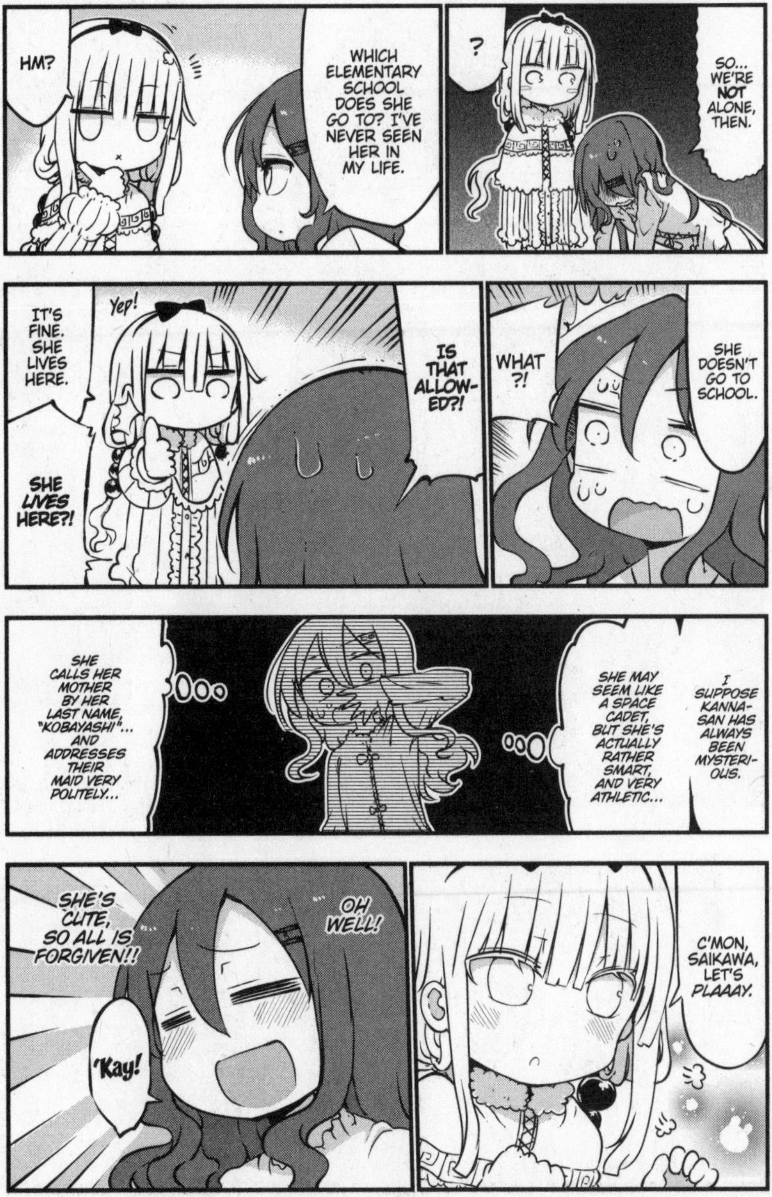
SO... WE'RE NOT ALONE, THEN.
?
WHICH ELEMENTARY SCHOOL DOES SHE GO TO? I'VE NEVER SEEN HER IN MY LIFE.
HM?
SHE DOESN'T GO TO SCHOOL.
WHAT?!
IS THAT ALLOW-ED?!
Yep!
IT'S FINE. SHE LIVES HERE.
SHE LIVES HERE?!
I SUPPOSE KANNA-SAN HAS ALWAYS BEEN MYSTERI-OUS.
SHE MAY SEEM LIKE A SPACE CADET, BUT SHE'S ACTUALLY RATHER SMART, AND VERY ATHLETIC...
SHE CALLS HER MOTHER BY HER LAST NAME, "KOBAYASHI"... AND ADDRESSES THEIR MAID VERY POLITELY...
C'MON, SAIKAWA, LET'S PLAAAY.
OH WELL!
SHE'S CUTE, SO ALL IS FORGIVEN!!
'Kay!

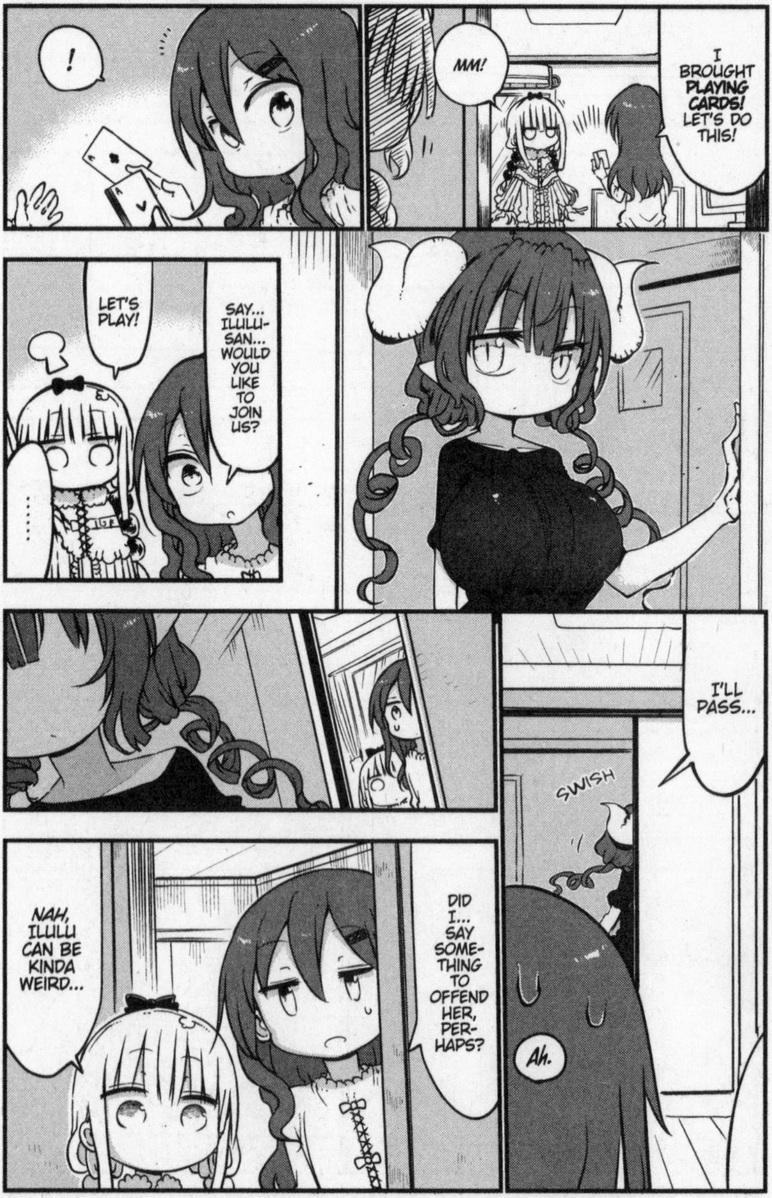
I BROUGHT PLAYING CARDS! LET'S DO THIS!
MM!
!
SAY... ILULU-SAN... WOULD YOU LIKE TO JOIN US?
LET'S PLAY!
......
I'LL PASS...
SWISH
Ah.
DID I... SAY SOMETHING TO OFFEND HER, PERHAPS?
NAH, ILULU CAN BE KINDA WEIRD...

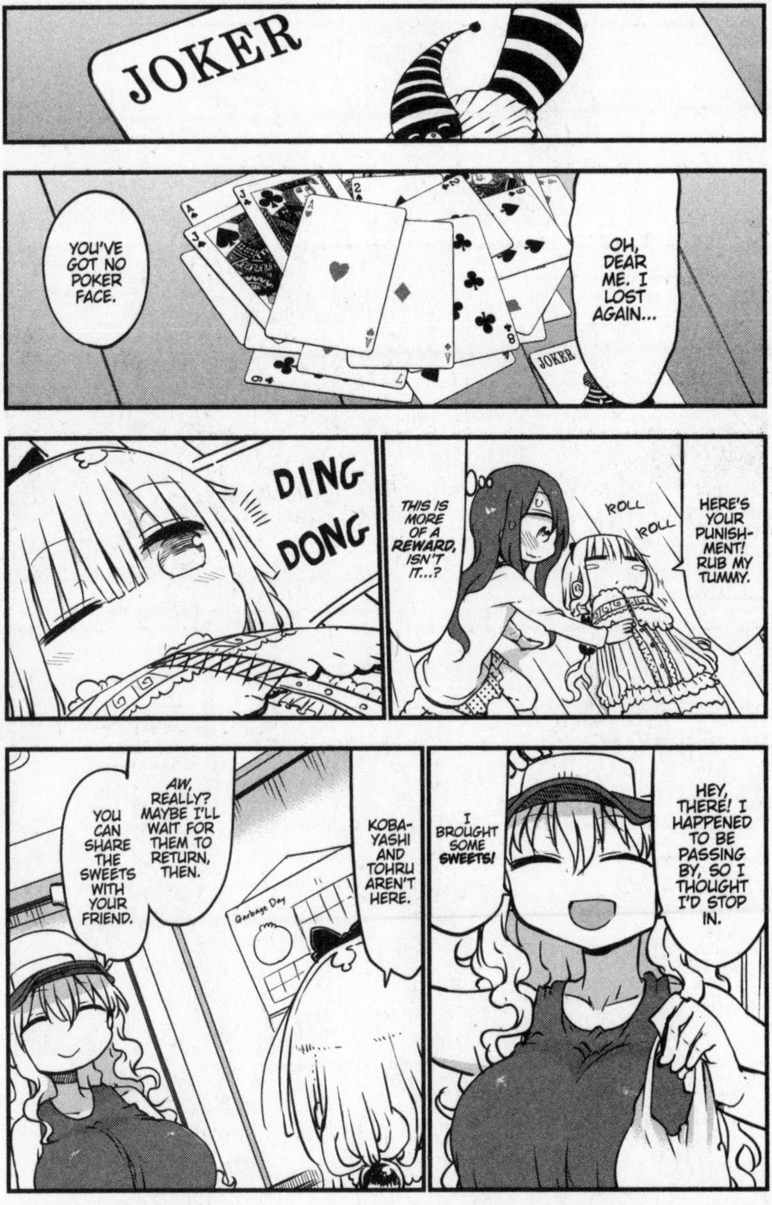
JOKER
OH, DEAR ME. I LOST AGAIN...
JOKER
YOU'VE GOT NO POKER FACE.
HERE'S YOUR PUNISHMENT! RUB MY TUMMY.
ROLL
ROLL
THIS IS MORE OF A REWARD, ISN'T IT...?
DING DONG
HEY, THERE! I HAPPENED TO BE PASSING BY, SO I THOUGHT I'D STOP IN.
I BROUGHT SOME SWEETS!
KOBAYASHI AND TOHRU AREN'T HERE.
Garbage Day
AW, REALLY? MAYBE I'LL WAIT FOR THEM TO RETURN, THEN.
YOU CAN SHARE THE SWEETS WITH YOUR FRIEND.

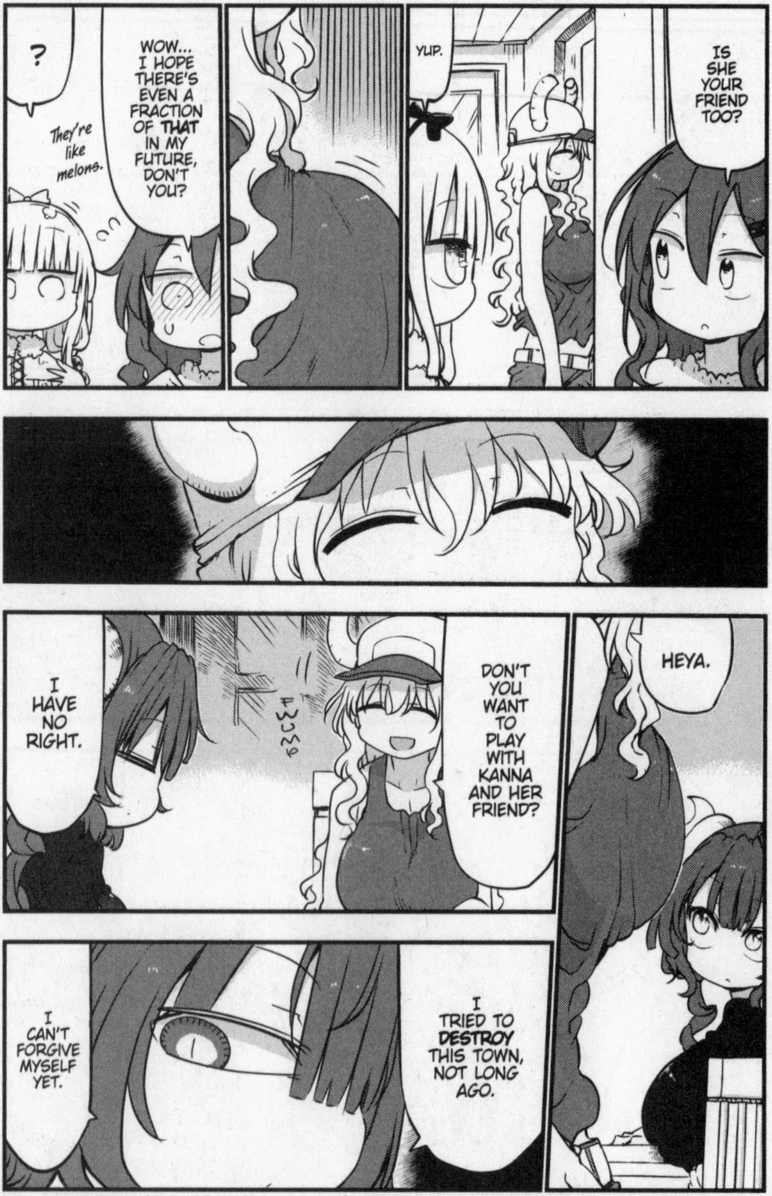
IS SHE YOUR FRIEND TOO?
YUP.
WOW... I HOPE THERE'S EVEN A FRACTION OF THAT IN MY FUTURE, DON'T YOU?
?
They're like melons.
HEYA.
DON'T YOU WANT TO PLAY WITH KANNA AND HER FRIEND?
FWUMP
I HAVE NO RIGHT.
I TRIED TO DESTROY THIS TOWN, NOT LONG AGO.
I CAN'T FORGIVE MYSELF YET.

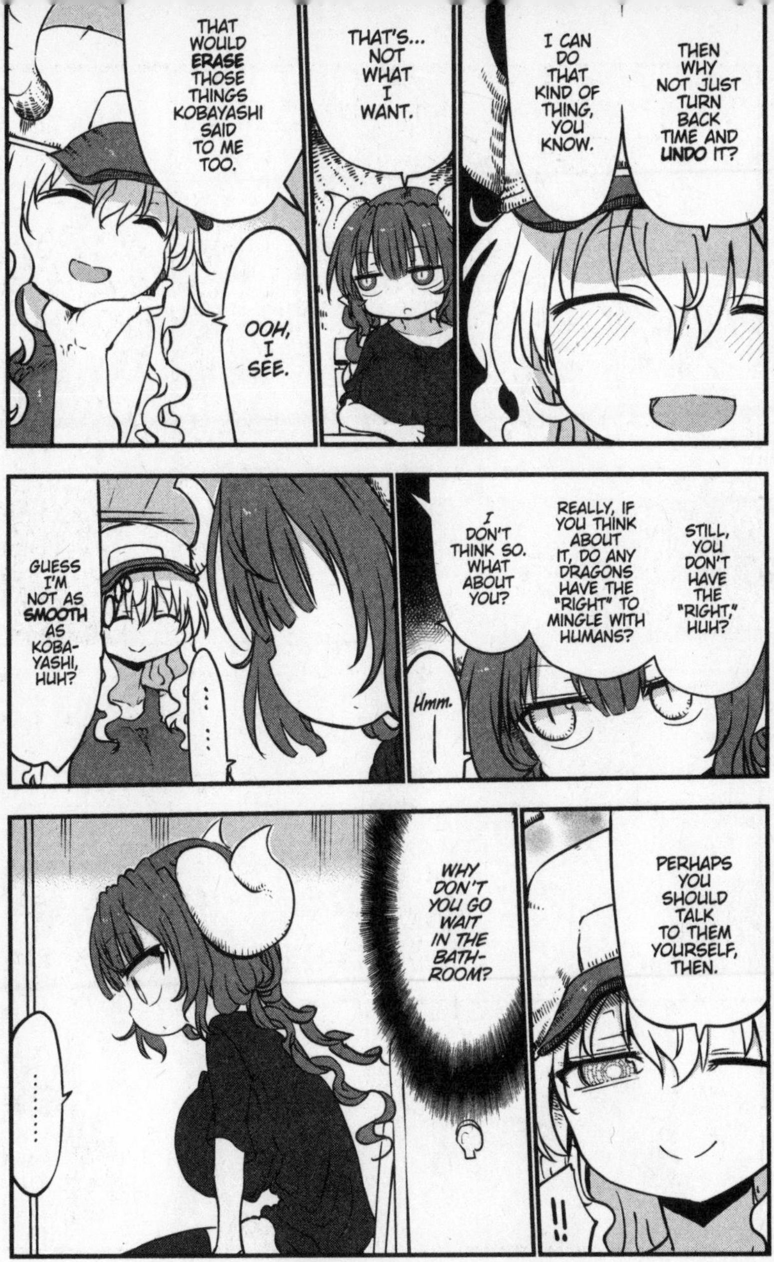
THEN WHY NOT JUST TURN BACK TIME AND UNDO IT?
I CAN DO THAT KIND OF THING, YOU KNOW.
THAT'S... NOT WHAT I WANT.
THAT WOULD ERASE THOSE THINGS KOBAYASHI SAID TO ME TOO.
OOH, I SEE.
STILL, YOU DON'T HAVE THE "RIGHT," HUH?
REALLY, IF YOU THINK ABOUT IT, DO ANY DRAGONS HAVE THE "RIGHT" TO MINGLE WITH HUMANS?
I DON'T THINK SO. WHAT ABOUT YOU?
Hmm.
GUESS I'M NOT AS SMOOTH AS KOBAYASHI, HUH?
......
PERHAPS YOU SHOULD TALK TO THEM YOURSELF, THEN.
!!
WHY DON'T YOU GO WAIT IN THE BATHROOM?
......

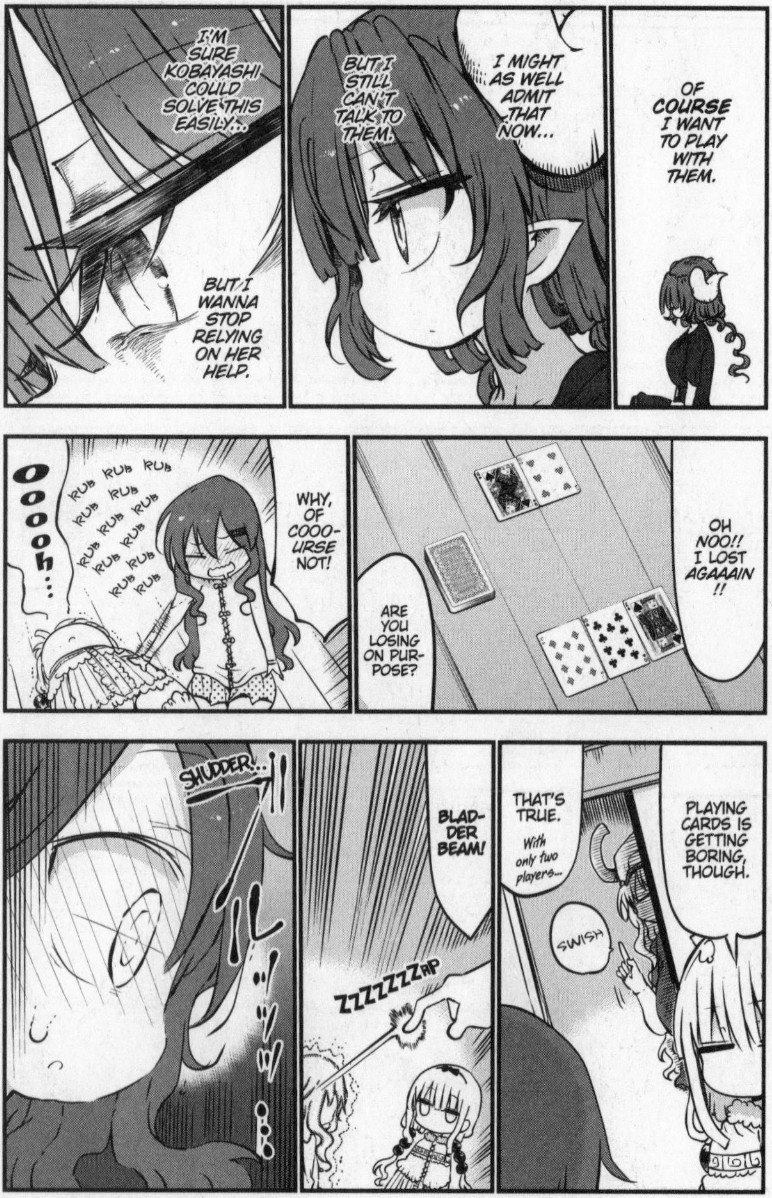
OF COURSE I WANT TO PLAY WITH THEM.
I MIGHT AS WELL ADMIT THAT NOW...
BUT I STILL CAN'T TALK TO THEM.
I'M SURE KOBAYASHI COULD SOLVE THIS EASILY...
BUT I WANNA STOP RELYING ON HER HELP.
OH NOO!! I LOST AGAAAIN!!
ARE YOU LOSING ON PURPOSE?
WHY, OF COOOURSE NOT!
RUB RUB RUB RUB RUB RUB RUB RUB RUB RUB RUB RUB RUB
Ooooh...
PLAYING CARDS IS GETTING BORING, THOUGH.
THAT'S TRUE.
With only two players...
SWISH
BLADDER BEAM!
ZZZZZZZRP
SHUDDER...!!

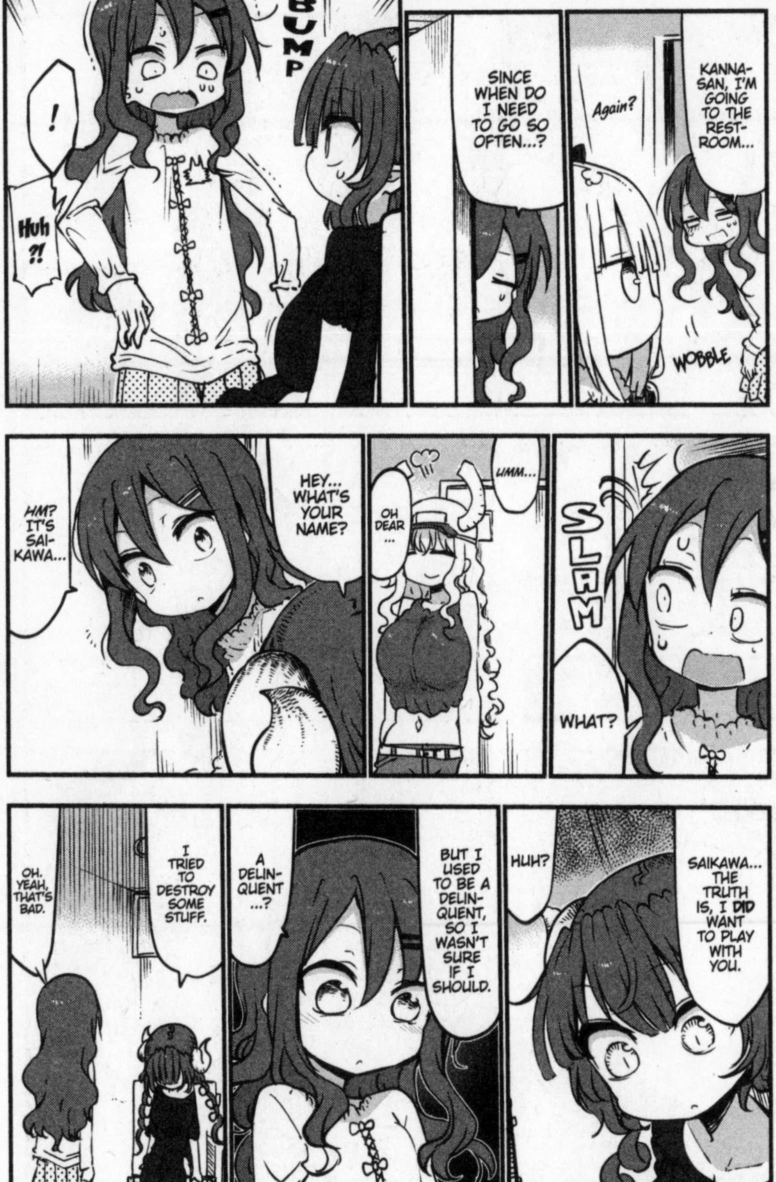
KANNA-SAN, I'M GOING TO THE REST-ROOM...
Again?
WOBBLE
SINCE WHEN DO I NEED TO GO SO OFTEN...?
BUMP
!
Huh ?!
SLAM
WHAT?
UMM...
OH DEAR ...
HEY... WHAT'S YOUR NAME?
HM? IT'S SAI-KAWA...
SAIKAWA... THE TRUTH IS, I DID WANT TO PLAY WITH YOU.
HUH?
BUT I USED TO BE A DELIN-QUENT, SO I WASN'T SURE IF I SHOULD.
A DELIN-QUENT ...?
I TRIED TO DESTROY SOME STUFF.
OH. YEAH, THAT'S BAD.

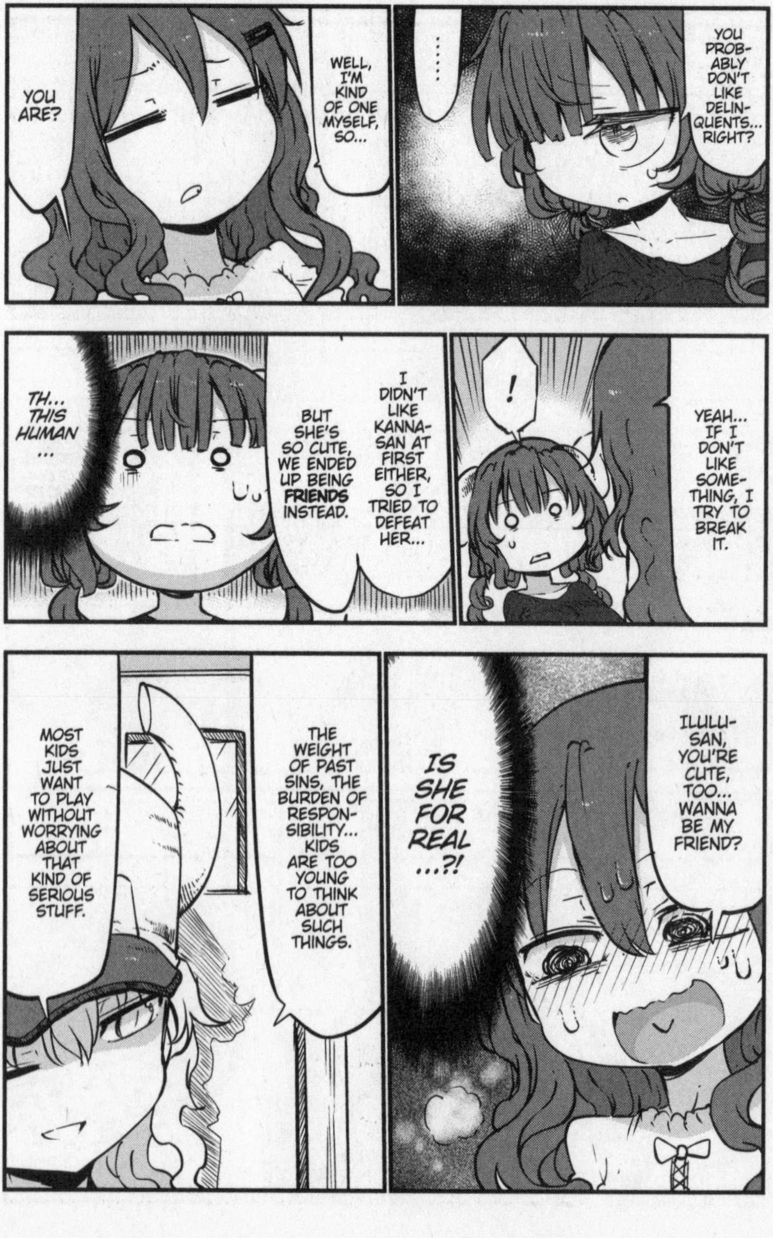
YOU PROBABLY DON'T LIKE DELINQUENTS... RIGHT?
......
WELL, I'M KIND OF ONE MYSELF, SO...
YOU ARE?
YEAH... IF I DON'T LIKE SOMETHING, I TRY TO BREAK IT.
!
I DIDN'T LIKE KANNA-SAN AT FIRST EITHER, SO I TRIED TO DEFEAT HER...
BUT SHE'S SO CUTE, WE ENDED UP BEING **FRIENDS** INSTEAD.
TH... THIS HUMAN...
ILULU-SAN, YOU'RE CUTE, TOO... WANNA BE MY FRIEND?
IS SHE FOR REAL...?!
THE WEIGHT OF PAST SINS, THE BURDEN OF RESPONSIBILITY... KIDS ARE TOO YOUNG TO THINK ABOUT SUCH THINGS.
MOST KIDS JUST WANT TO PLAY WITHOUT WORRYING ABOUT THAT KIND OF SERIOUS STUFF.

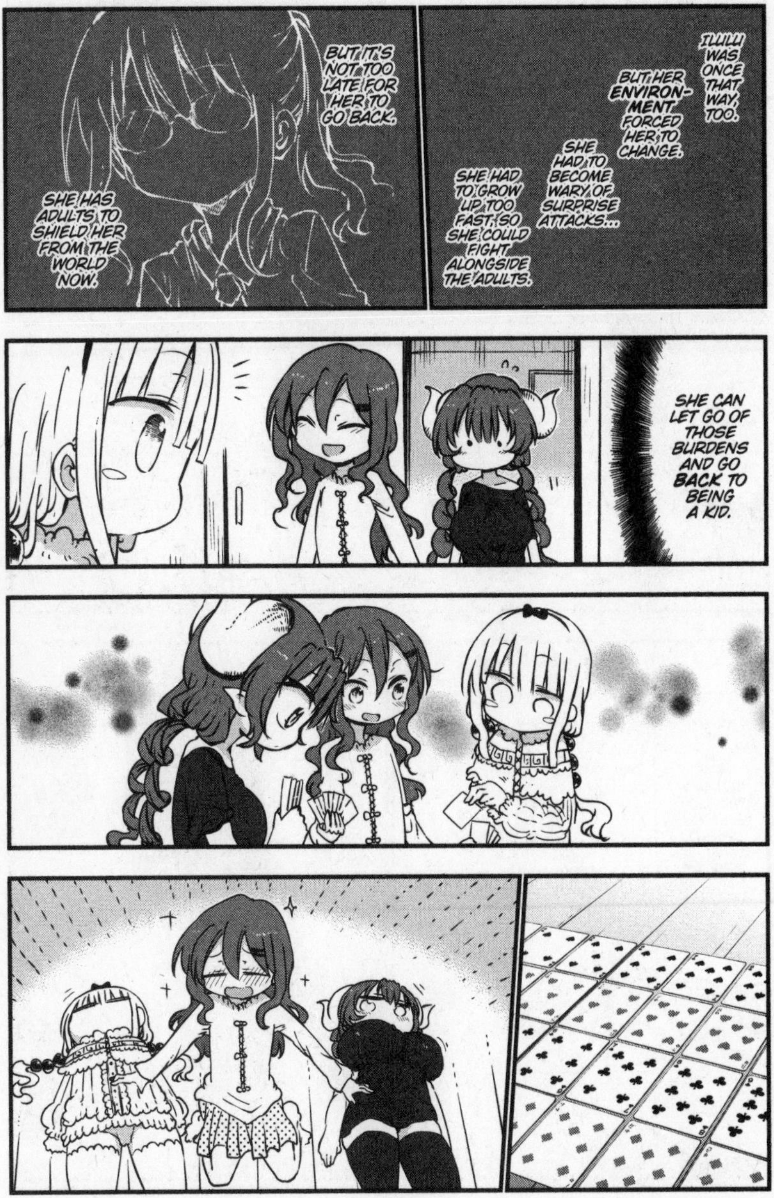
ILULU WAS ONCE THAT WAY, TOO.
BUT HER ENVIRONMENT FORCED HER TO CHANGE.
SHE HAD TO BECOME WARY OF SURPRISE ATTACKS...
SHE HAD TO GROW UP TOO FAST, SO SHE COULD FIGHT ALONGSIDE THE ADULTS.
BUT IT'S NOT TOO LATE FOR HER TO GO BACK.
SHE HAS ADULTS TO SHIELD HER FROM THE WORLD NOW.
SHE CAN LET GO OF THOSE BURDENS AND GO BACK TO BEING A KID.

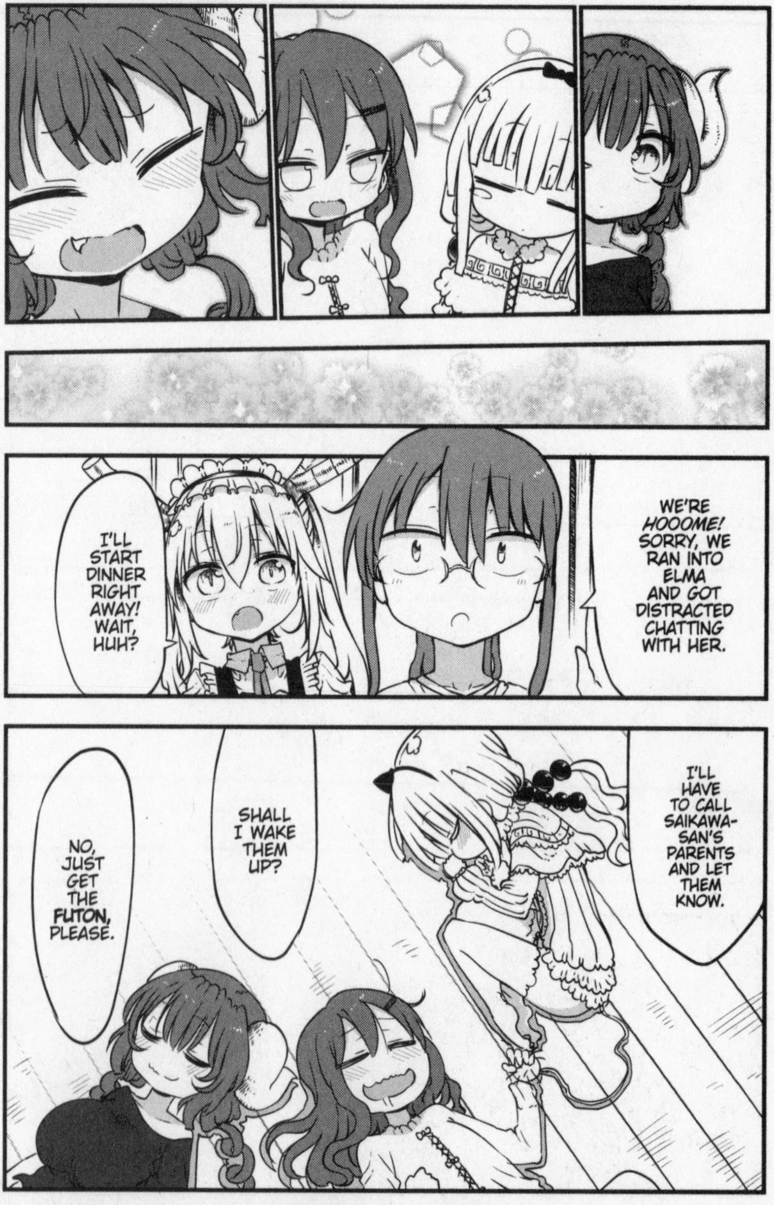
WE'RE *HOOOME!* SORRY, WE RAN INTO ELMA AND GOT DISTRACTED CHATTING WITH HER.
I'LL START DINNER RIGHT AWAY! WAIT, HUH?
I'LL HAVE TO CALL SAIKAWA-SAN'S PARENTS AND LET THEM KNOW.
SHALL I WAKE THEM UP?
NO, JUST GET THE FUTON, PLEASE.

CHAPTER 45/END

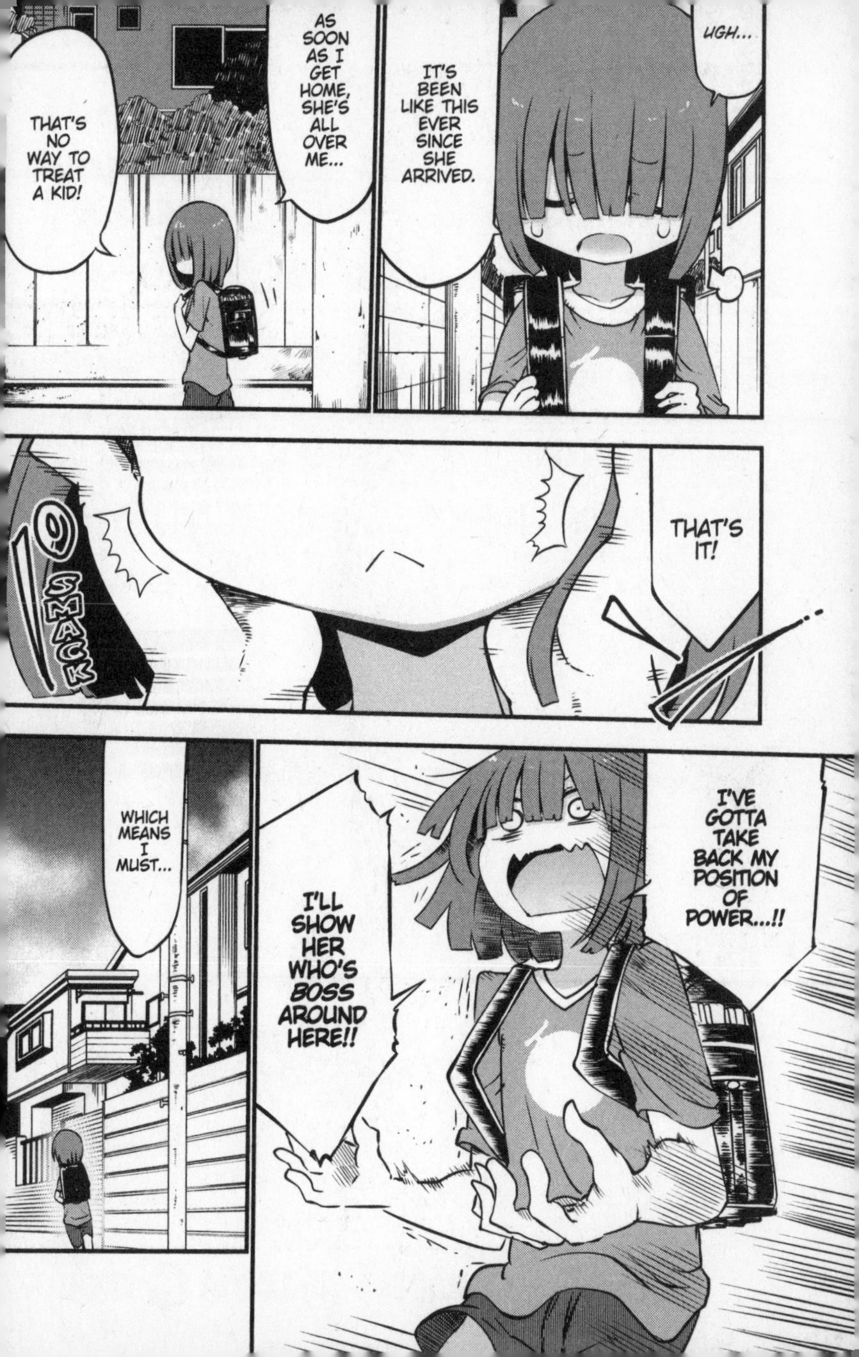
UGH...
IT'S BEEN LIKE THIS EVER SINCE SHE ARRIVED.
AS SOON AS I GET HOME, SHE'S ALL OVER ME...
THAT'S NO WAY TO TREAT A KID!
THAT'S IT!
SMACK
I'VE GOTTA TAKE BACK MY POSITION OF POWER...!!
I'LL SHOW HER WHO'S *BOSS* AROUND HERE!!
WHICH MEANS I MUST...

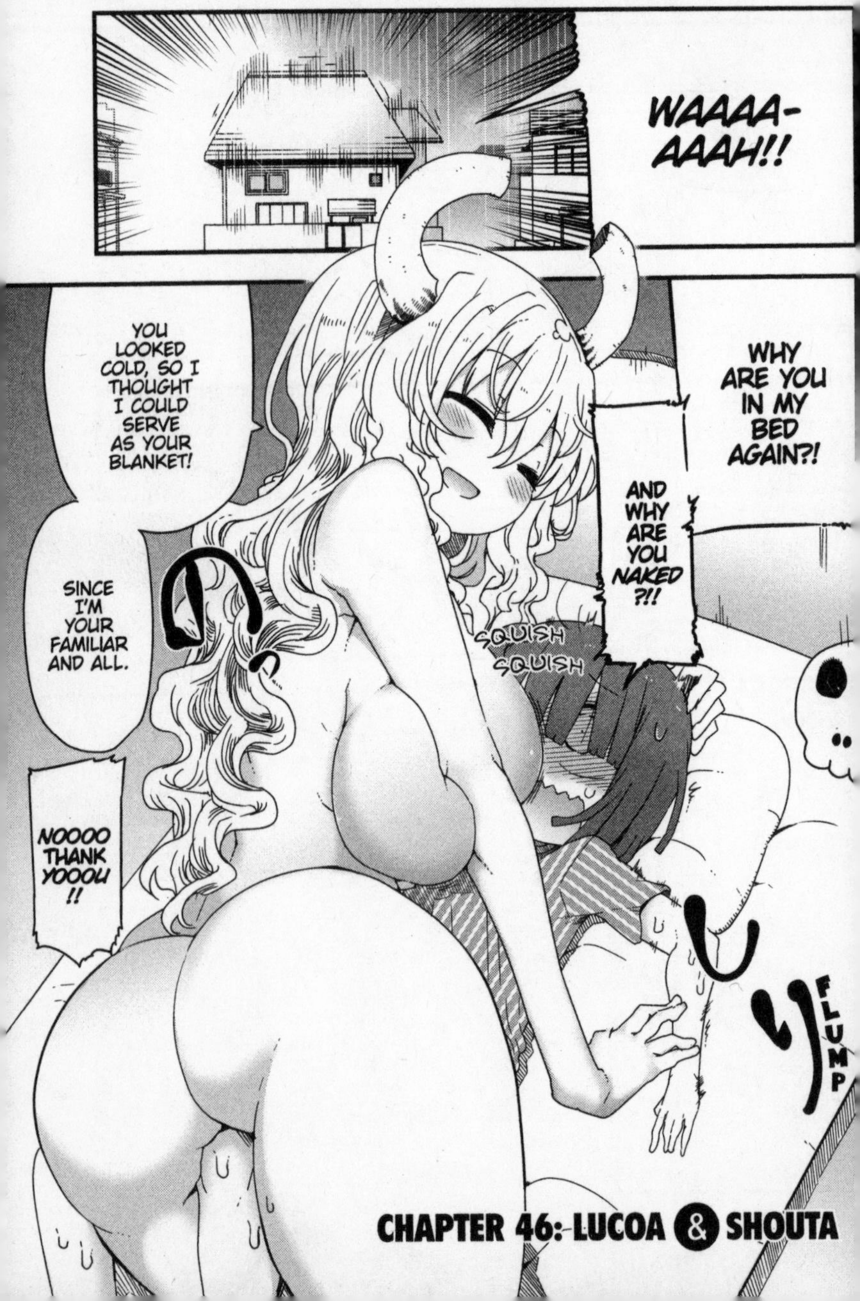
WAAAA-AAAH!!
WHY ARE YOU IN MY BED AGAIN?!
AND WHY ARE YOU NAKED?!!
SQUISH SQUISH
YOU LOOKED COLD, SO I THOUGHT I COULD SERVE AS YOUR BLANKET!
SINCE I'M YOUR FAMILIAR AND ALL.
NOOOO THANK YOOOU!!
FLUMP

CHAPTER 46: LUCOA & SHOUTA

Miss Kobayashi's
Dragon Maid

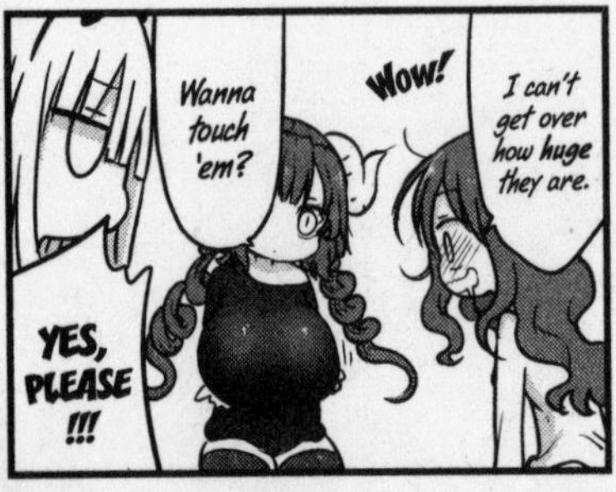
I can't get over how huge they are.
WOW!
Wanna touch 'em?
YES, PLEASE!!!

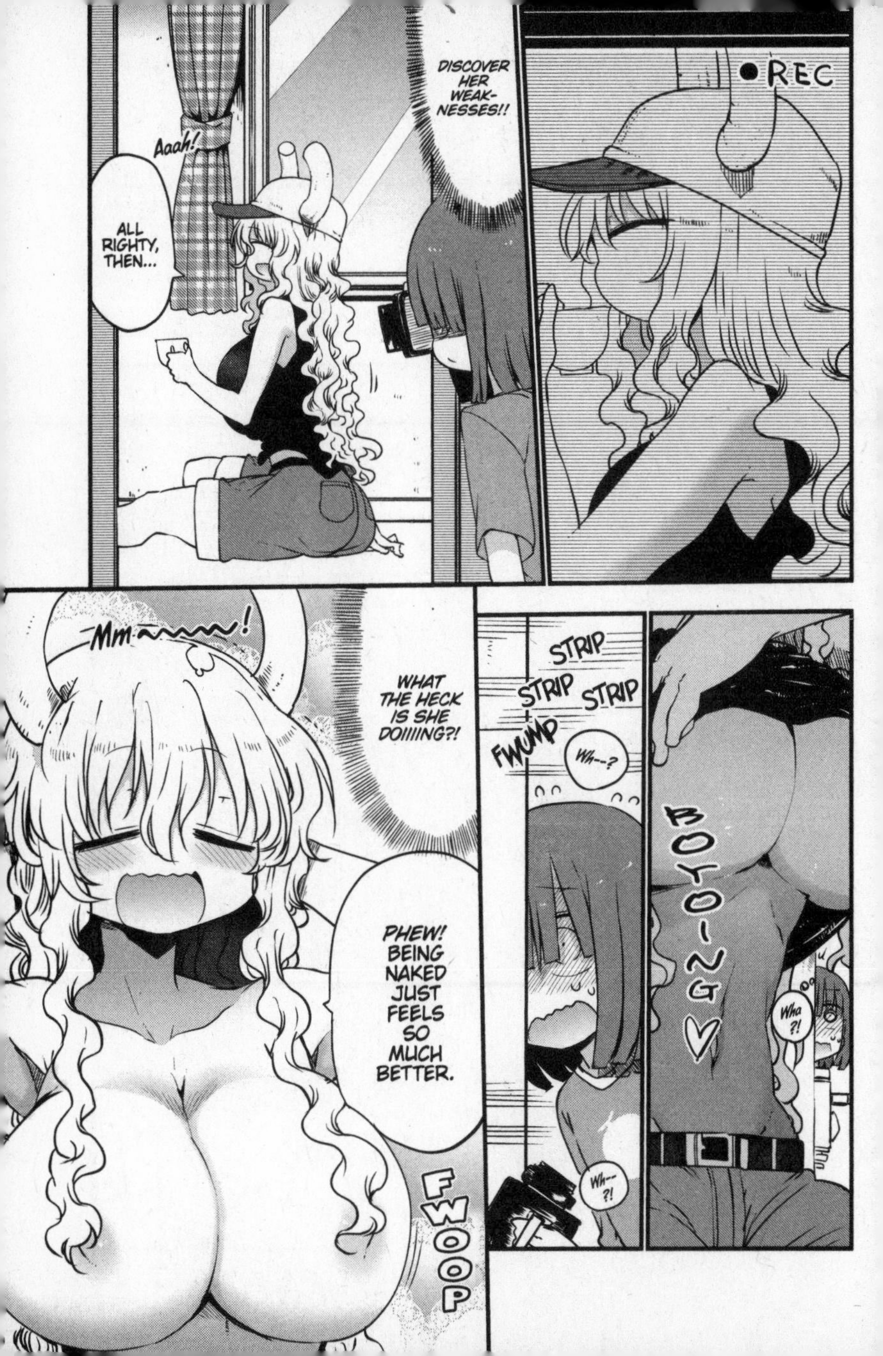

●REC
DISCOVER HER WEAK-NESSES!!
Aaah!
ALL RIGHTY, THEN...
BOYOING ♥
Wha ?!
Wh-- ?!
STRIP
STRIP STRIP
FWUMP
Wh--?
Mm~~~!
WHAT THE HECK IS SHE DOIIIING?!
PHEW! BEING NAKED JUST FEELS SO MUCH BETTER.
FWOOP

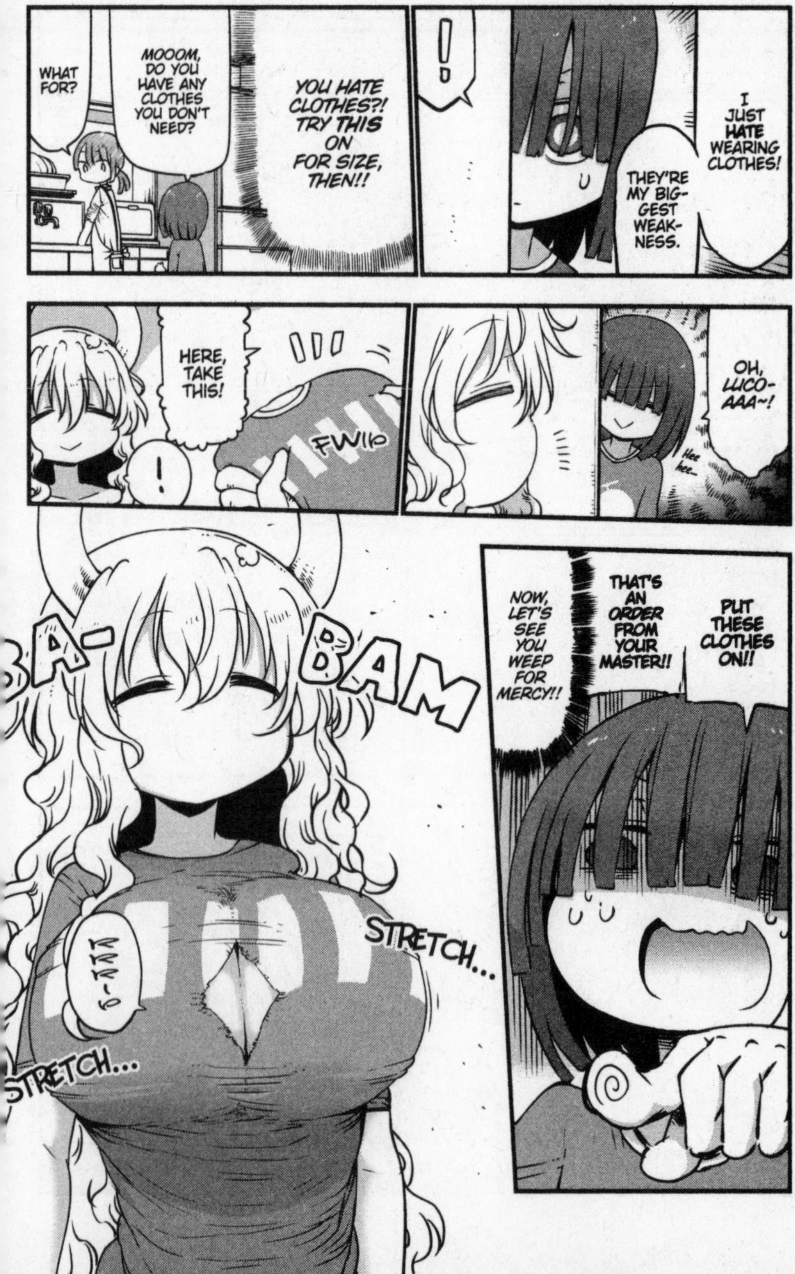
I JUST HATE WEARING CLOTHES!
THEY'RE MY BIG-GEST WEAK-NESS.
!
YOU HATE CLOTHES?! TRY THIS ON FOR SIZE, THEN!!
MOOOM, DO YOU HAVE ANY CLOTHES YOU DON'T NEED?
WHAT FOR?
OH, LUCO-AAA~!
Hee hee...
HERE, TAKE THIS!
FWIP
!
PUT THESE CLOTHES ON!!
THAT'S AN ORDER FROM YOUR MASTER!!
NOW, LET'S SEE YOU WEEP FOR MERCY!!
BA-BAM
STRETCH...
STRETCH...

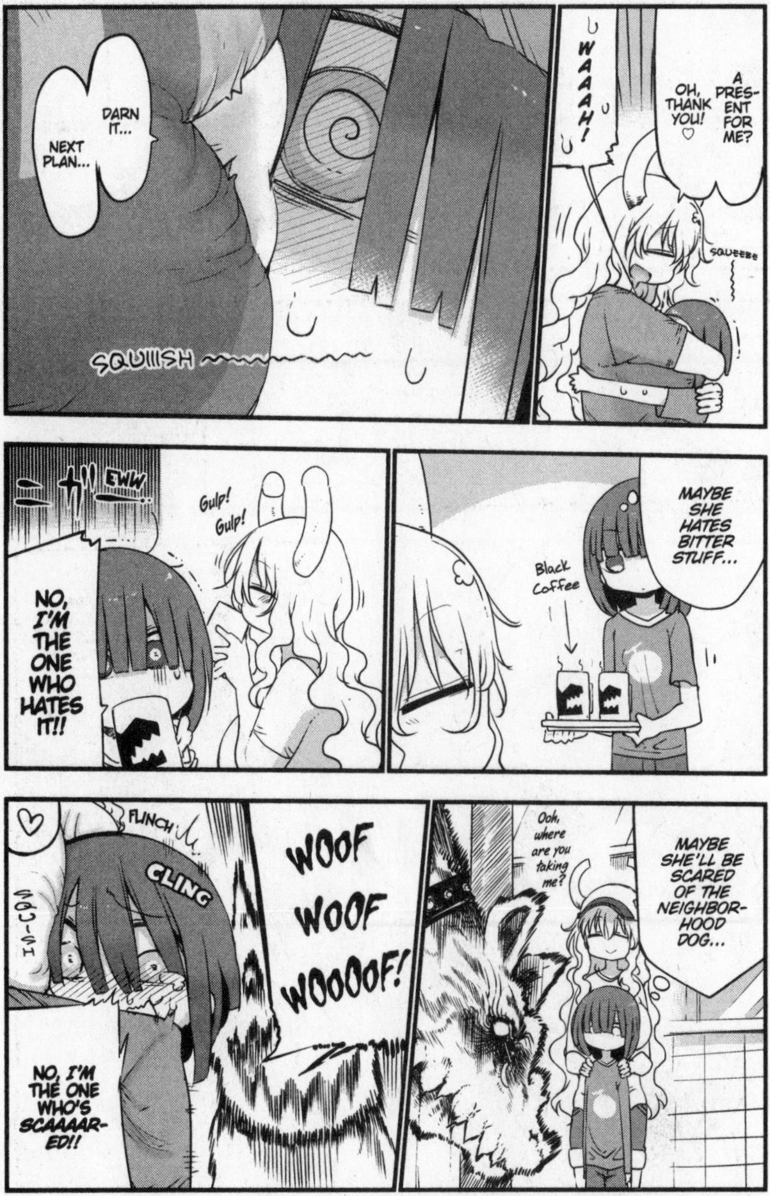
A PRESENT FOR ME?
OH, THANK YOU! ♡
WAAAAH!
SQUEEEE
SQUIIISH
DARN IT... NEXT PLAN...
MAYBE SHE HATES BITTER STUFF...
Black Coffee
Gulp! Gulp!
EWW
NO, I'M THE ONE WHO HATES IT!!
MAYBE SHE'LL BE SCARED OF THE NEIGHBORHOOD DOG...
Ooh, where are you taking me?
WOOF WOOF WOOOOF!
FLINCH
CLING
SQUISH
NO, I'M THE ONE WHO'S SCAAAARED!!

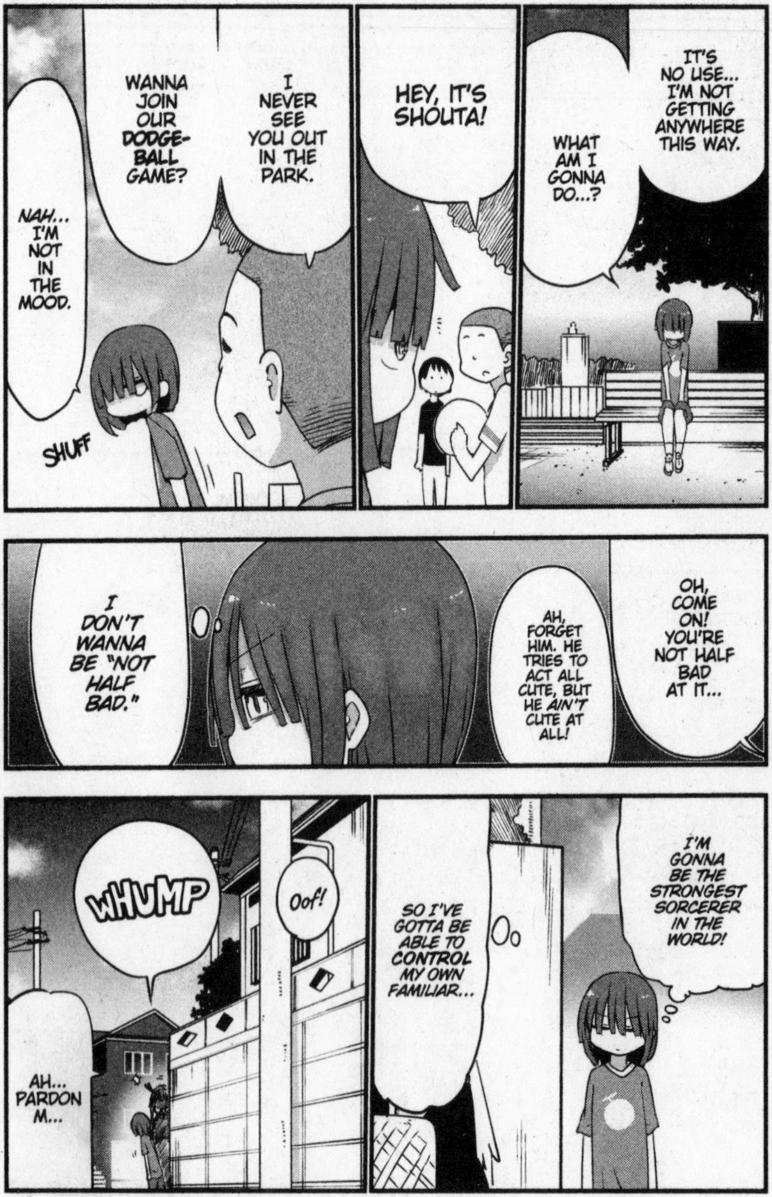
IT'S NO USE... I'M NOT GETTING ANYWHERE THIS WAY.
WHAT AM I GONNA DO...?
HEY, IT'S SHOUTA!
I NEVER SEE YOU OUT IN THE PARK.
WANNA JOIN OUR DODGE-BALL GAME?
NAH... I'M NOT IN THE MOOD.
SHUFF
OH, COME ON! YOU'RE NOT HALF BAD AT IT...
AH, FORGET HIM. HE TRIES TO ACT ALL CUTE, BUT HE AIN'T CUTE AT ALL!
I DON'T WANNA BE "NOT HALF BAD."
I'M GONNA BE THE STRONGEST SORCERER IN THE WORLD!
SO I'VE GOTTA BE ABLE TO CONTROL MY OWN FAMILIAR...
Oof!
WHUMP
AH... PARDON M...

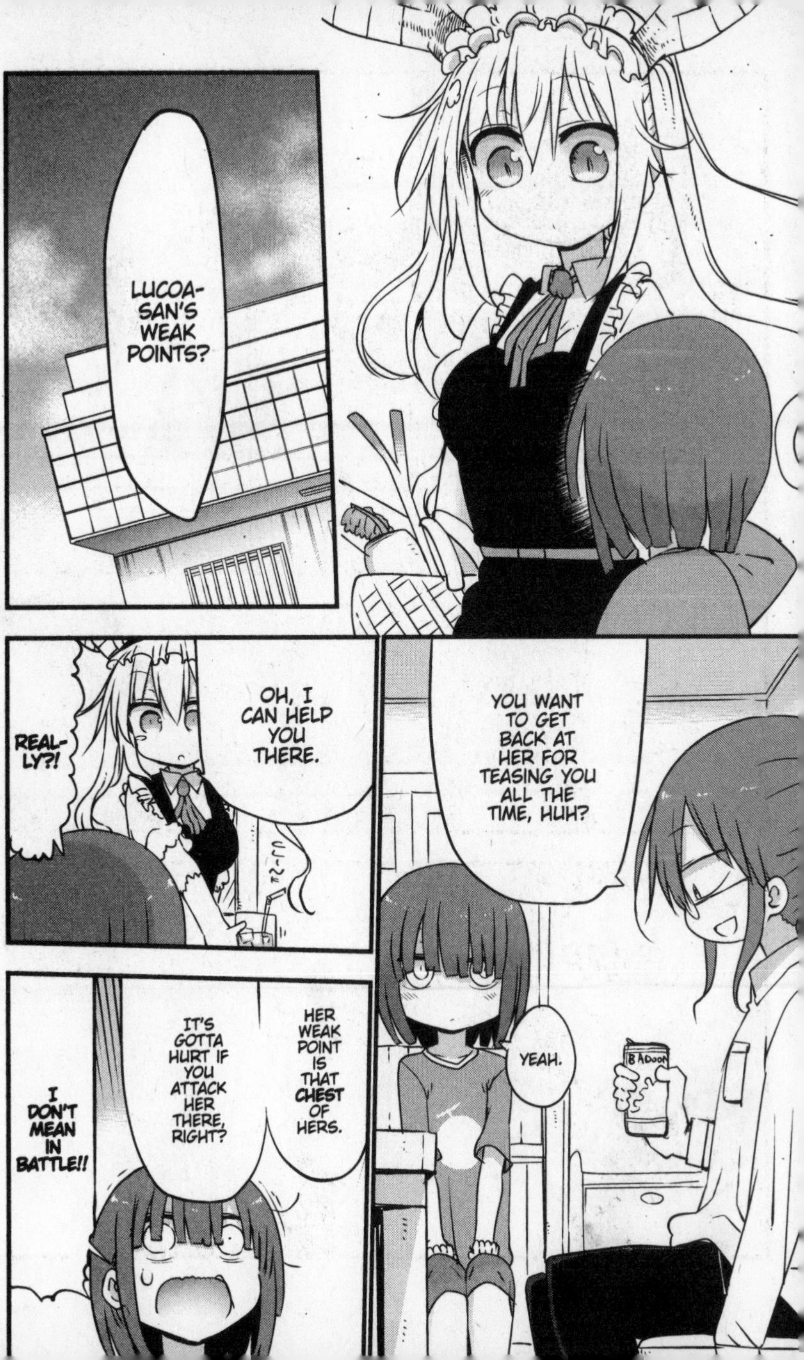

LUCOA-SAN'S WEAK POINTS?
YOU WANT TO GET BACK AT HER FOR TEASING YOU ALL THE TIME, HUH?
YEAH.
OH, I CAN HELP YOU THERE.
REAL-LY?!
HER WEAK POINT IS THAT CHEST OF HERS.
IT'S GOTTA HURT IF YOU ATTACK HER THERE, RIGHT?
I DON'T MEAN IN BATTLE!!

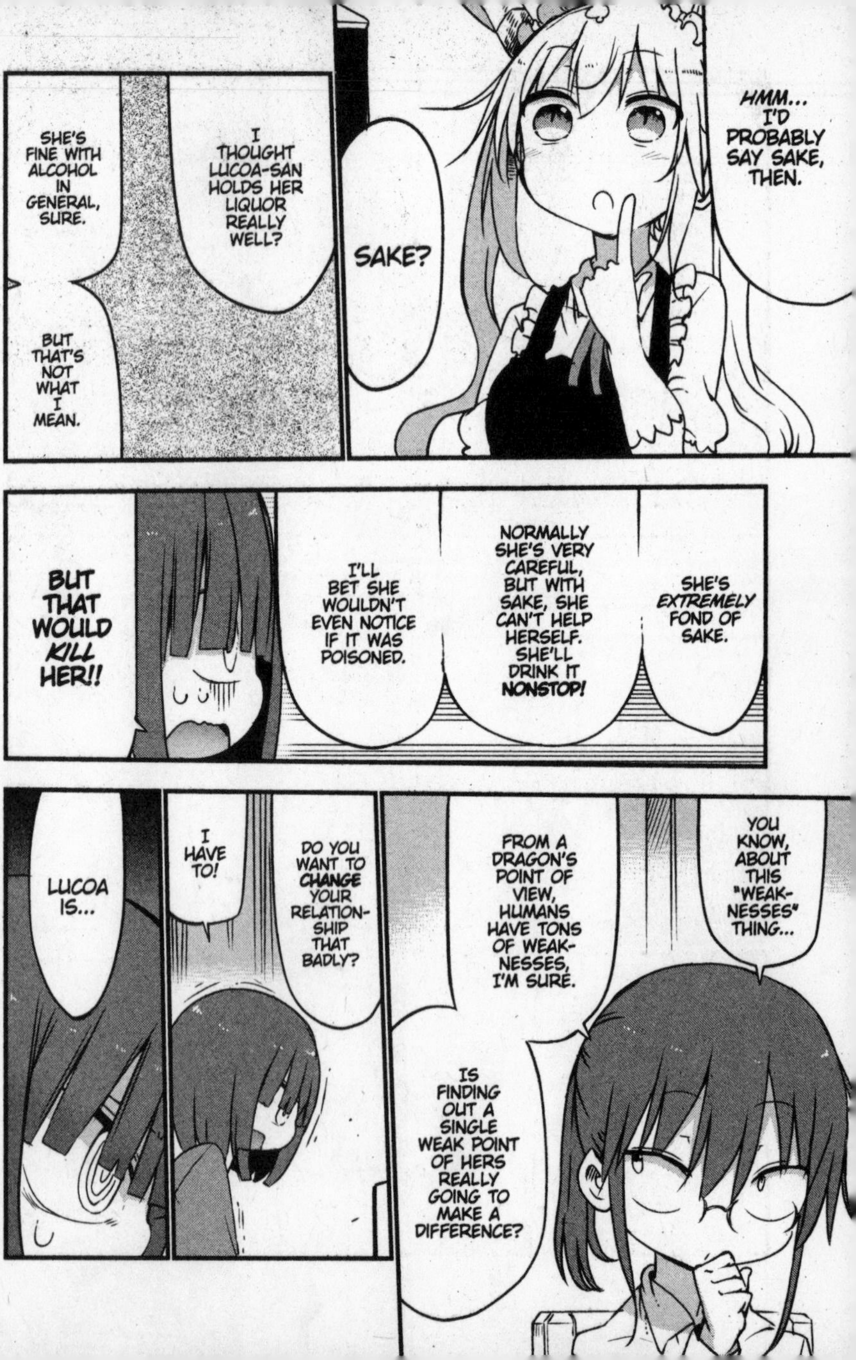
HMM... I'D PROBABLY SAY SAKE, THEN.
SAKE?
I THOUGHT LUCOA-SAN HOLDS HER LIQUOR REALLY WELL?
SHE'S FINE WITH ALCOHOL IN GENERAL, SURE.
BUT THAT'S NOT WHAT I MEAN.
SHE'S EXTREMELY FOND OF SAKE.
NORMALLY SHE'S VERY CAREFUL, BUT WITH SAKE, SHE CAN'T HELP HERSELF. SHE'LL DRINK IT NONSTOP!
I'LL BET SHE WOULDN'T EVEN NOTICE IF IT WAS POISONED.
BUT THAT WOULD KILL HER!!
YOU KNOW, ABOUT THIS "WEAKNESSES" THING...
FROM A DRAGON'S POINT OF VIEW, HUMANS HAVE TONS OF WEAKNESSES, I'M SURE.
IS FINDING OUT A SINGLE WEAK POINT OF HERS REALLY GOING TO MAKE A DIFFERENCE?
DO YOU WANT TO CHANGE YOUR RELATIONSHIP THAT BADLY?
I HAVE TO!
LUCOA IS...

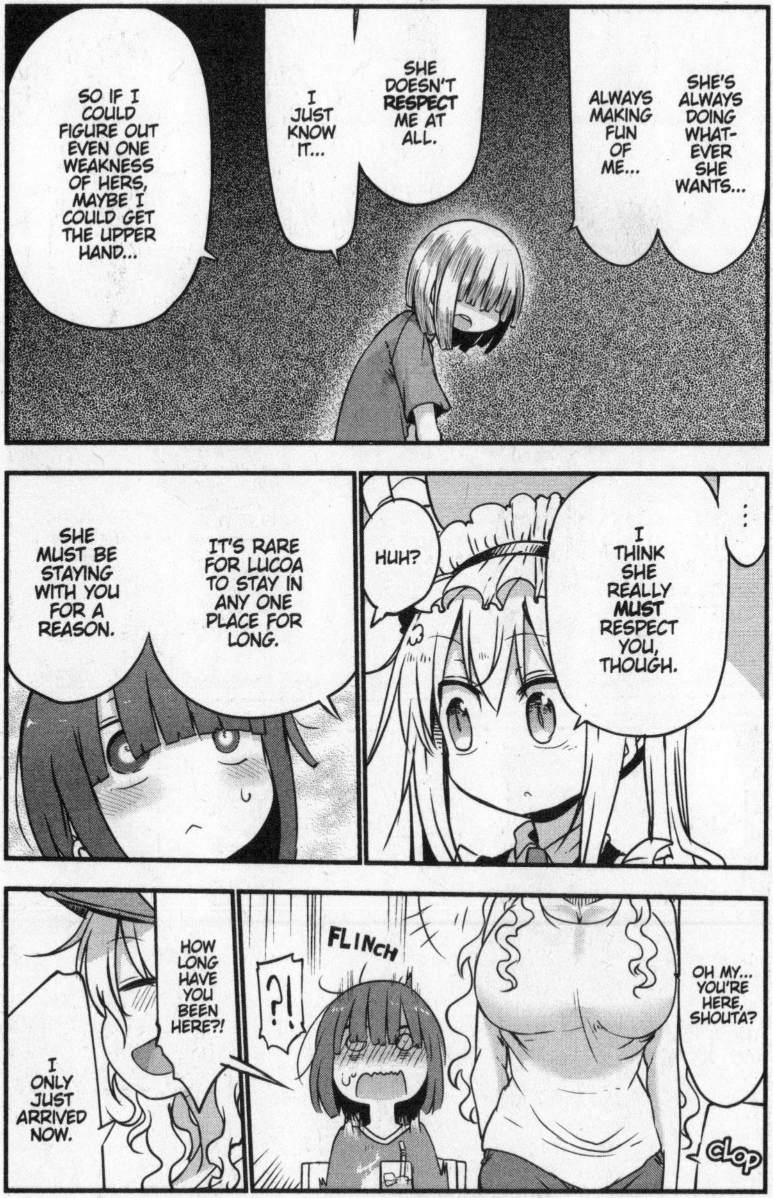

SHE'S ALWAYS DOING WHAT-EVER SHE WANTS...
ALWAYS MAKING FUN OF ME...
SHE DOESN'T RESPECT ME AT ALL.
I JUST KNOW IT...
SO IF I COULD FIGURE OUT EVEN ONE WEAKNESS OF HERS, MAYBE I COULD GET THE UPPER HAND...
...
I THINK SHE REALLY MUST RESPECT YOU, THOUGH.
HUH?
IT'S RARE FOR LUCOA TO STAY IN ANY ONE PLACE FOR LONG.
SHE MUST BE STAYING WITH YOU FOR A REASON.
OH MY... YOU'RE HERE, SHOUTA?
CLOP
FLINCH
?!
HOW LONG HAVE YOU BEEN HERE?!
I ONLY JUST ARRIVED NOW.

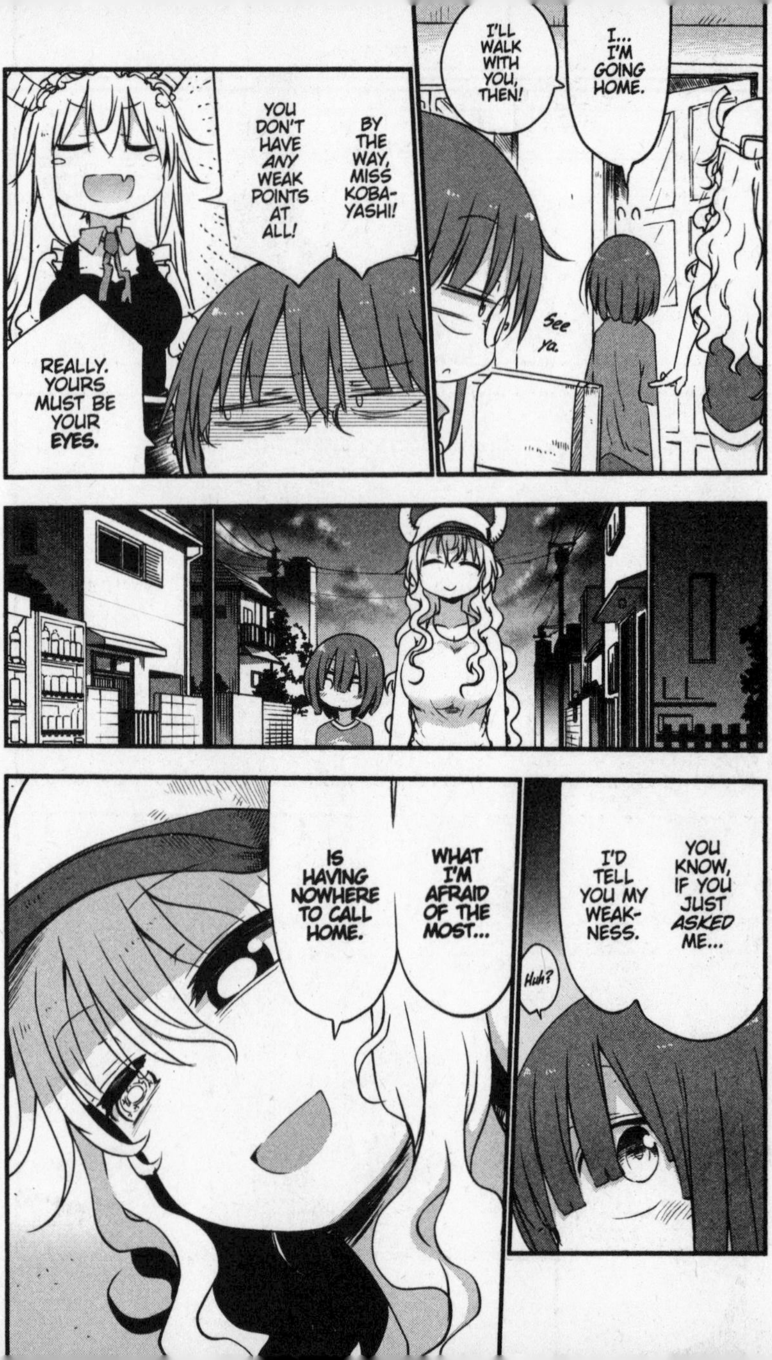
I... I'M GOING HOME.
I'LL WALK WITH YOU, THEN!
See ya.
BY THE WAY, MISS KOBAYASHI!
YOU DON'T HAVE ANY WEAK POINTS AT ALL!
REALLY. YOURS MUST BE YOUR EYES.
YOU KNOW, IF YOU JUST ASKED ME...
I'D TELL YOU MY WEAKNESS.
Huh?
WHAT I'M AFRAID OF THE MOST...
IS HAVING NOWHERE TO CALL HOME.

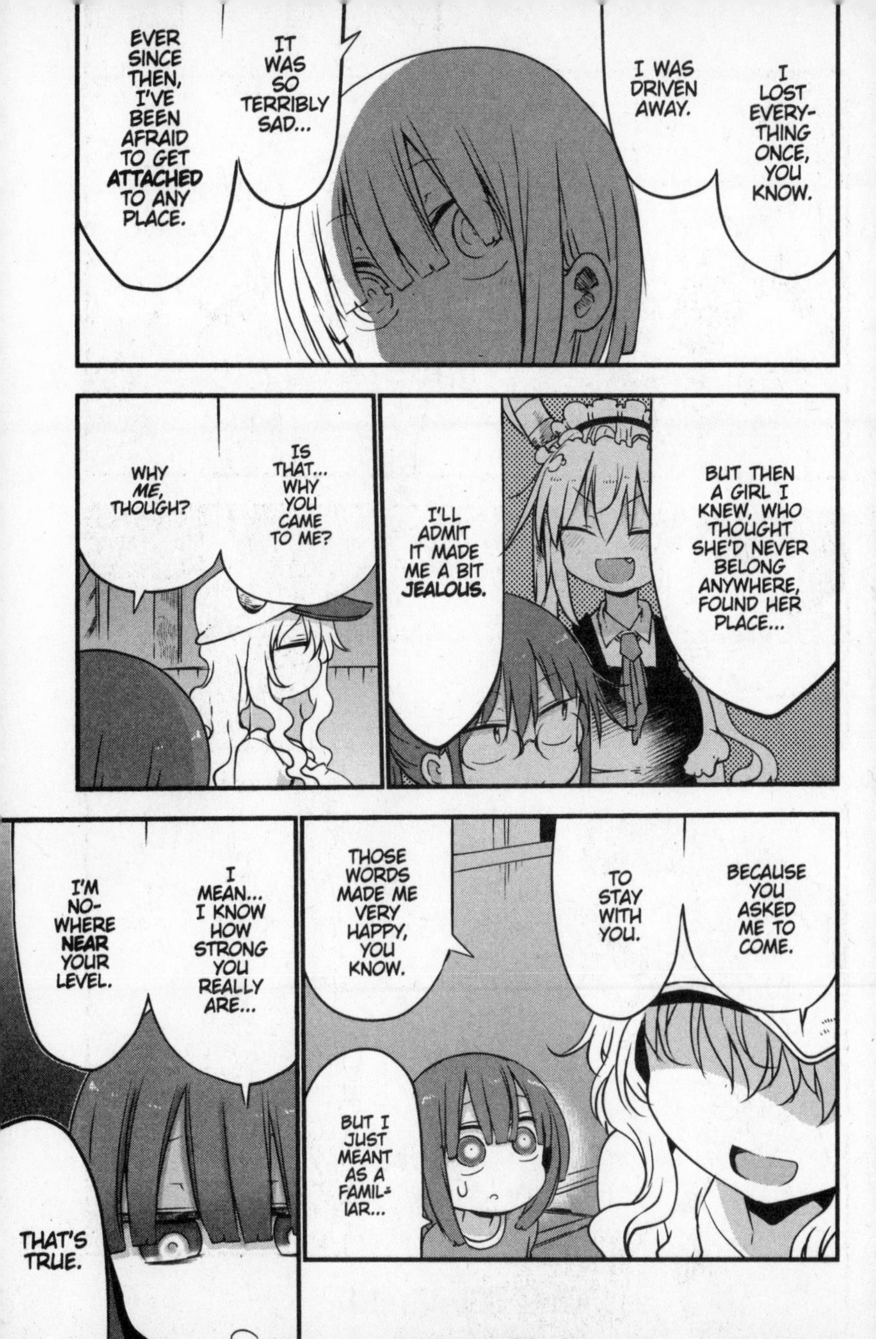
I LOST EVERYTHING ONCE, YOU KNOW.
I WAS DRIVEN AWAY.
IT WAS SO TERRIBLY SAD...
EVER SINCE THEN, I'VE BEEN AFRAID TO GET ATTACHED TO ANY PLACE.
BUT THEN A GIRL I KNEW, WHO THOUGHT SHE'D NEVER BELONG ANYWHERE, FOUND HER PLACE...
I'LL ADMIT IT MADE ME A BIT JEALOUS.
IS THAT... WHY YOU CAME TO ME?
WHY ME, THOUGH?
BECAUSE YOU ASKED ME TO COME.
TO STAY WITH YOU.
THOSE WORDS MADE ME VERY HAPPY, YOU KNOW.
BUT I JUST MEANT AS A FAMILIAR...
I MEAN... I KNOW HOW STRONG YOU REALLY ARE...
I'M NOWHERE NEAR YOUR LEVEL.
THAT'S TRUE.

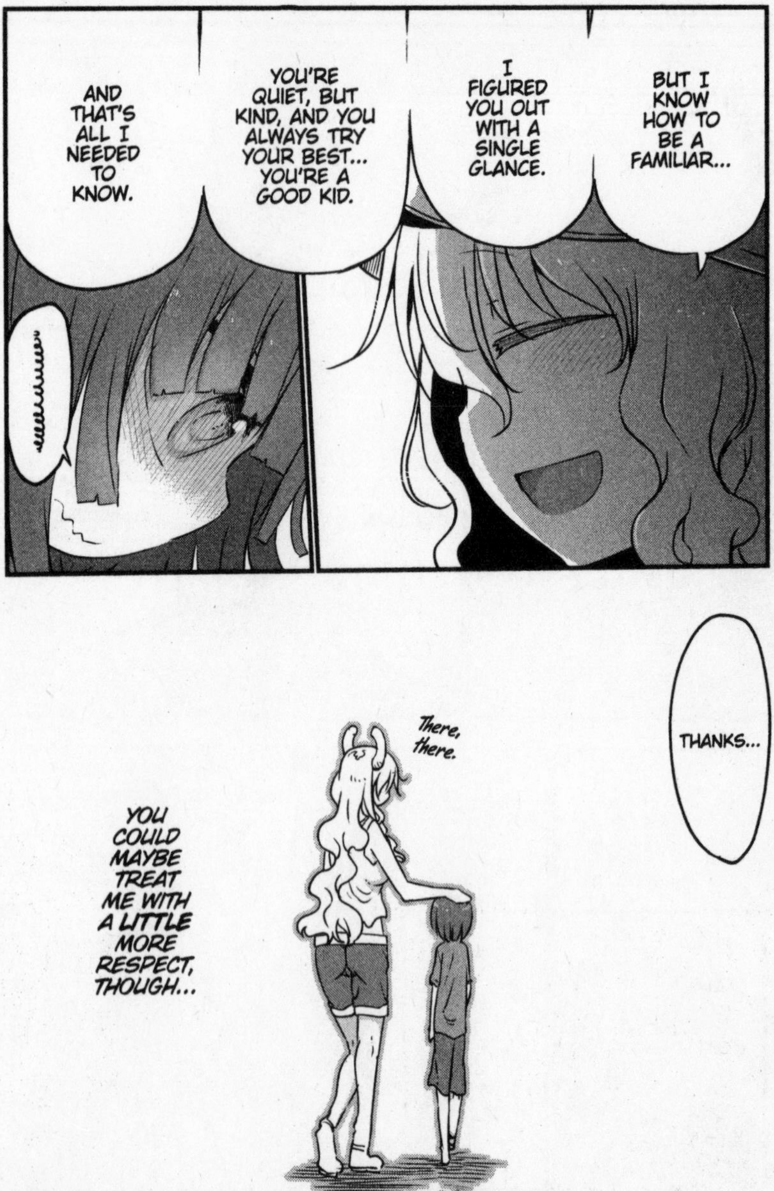
BUT I KNOW HOW TO BE A FAMILIAR...
I FIGURED YOU OUT WITH A SINGLE GLANCE.
YOU'RE QUIET, BUT KIND, AND YOU ALWAYS TRY YOUR BEST... YOU'RE A GOOD KID.
AND THAT'S ALL I NEEDED TO KNOW.
THANKS...
There, there.
YOU COULD MAYBE TREAT ME WITH A LITTLE MORE RESPECT, THOUGH...

CHAPTER 46/END

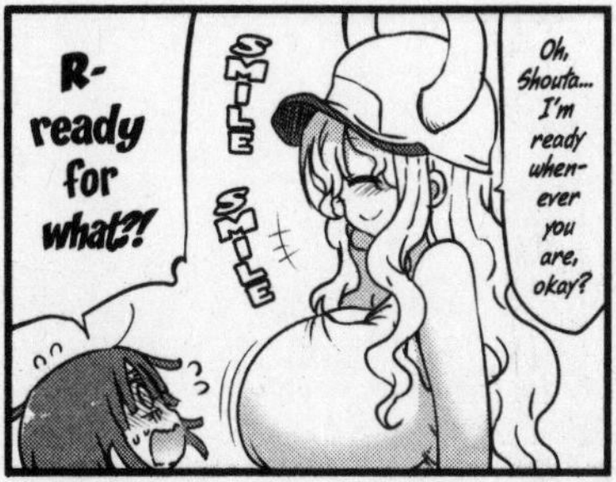
Oh, Shouta... I'm ready whenever you are, okay?
SMILE SMILE
R-ready for what?!

Miss Kobayashi's Dragon Maid

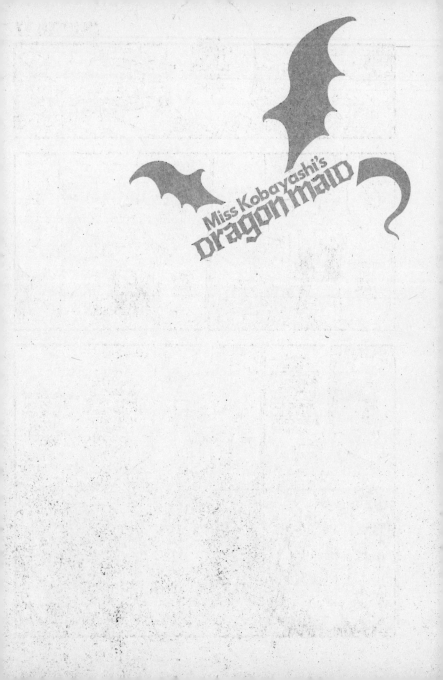

CHAPTER 47

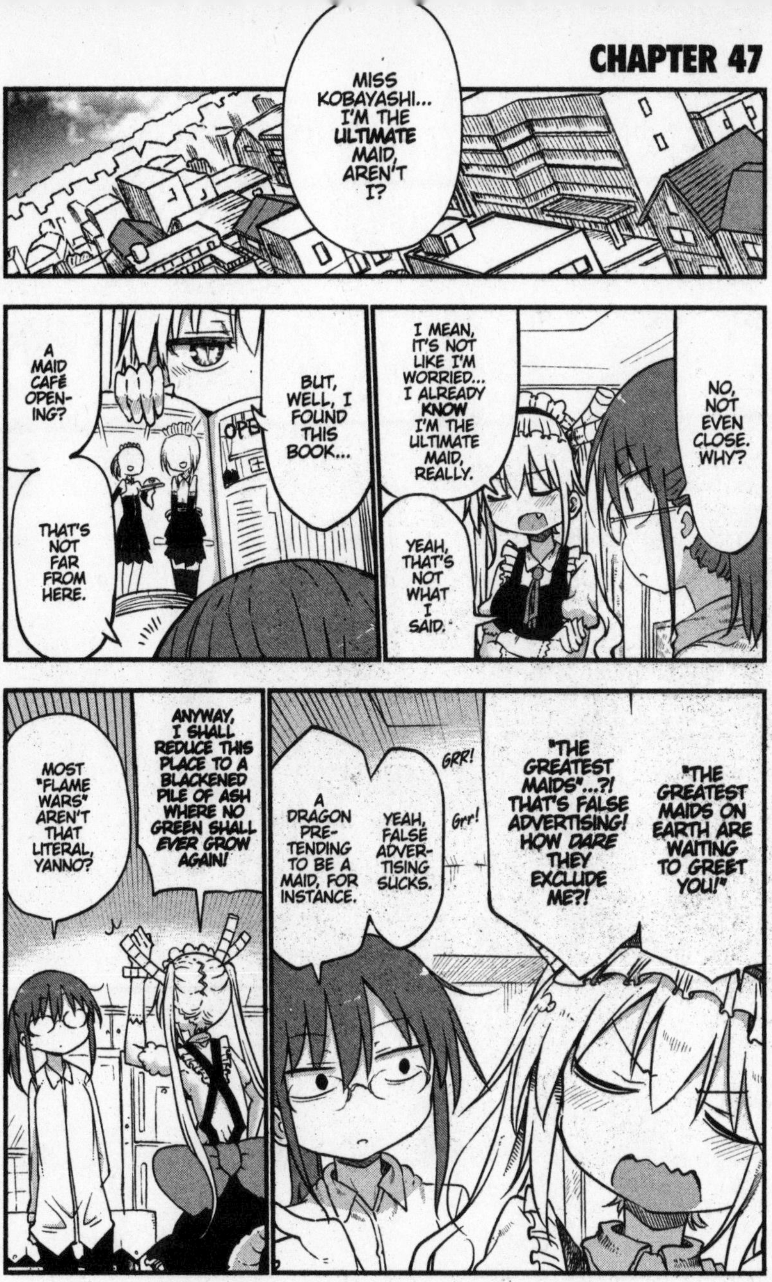
MISS KOBAYASHI... I'M THE ULTIMATE MAID, AREN'T I?
NO, NOT EVEN CLOSE. WHY?
I MEAN, IT'S NOT LIKE I'M WORRIED... I ALREADY KNOW I'M THE ULTIMATE MAID, REALLY.
YEAH, THAT'S NOT WHAT I SAID.
BUT, WELL, I FOUND THIS BOOK...
A MAID CAFÉ OPENING?
THAT'S NOT FAR FROM HERE.
"THE GREATEST MAIDS ON EARTH ARE WAITING TO GREET YOU!"
"THE GREATEST MAIDS"...?! THAT'S FALSE ADVERTISING! HOW DARE THEY EXCLUDE ME?!
GRR!
Grr!
YEAH, FALSE ADVERTISING SUCKS.
A DRAGON PRETENDING TO BE A MAID, FOR INSTANCE.
ANYWAY, I SHALL REDUCE THIS PLACE TO A BLACKENED PILE OF ASH WHERE NO GREEN SHALL EVER GROW AGAIN!
MOST "FLAME WARS" AREN'T THAT LITERAL, YANNO?

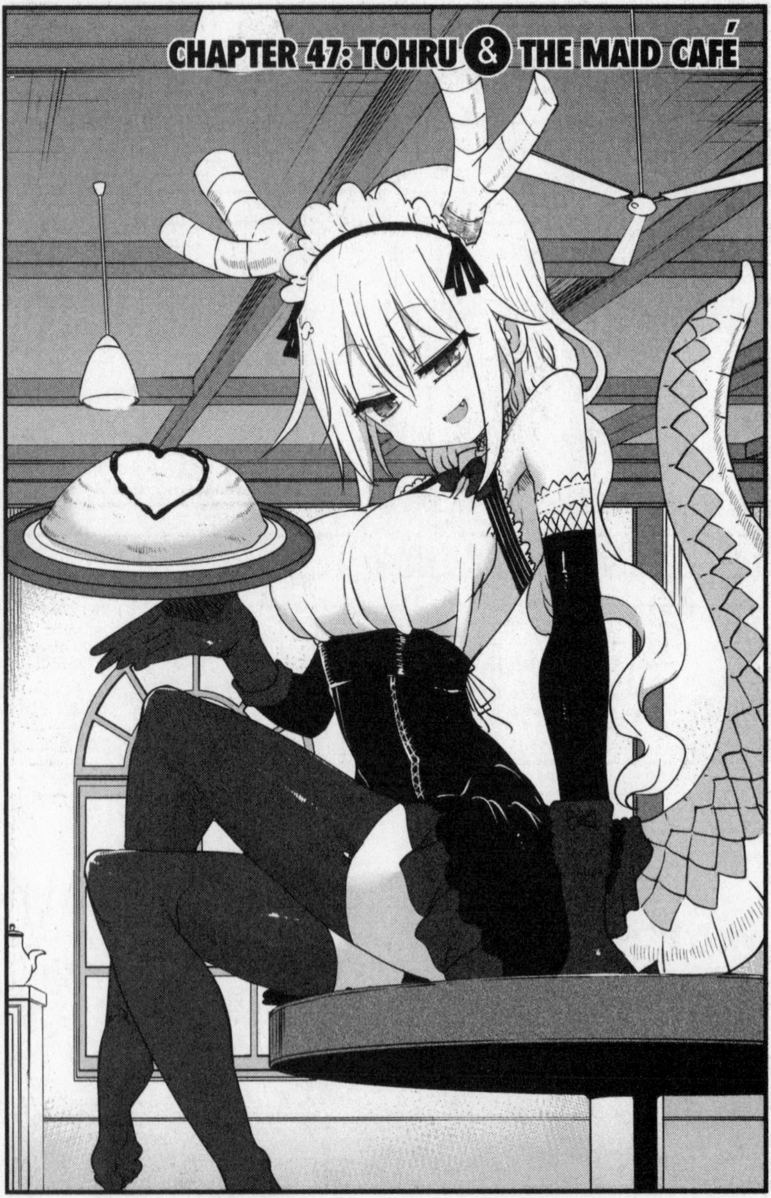
CHAPTER 47: TOHRU & THE MAID CAFÉ

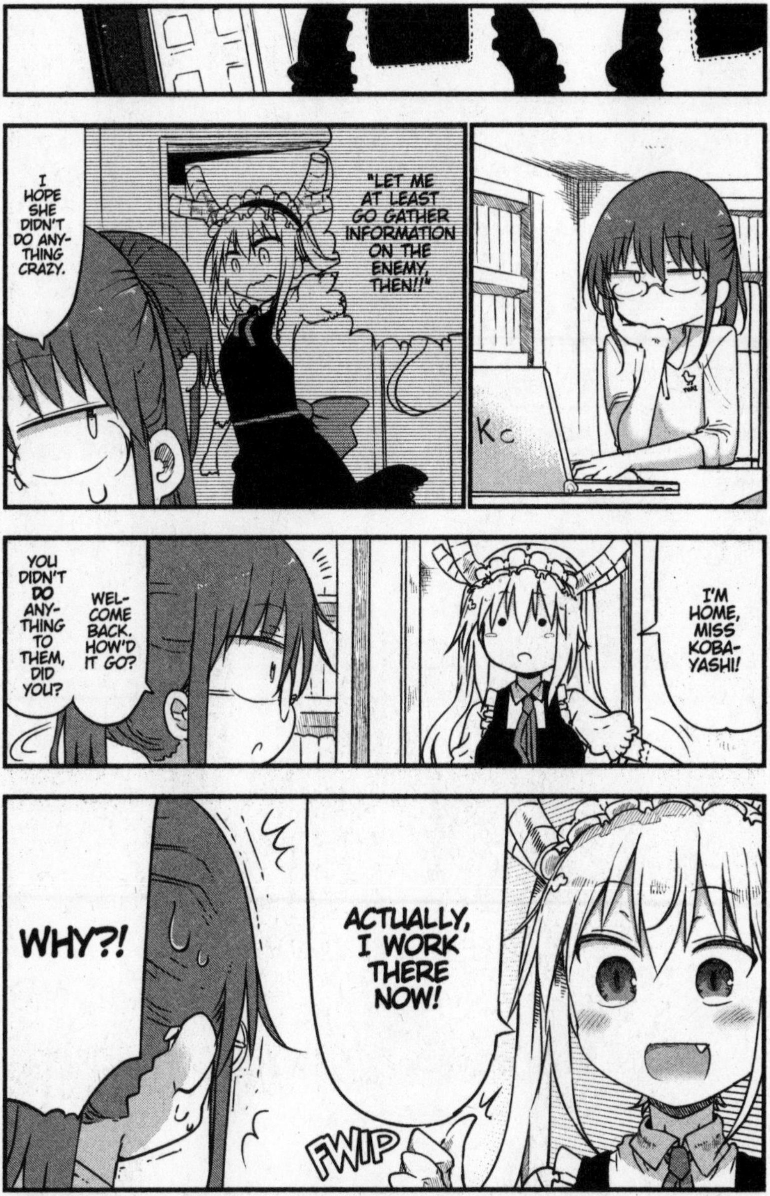
...
"LET ME AT LEAST GO GATHER INFORMATION ON THE ENEMY, THEN!!"
I HOPE SHE DIDN'T DO ANYTHING CRAZY.
I'M HOME, MISS KOBAYASHI!
WELCOME BACK. HOW'D IT GO?
YOU DIDN'T DO ANYTHING TO THEM, DID YOU?
ACTUALLY, I WORK THERE NOW!
FWIP
WHY?!

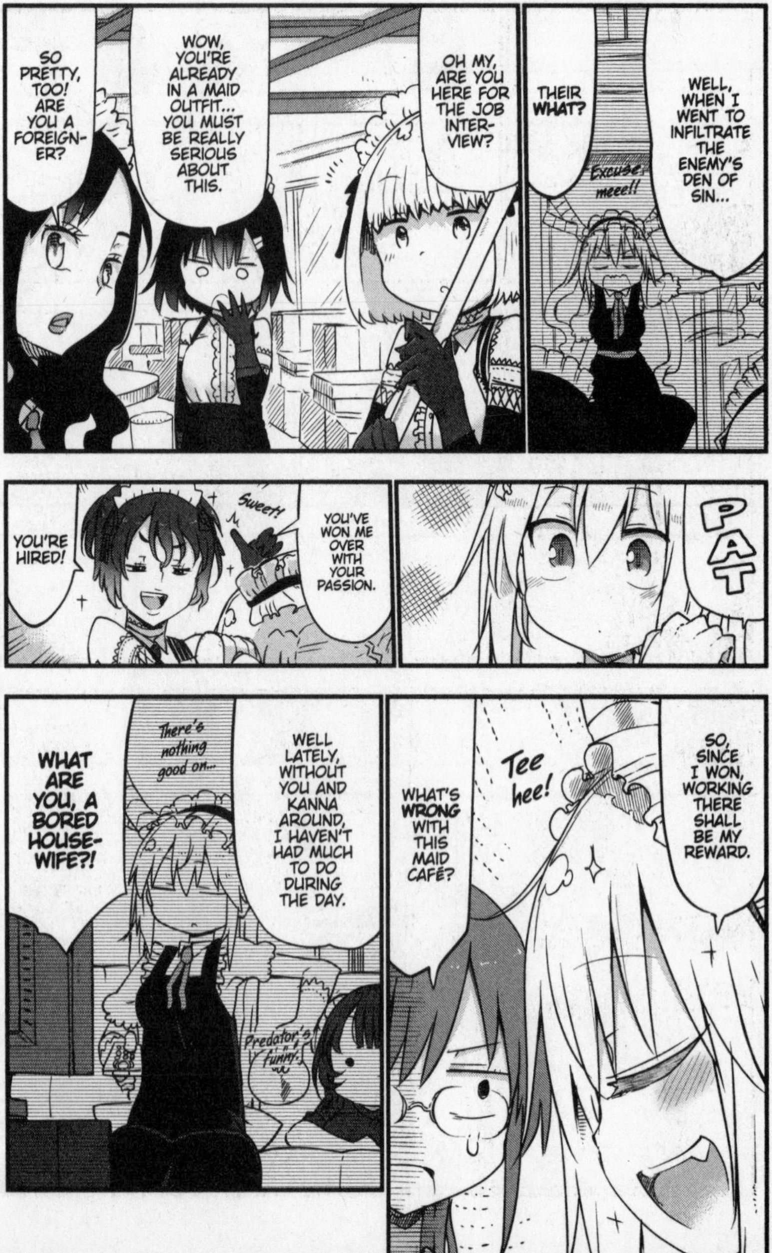
WELL, WHEN I WENT TO INFILTRATE THE ENEMY'S DEN OF SIN...
THEIR WHAT?
Excuse meee!!
OH MY, ARE YOU HERE FOR THE JOB INTERVIEW?
WOW, YOU'RE ALREADY IN A MAID OUTFIT... YOU MUST BE REALLY SERIOUS ABOUT THIS.
SO PRETTY, TOO! ARE YOU A FOREIGNER?
PAT
YOU'VE WON ME OVER WITH YOUR PASSION.
Sweet!
YOU'RE HIRED!
SO, SINCE I WON, WORKING THERE SHALL BE MY REWARD.
Tee hee!
WHAT'S WRONG WITH THIS MAID CAFÉ?
WELL LATELY, WITHOUT YOU AND KANNA AROUND, I HAVEN'T HAD MUCH TO DO DURING THE DAY.
There's nothing good on...
WHAT ARE YOU, A BORED HOUSEWIFE?!
Predator's funny.

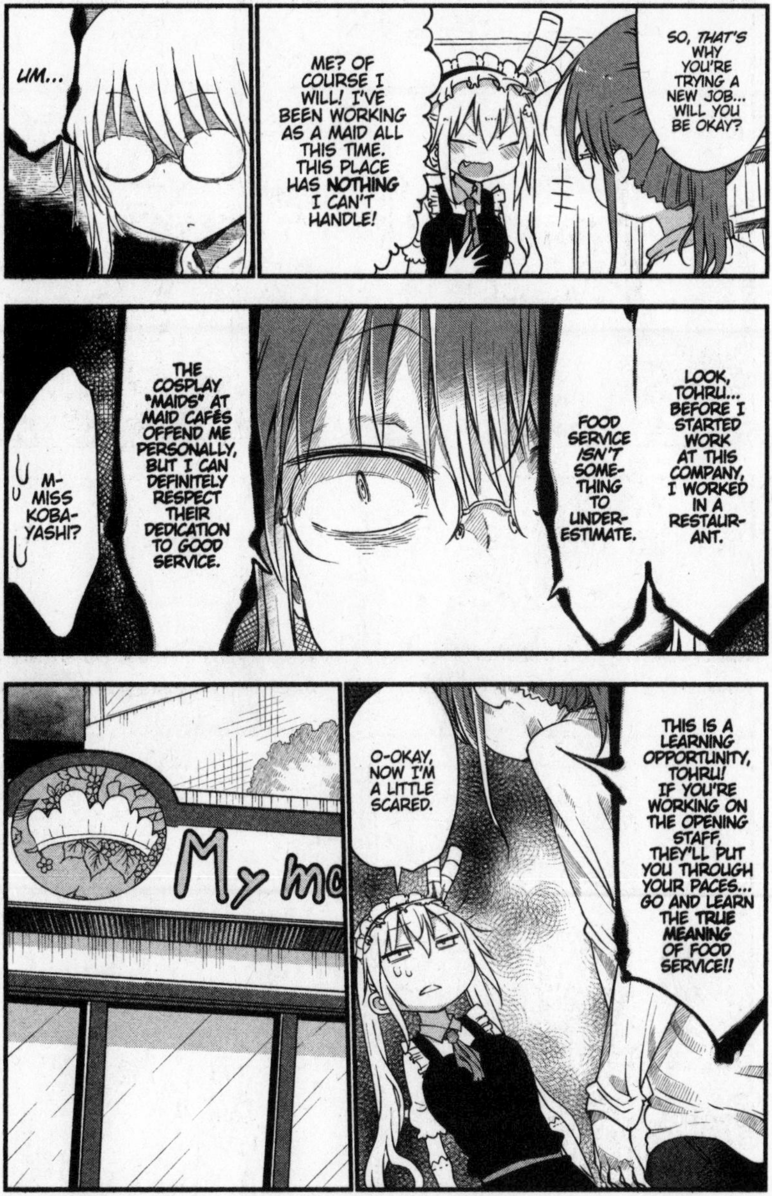
SO, THAT'S WHY YOU'RE TRYING A NEW JOB... WILL YOU BE OKAY?
ME? OF COURSE I WILL! I'VE BEEN WORKING AS A MAID ALL THIS TIME. THIS PLACE HAS **NOTHING** I CAN'T HANDLE!
UM...
LOOK, TOHRU... BEFORE I STARTED WORK AT THIS COMPANY, I WORKED IN A RESTAURANT.
FOOD SERVICE *ISN'T* SOMETHING TO UNDERESTIMATE.
THE COSPLAY "MAIDS" AT MAID CAFÉS OFFEND ME PERSONALLY, BUT I CAN DEFINITELY RESPECT THEIR DEDICATION TO GOOD SERVICE.
M-MISS KOBAYASHI?
THIS IS A LEARNING OPPORTUNITY, TOHRU! IF YOU'RE WORKING ON THE OPENING STAFF, THEY'LL PUT YOU THROUGH YOUR PACES... GO AND LEARN THE TRUE MEANING OF FOOD SERVICE!!
O-OKAY, NOW I'M A LITTLE SCARED.

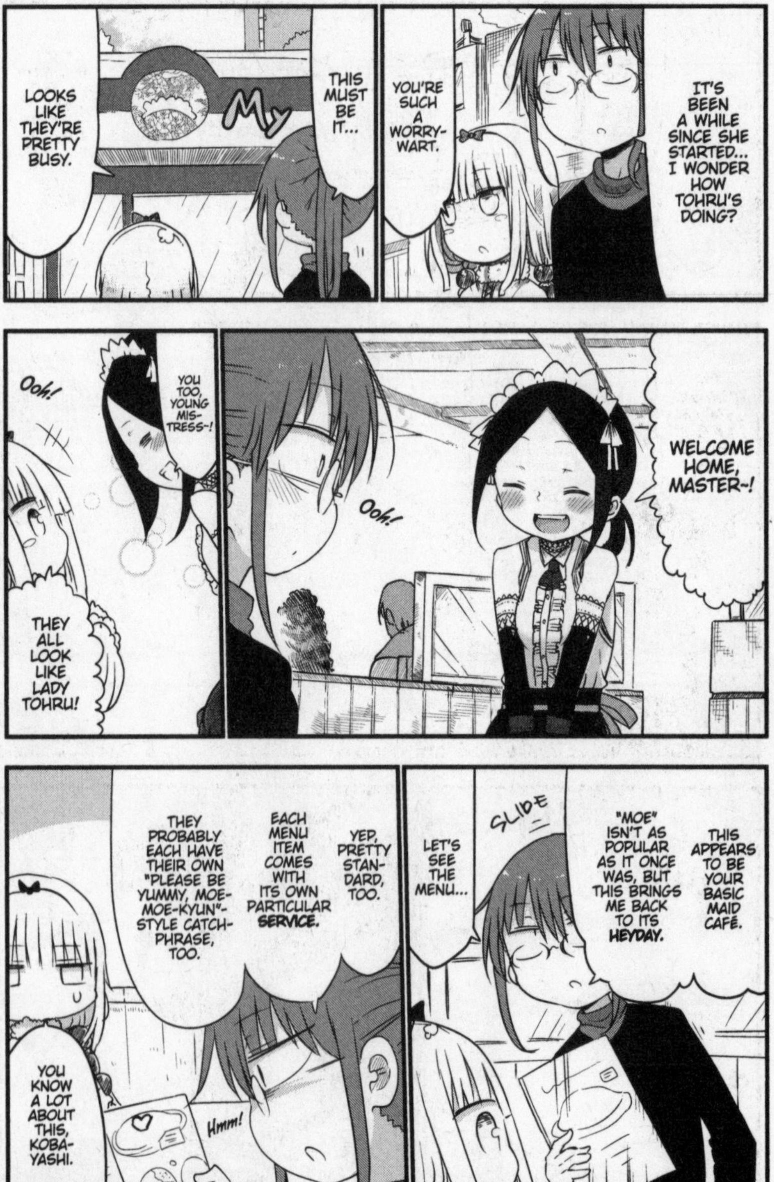
IT'S BEEN A WHILE SINCE SHE STARTED... I WONDER HOW TOHRU'S DOING?
YOU'RE SUCH A WORRY-WART.
THIS MUST BE IT...
My
LOOKS LIKE THEY'RE PRETTY BUSY.
WELCOME HOME, MASTER~!
Ooh!
YOU TOO, YOUNG MIS-TRESS~!
Ooh!
THEY ALL LOOK LIKE LADY TOHRU!
THIS APPEARS TO BE YOUR BASIC MAID CAFÉ.
"MOE" ISN'T AS POPULAR AS IT ONCE WAS, BUT THIS BRINGS ME BACK TO ITS HEYDAY.
SLIDE
LET'S SEE THE MENU...
YEP, PRETTY STAN-DARD, TOO.
EACH MENU ITEM COMES WITH ITS OWN PARTICULAR SERVICE.
THEY PROBABLY EACH HAVE THEIR OWN "PLEASE BE YUMMY, MOE-MOE-KYUN"-STYLE CATCH-PHRASE, TOO.
Hmm!
YOU KNOW A LOT ABOUT THIS, KOBA-YASHI.

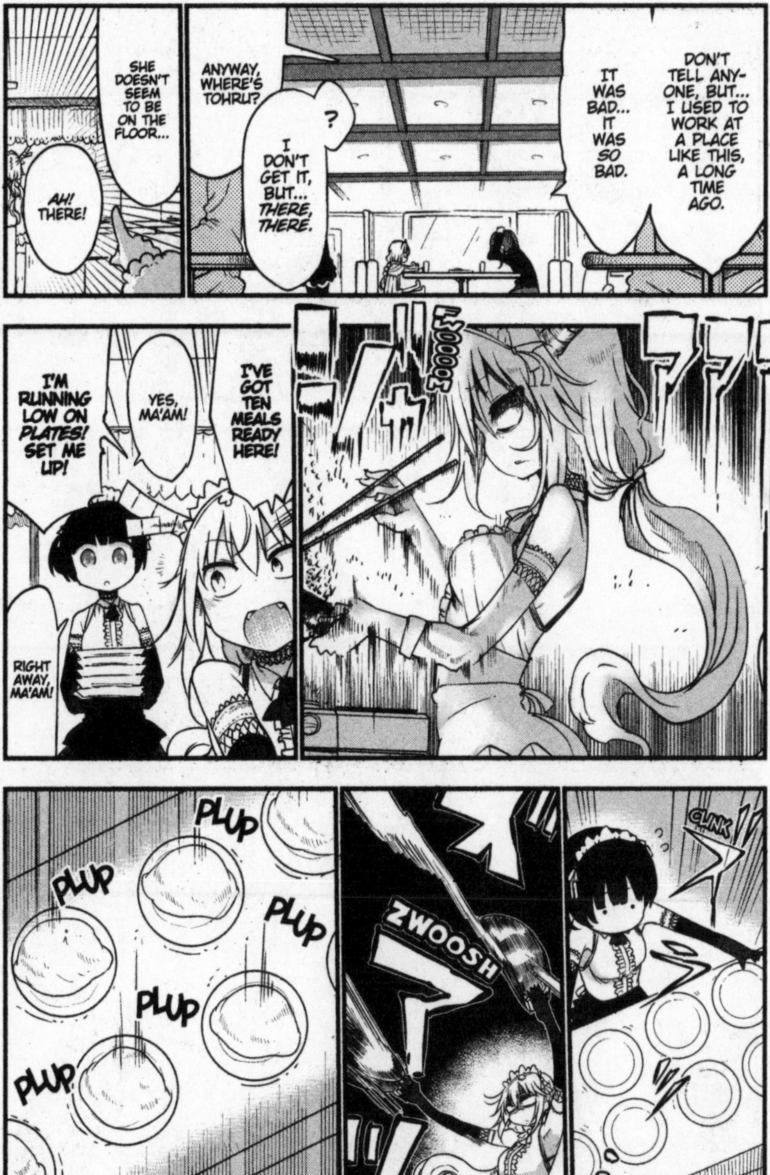
DON'T TELL ANYONE, BUT... I USED TO WORK AT A PLACE LIKE THIS, A LONG TIME AGO.
IT WAS BAD... IT WAS SO BAD.
ANYWAY, WHERE'S TOHRU?
?
I DON'T GET IT, BUT... THERE, THERE.
SHE DOESN'T SEEM TO BE ON THE FLOOR...
AH! THERE!
WOOOOM
I'VE GOT TEN MEALS READY HERE!
YES, MA'AM!
I'M RUNNING LOW ON PLATES! SET ME UP!
RIGHT AWAY, MA'AM!
CLINK
ZWOOSH
PLUP
PLUP
PLUP
PLUP
PLUP

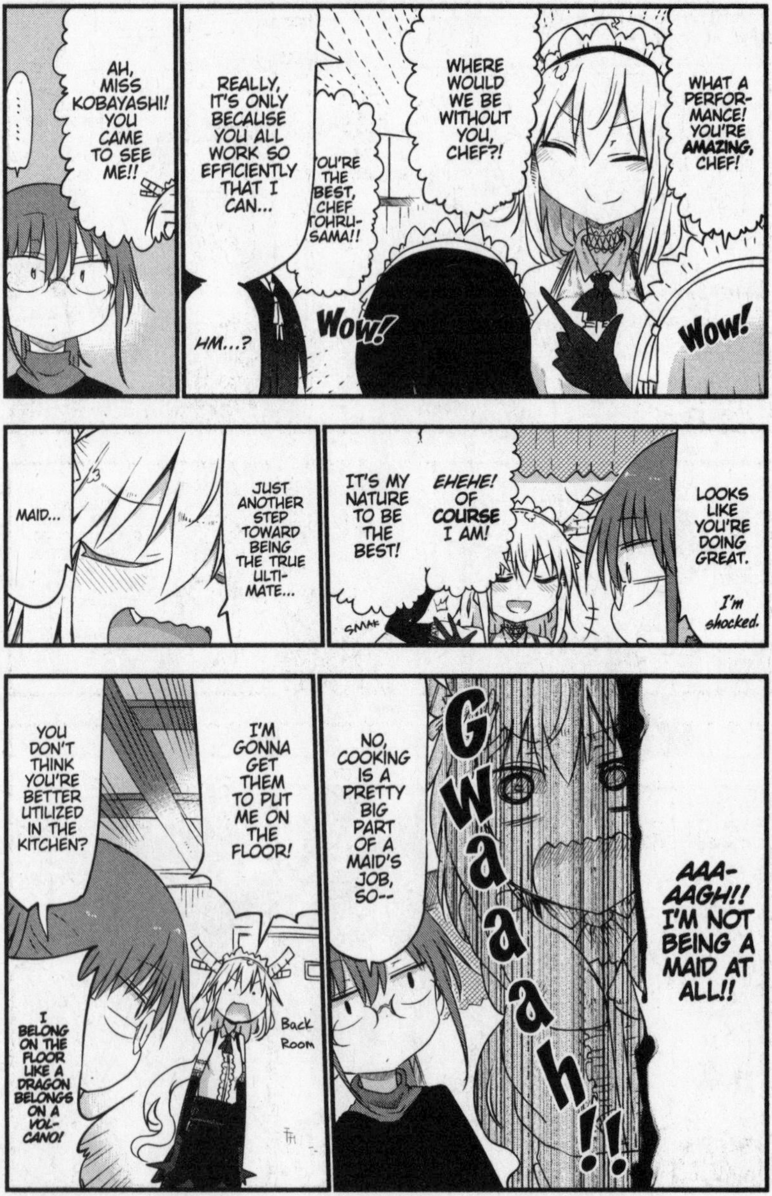
WHAT A PERFORMANCE! YOU'RE AMAZING, CHEF!
WHERE WOULD WE BE WITHOUT YOU, CHEF?!
WOW!
WOW!
YOU'RE THE BEST, CHEF TOHRU-SAMA!!
REALLY, IT'S ONLY BECAUSE YOU ALL WORK SO EFFICIENTLY THAT I CAN...
HM...?
AH, MISS KOBAYASHI! YOU CAME TO SEE ME!!
......
LOOKS LIKE YOU'RE DOING GREAT.
I'm shocked.
EHEHE! OF COURSE I AM!
IT'S MY NATURE TO BE THE BEST!
SMAK
JUST ANOTHER STEP TOWARD BEING THE TRUE ULTIMATE...
MAID...
AAA-AAGH!! I'M NOT BEING A MAID AT ALL!!
Gwaaah!!
NO, COOKING IS A PRETTY BIG PART OF A MAID'S JOB, SO--
I'M GONNA GET THEM TO PUT ME ON THE FLOOR!
YOU DON'T THINK YOU'RE BETTER UTILIZED IN THE KITCHEN?
Back Room
I BELONG ON THE FLOOR LIKE A DRAGON BELONGS ON A VOLCANO!

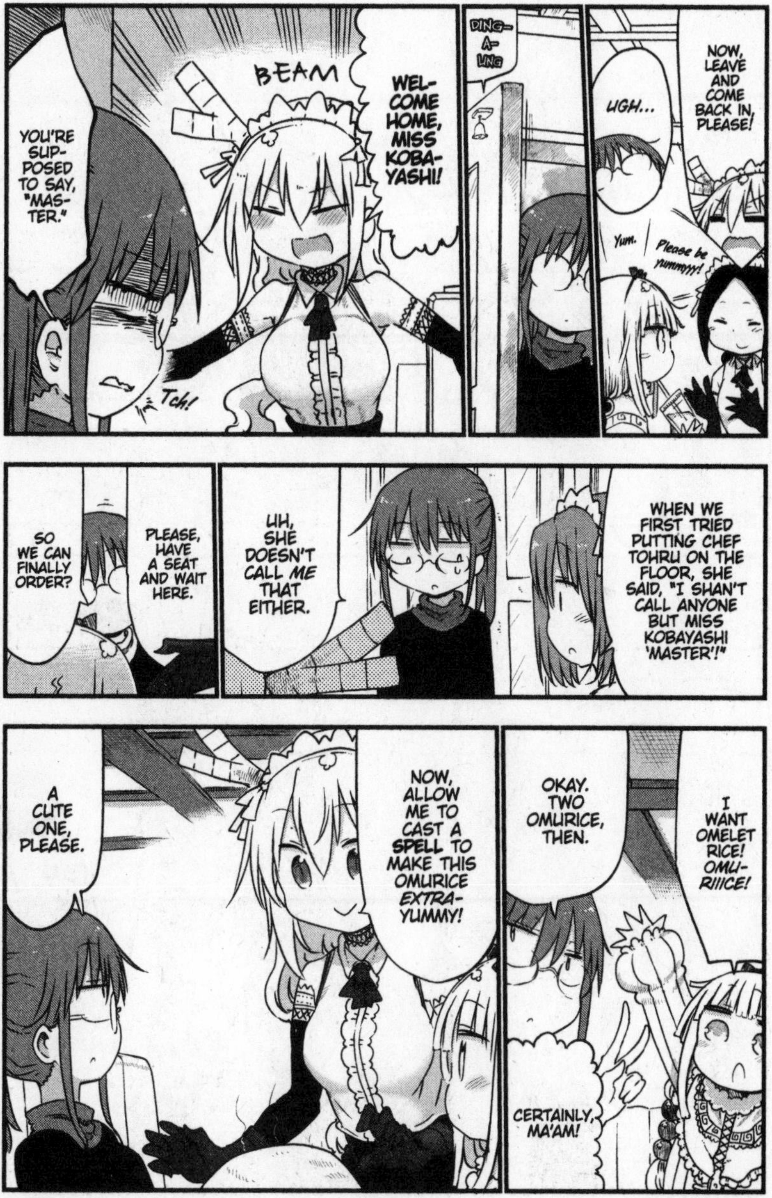
NOW, LEAVE AND COME BACK IN, PLEASE!
UGH...
Please be yummyyy!
Yum.
DING-A-LING
WELCOME HOME, MISS KOBAYASHI!
BEAM
YOU'RE SUPPOSED TO SAY, "MASTER."
Tch!
WHEN WE FIRST TRIED PUTTING CHEF TOHRU ON THE FLOOR, SHE SAID, "I SHAN'T CALL ANYONE BUT MISS KOBAYASHI 'MASTER'!"
UH, SHE DOESN'T CALL *ME* THAT EITHER.
PLEASE, HAVE A SEAT AND WAIT HERE.
SO WE CAN FINALLY ORDER?
I WANT OMELET RICE! OMURIIICE!
OKAY. TWO OMURICE, THEN.
CERTAINLY, MA'AM!
NOW, ALLOW ME TO CAST A **SPELL** TO MAKE THIS OMURICE *EXTRA-YUMMY*!
A CUTE ONE, PLEASE.

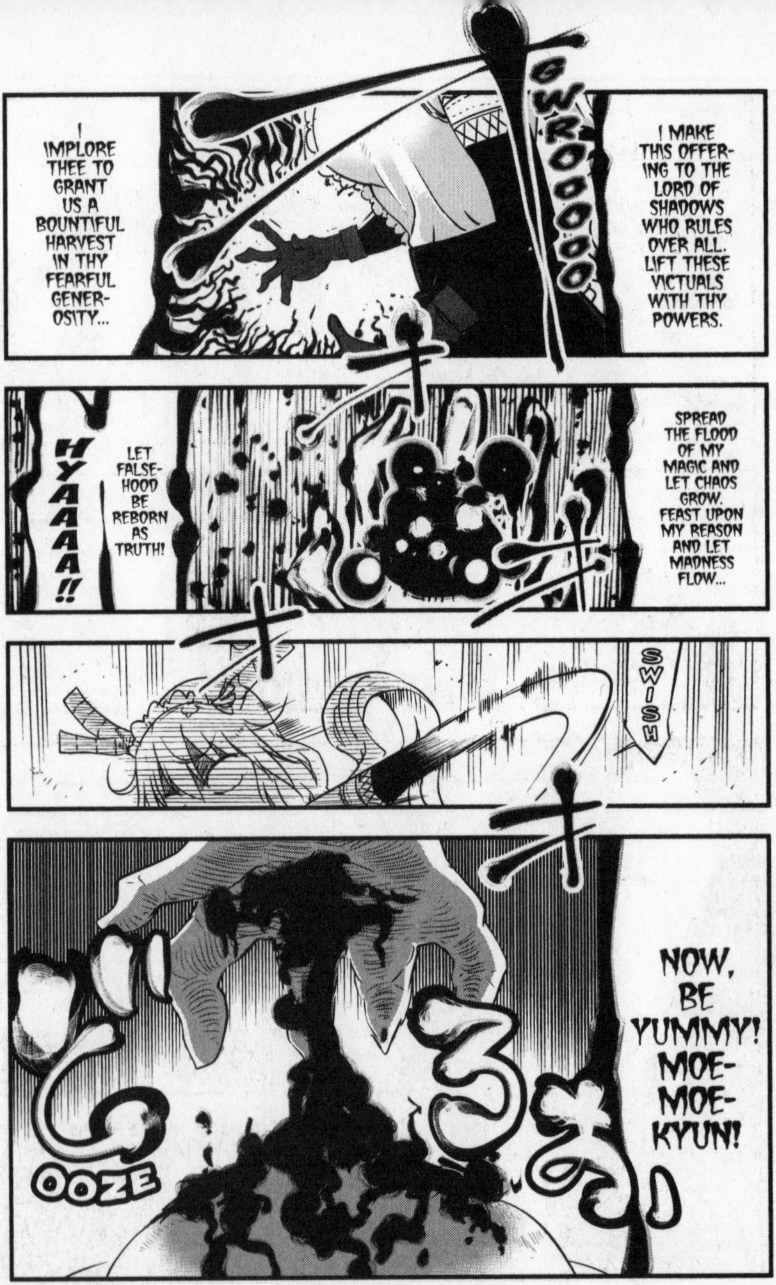
I MAKE THIS OFFERING TO THE LORD OF SHADOWS WHO RULES OVER ALL. LIFT THESE VICTUALS WITH THY POWERS.
GWROOOOOO
I IMPLORE THEE TO GRANT US A BOUNTIFUL HARVEST IN THY FEARFUL GENEROSITY...
SPREAD THE FLOOD OF MY MAGIC AND LET CHAOS GROW. FEAST UPON MY REASON AND LET MADNESS FLOW...
LET FALSEHOOD BE REBORN AS TRUTH!
HYAAAA!!
SWISH
NOW, BE YUMMY! MOE-MOE-KYUN!
OOZE

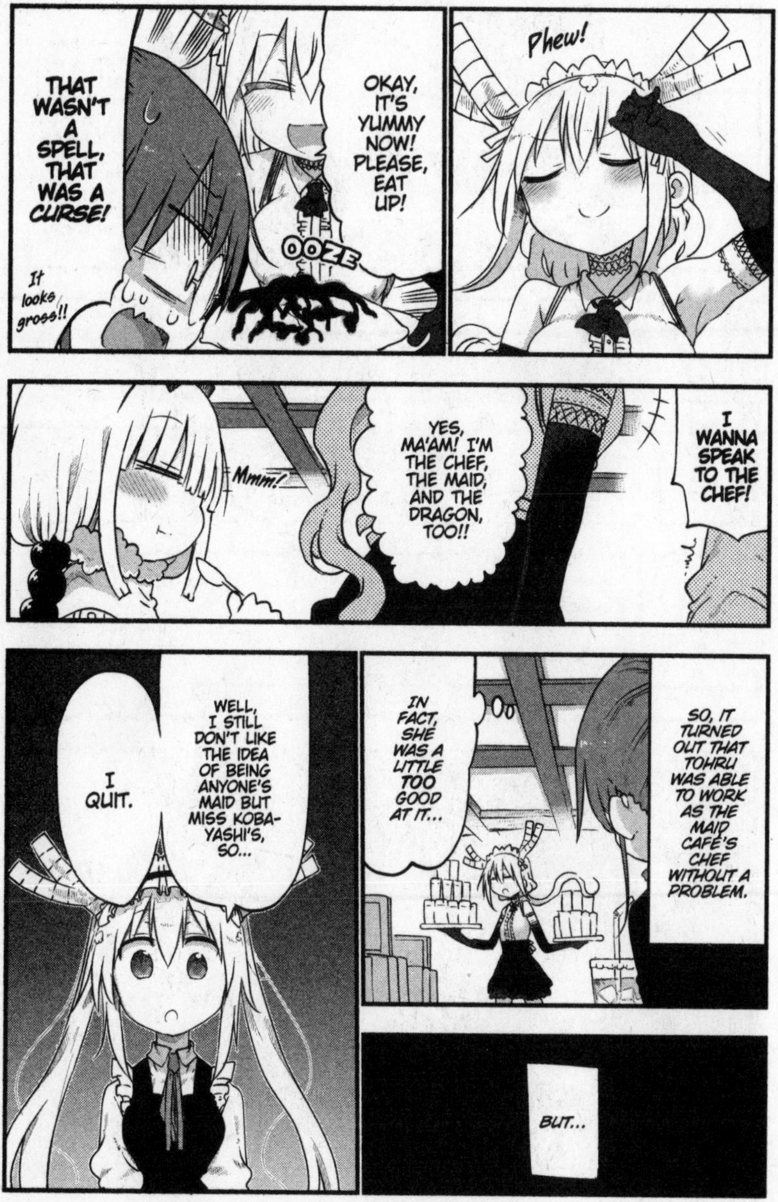
Phew!
OKAY, IT'S YUMMY NOW! PLEASE, EAT UP!
THAT WASN'T A SPELL, THAT WAS A CURSE!
OOZE
It looks gross!!
I WANNA SPEAK TO THE CHEF!
YES, MA'AM! I'M THE CHEF, THE MAID, AND THE DRAGON, TOO!!
Mmm!
SO, IT TURNED OUT THAT TOHRU WAS ABLE TO WORK AS THE MAID CAFÉ'S CHEF WITHOUT A PROBLEM.
IN FACT, SHE WAS A LITTLE TOO GOOD AT IT...
BUT...
WELL, I STILL DON'T LIKE THE IDEA OF BEING ANYONE'S MAID BUT MISS KOBAYASHI'S, SO...
I QUIT.

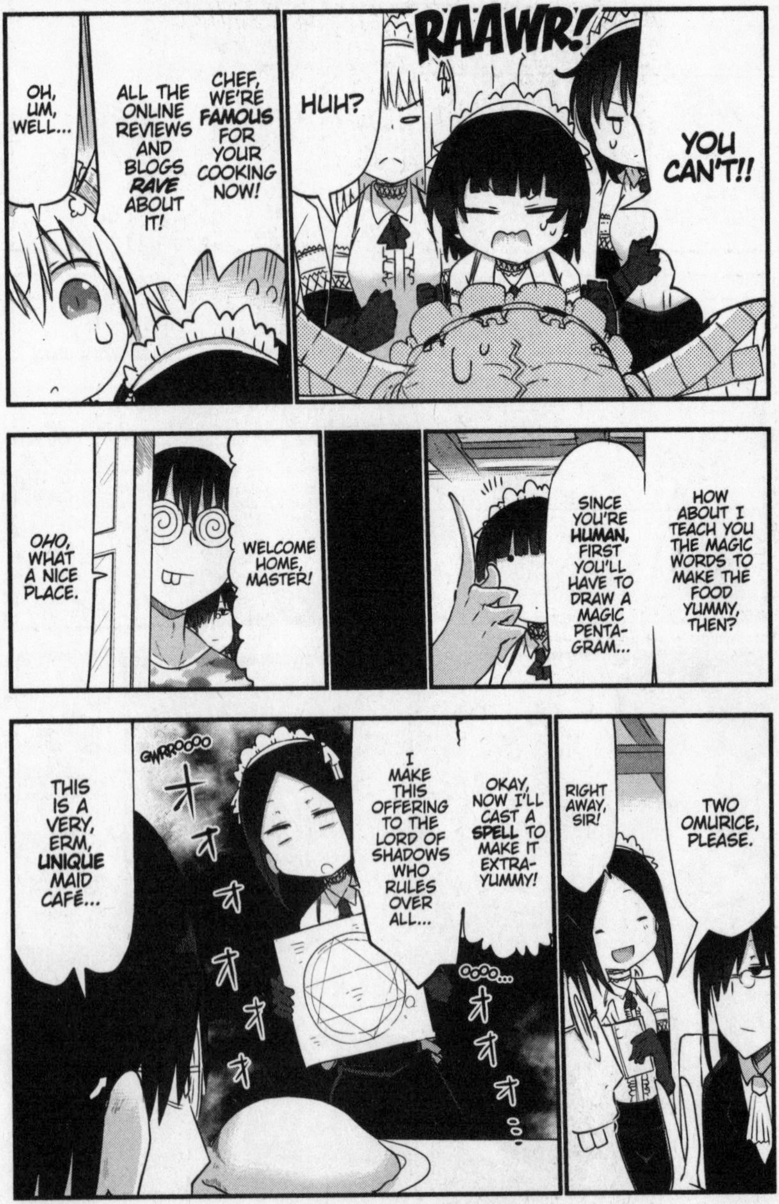
RAAWR!
YOU CAN'T!!
HUH?
CHEF, WE'RE FAMOUS FOR YOUR COOKING NOW!
ALL THE ONLINE REVIEWS AND BLOGS RAVE ABOUT IT!
OH, UM, WELL...
HOW ABOUT I TEACH YOU THE MAGIC WORDS TO MAKE THE FOOD YUMMY, THEN?
SINCE YOU'RE HUMAN, FIRST YOU'LL HAVE TO DRAW A MAGIC PENTAGRAM...
WELCOME HOME, MASTER!
OHO, WHAT A NICE PLACE.
TWO OMURICE, PLEASE.
RIGHT AWAY, SIR!
OKAY, NOW I'LL CAST A SPELL TO MAKE IT EXTRA-YUMMY!
I MAKE THIS OFFERING TO THE LORD OF SHADOWS WHO RULES OVER ALL...
OOOO...
GWRRROOOO
THIS IS A VERY, ERM, UNIQUE MAID CAFÉ...

CHAPTER 47/END

CHAPTER 48

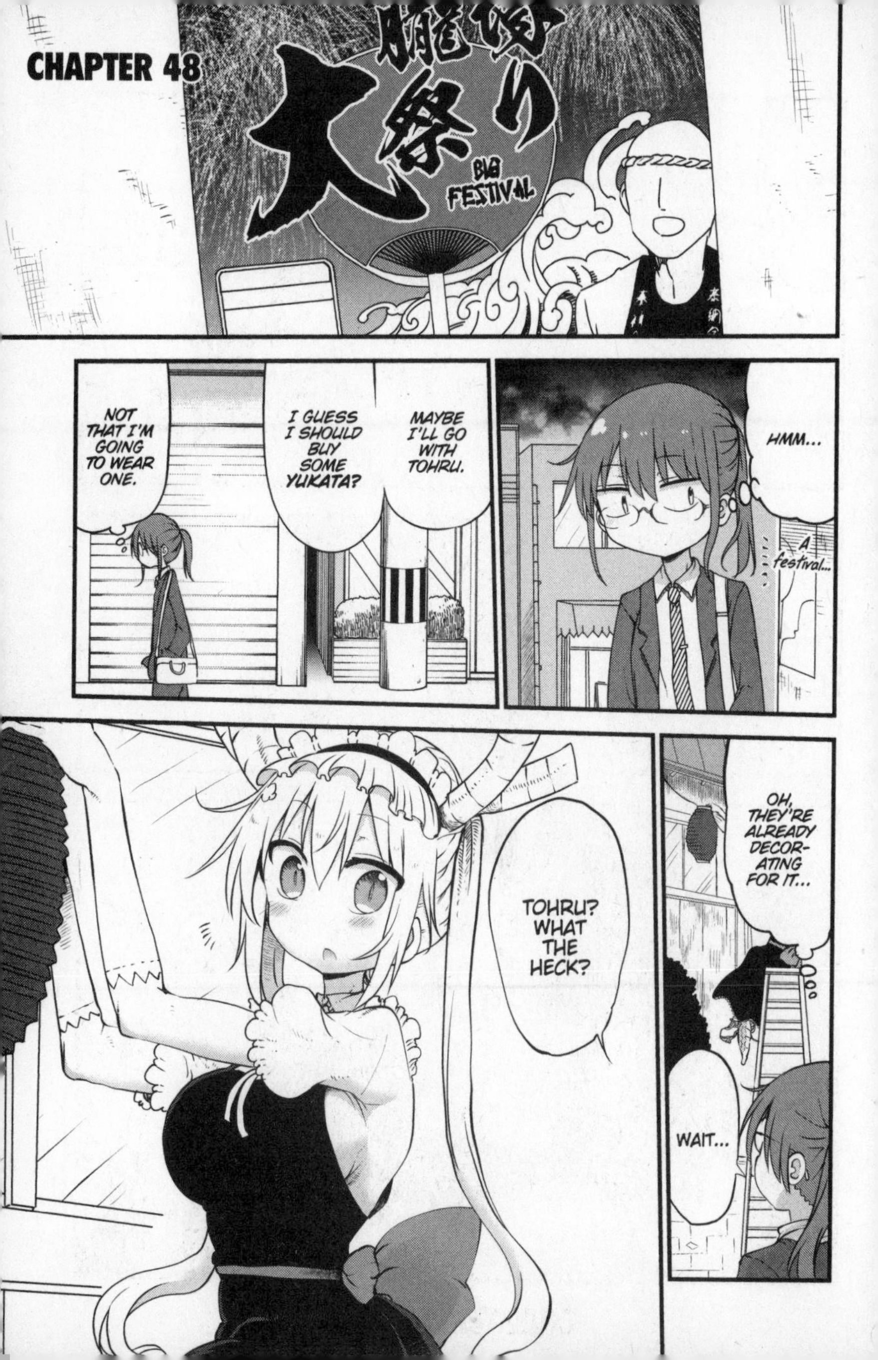
大祭り
BIG FESTIVAL
HMM...
A festival...
MAYBE I'LL GO WITH TOHRU.
I GUESS I SHOULD BUY SOME YUKATA?
NOT THAT I'M GOING TO WEAR ONE.
OH, THEY'RE ALREADY DECOR-ATING FOR IT...
WAIT...
TOHRU? WHAT THE HECK?

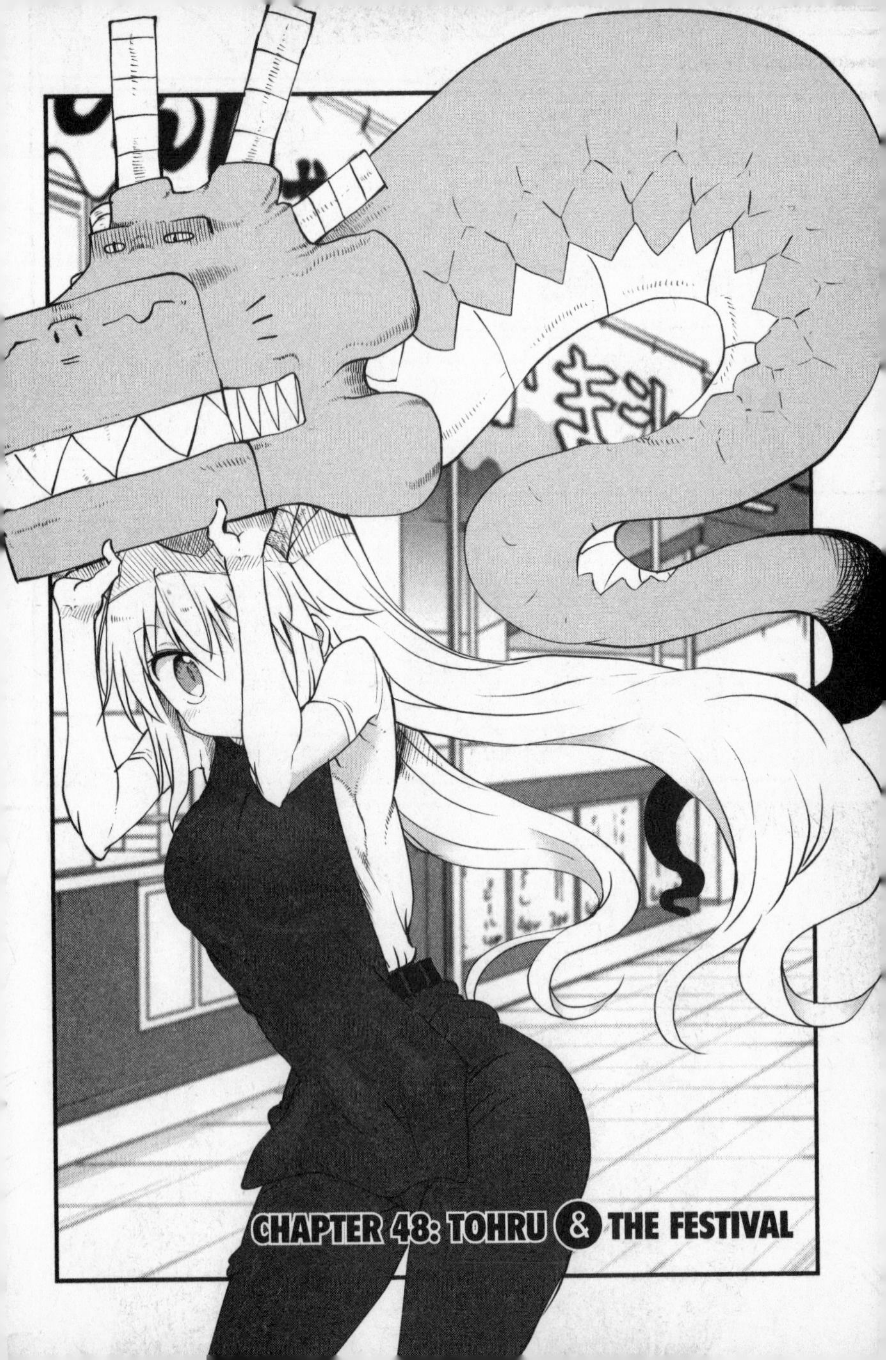
CHAPTER 48: TOHRU & THE FESTIVAL

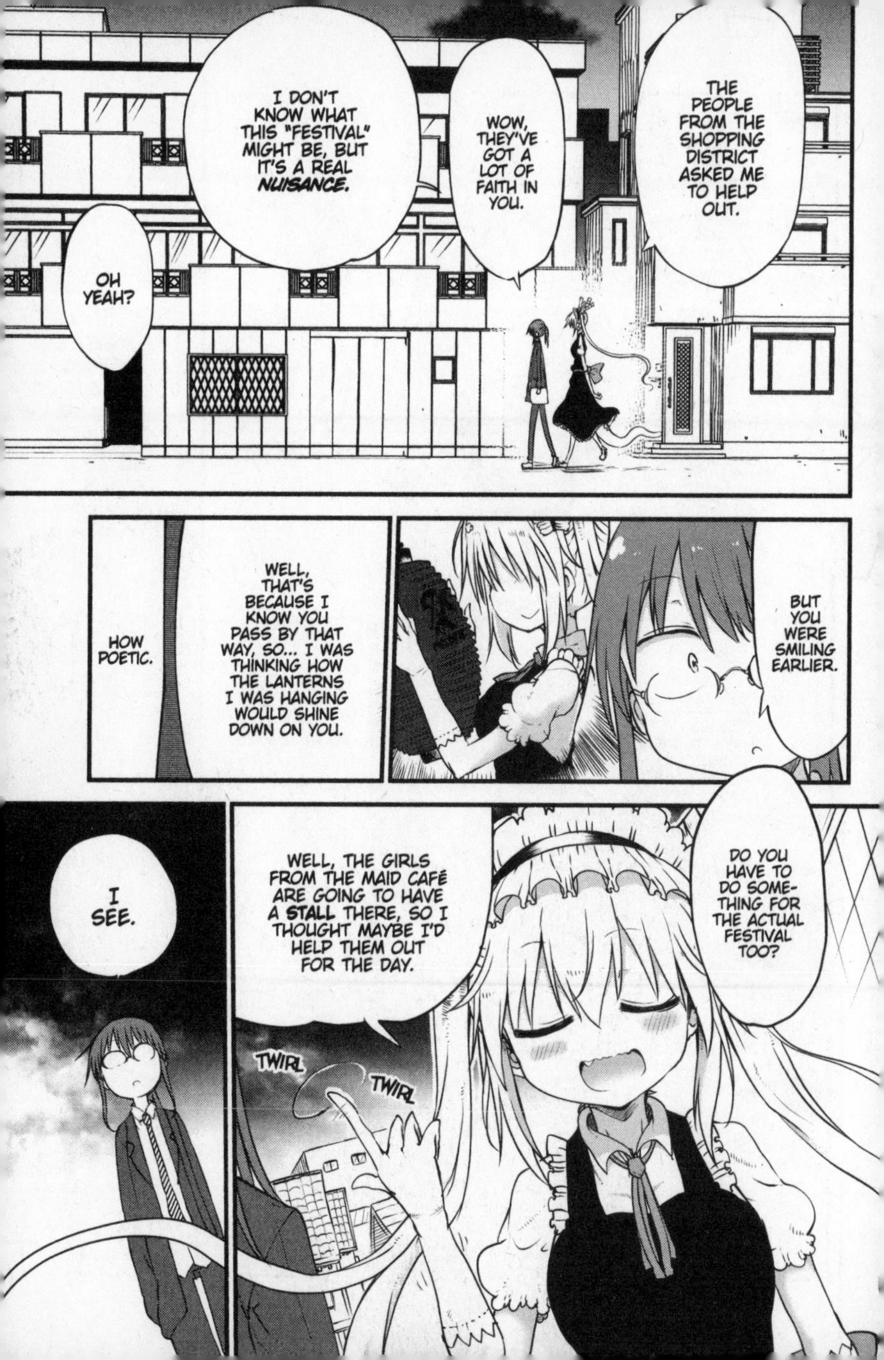
THE PEOPLE FROM THE SHOPPING DISTRICT ASKED ME TO HELP OUT.
WOW, THEY'VE GOT A LOT OF FAITH IN YOU.
I DON'T KNOW WHAT THIS "FESTIVAL" MIGHT BE, BUT IT'S A REAL ***NUISANCE.***
OH YEAH?
BUT YOU WERE SMILING EARLIER.
WELL, THAT'S BECAUSE I KNOW YOU PASS BY THAT WAY, SO... I WAS THINKING HOW THE LANTERNS I WAS HANGING WOULD SHINE DOWN ON YOU.
HOW POETIC.
DO YOU HAVE TO DO SOME-THING FOR THE ACTUAL FESTIVAL TOO?
WELL, THE GIRLS FROM THE MAID CAFÉ ARE GOING TO HAVE A **STALL** THERE, SO I THOUGHT MAYBE I'D HELP THEM OUT FOR THE DAY.
TWIRL
TWIRL
I SEE.

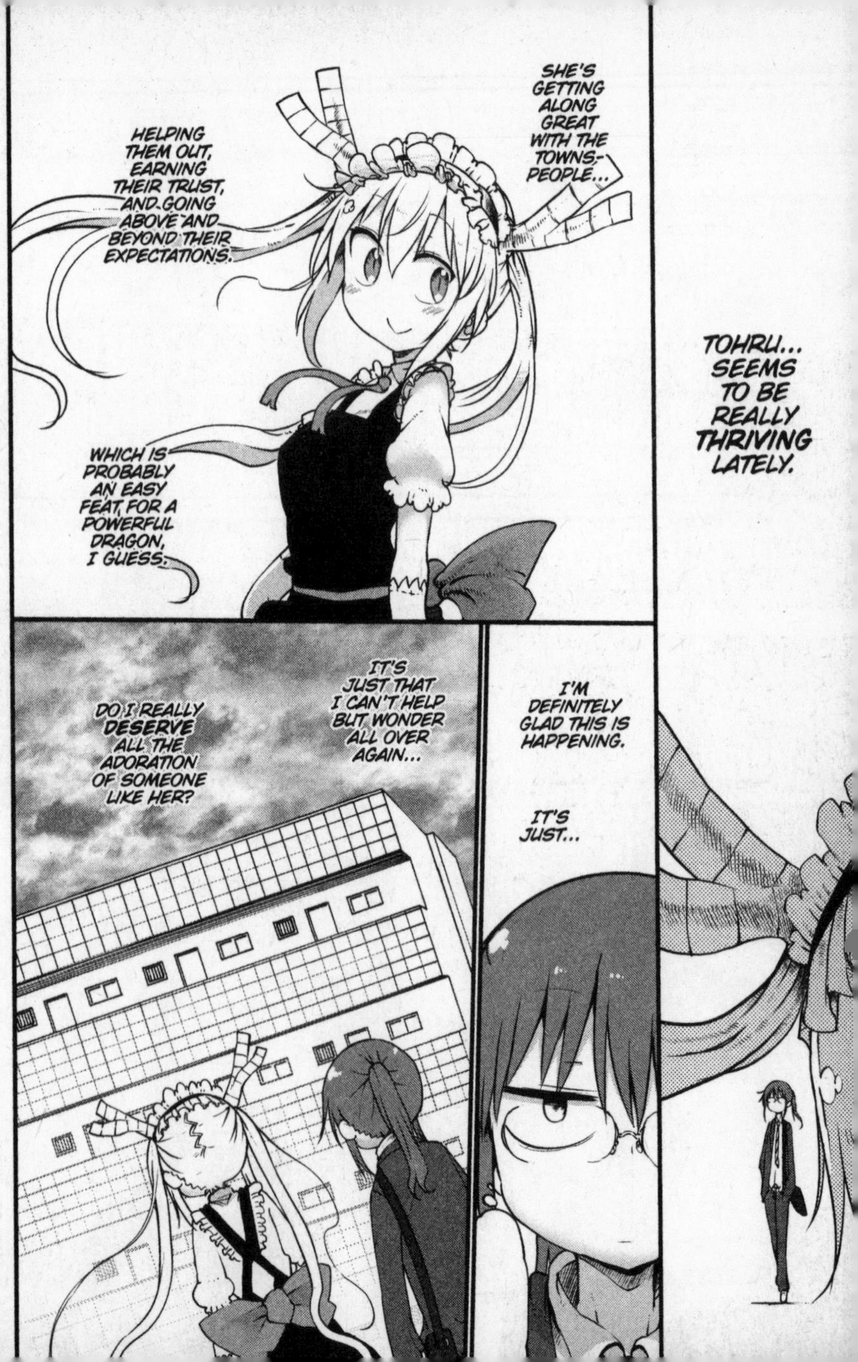
TOHRU... SEEMS TO BE REALLY THRIVING LATELY.
SHE'S GETTING ALONG GREAT WITH THE TOWNS-PEOPLE...
HELPING THEM OUT, EARNING THEIR TRUST, AND GOING ABOVE AND BEYOND THEIR EXPECTATIONS.
WHICH IS PROBABLY AN EASY FEAT FOR A POWERFUL DRAGON, I GUESS.
I'M DEFINITELY GLAD THIS IS HAPPENING.
IT'S JUST...
IT'S JUST THAT I CAN'T HELP BUT WONDER ALL OVER AGAIN...
DO I REALLY DESERVE ALL THE ADORATION OF SOMEONE LIKE HER?

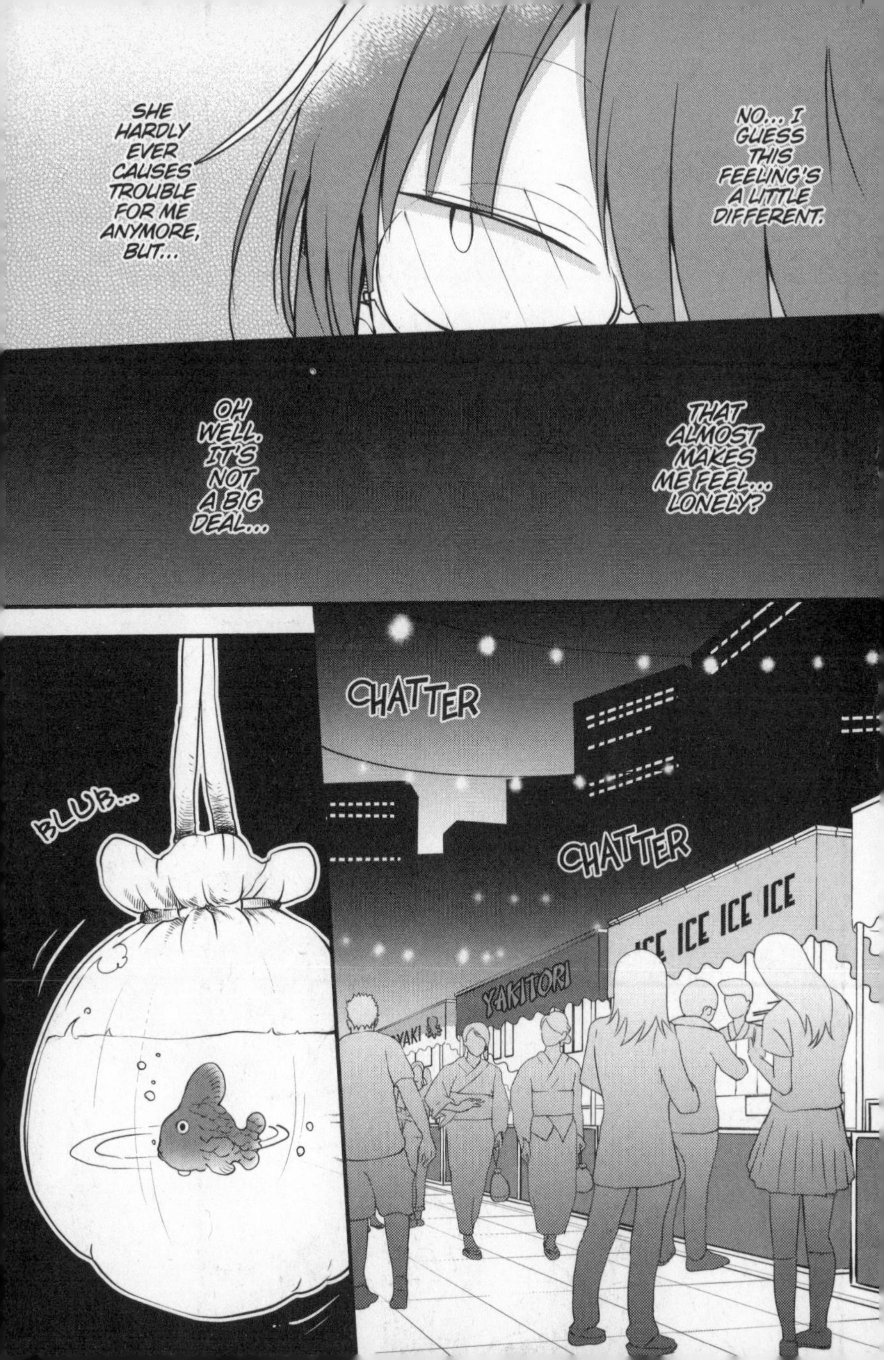
NO... I GUESS THIS FEELING'S A LITTLE DIFFERENT.
SHE HARDLY EVER CAUSES TROUBLE FOR ME ANYMORE, BUT...
THAT ALMOST MAKES ME FEEL... LONELY?
OH WELL. IT'S NOT A BIG DEAL...
CHATTER
CHATTER
ICE ICE ICE ICE
YAKITORI
BLUB...

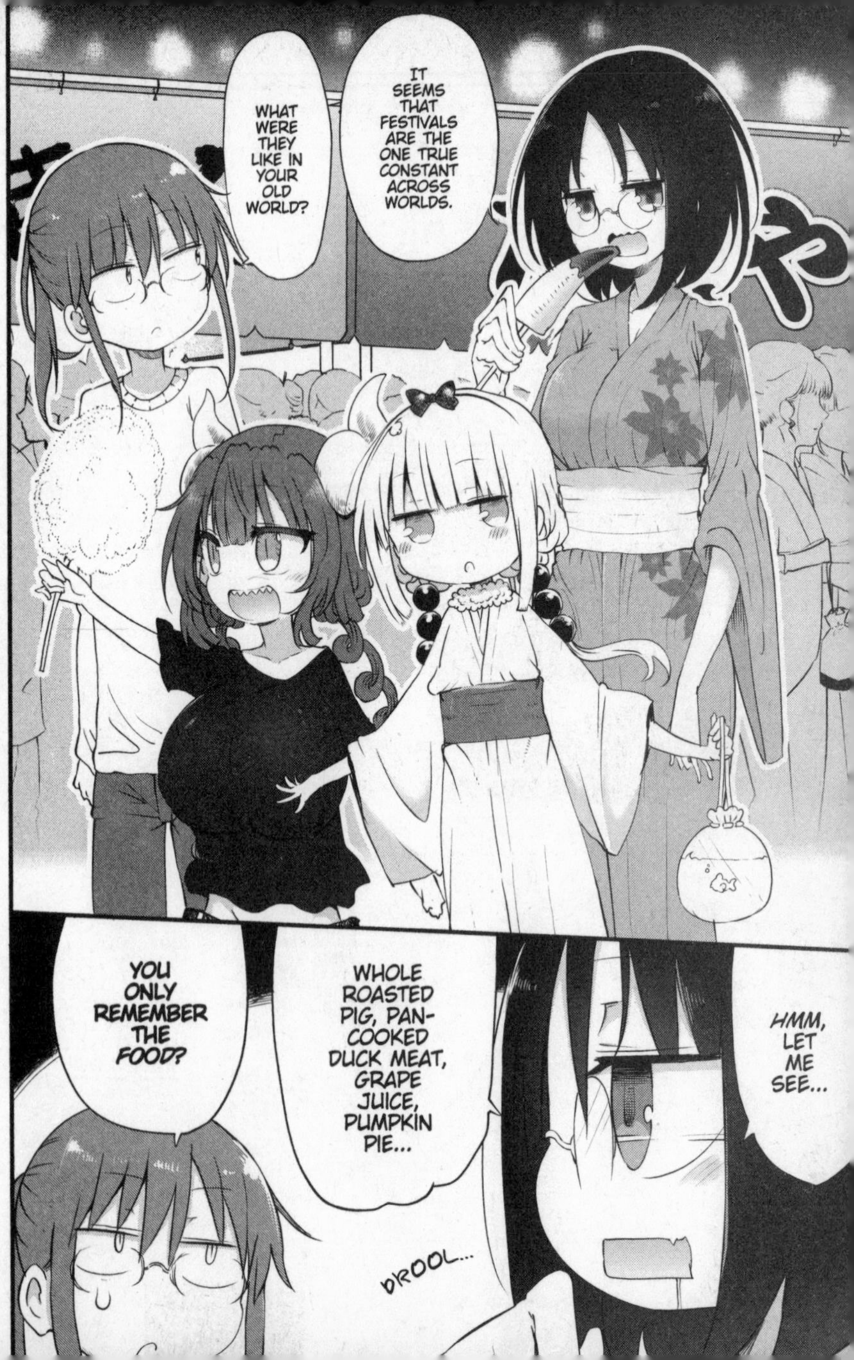
IT SEEMS THAT FESTIVALS ARE THE ONE TRUE CONSTANT ACROSS WORLDS.
WHAT WERE THEY LIKE IN YOUR OLD WORLD?
HMM, LET ME SEE...
WHOLE ROASTED PIG, PAN-COOKED DUCK MEAT, GRAPE JUICE, PUMPKIN PIE...
DROOL...
YOU ONLY REMEMBER THE *FOOD*?

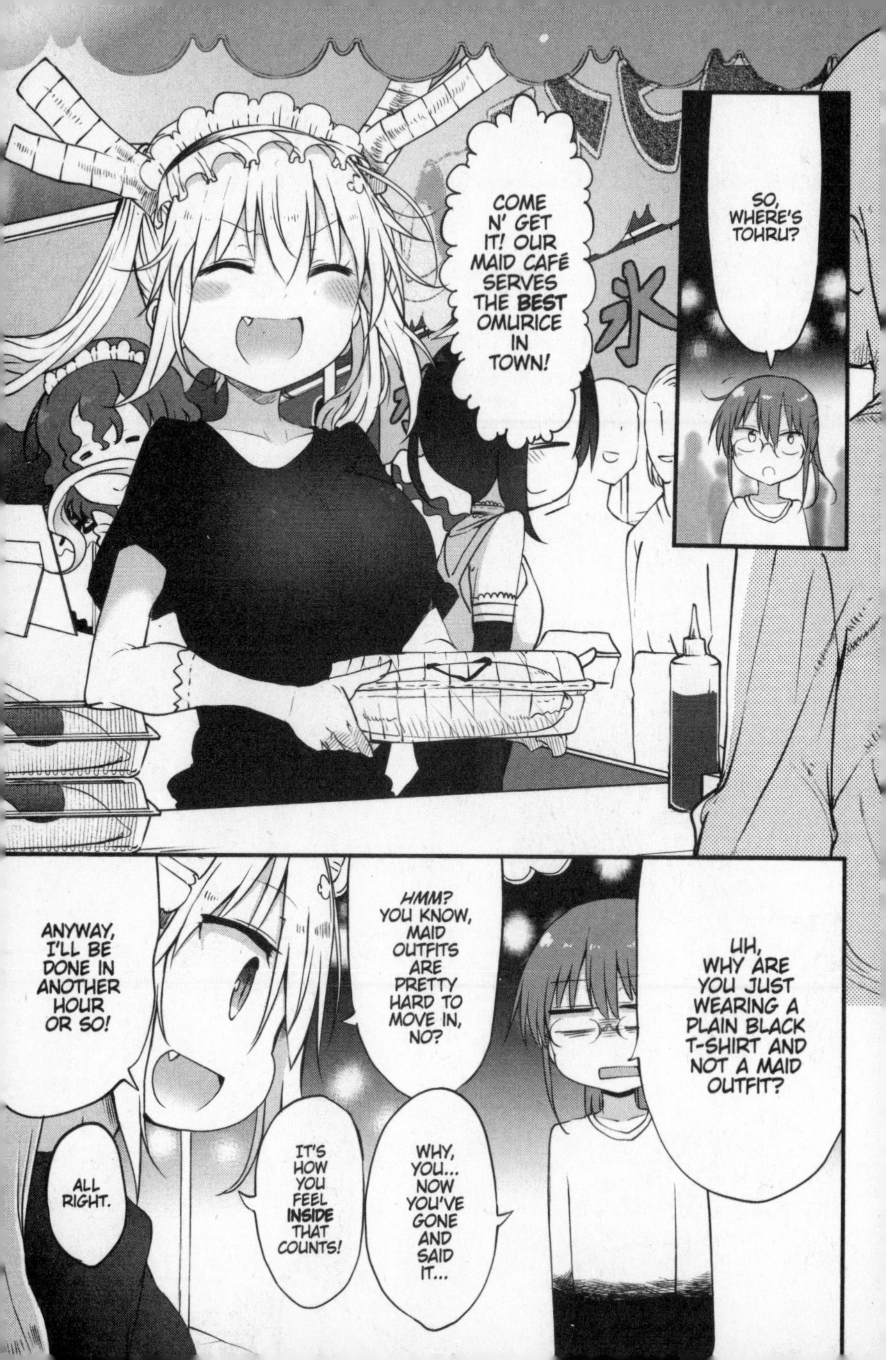
SO, WHERE'S TOHRU?
COME N' GET IT! OUR MAID CAFÉ SERVES THE **BEST** OMURICE IN TOWN!
UH, WHY ARE YOU JUST WEARING A PLAIN BLACK T-SHIRT AND NOT A MAID OUTFIT?
HMM? YOU KNOW, MAID OUTFITS ARE PRETTY HARD TO MOVE IN, NO?
WHY, YOU... NOW YOU'VE GONE AND SAID IT...
IT'S HOW YOU FEEL **INSIDE** THAT COUNTS!
ANYWAY, I'LL BE DONE IN ANOTHER HOUR OR SO!
ALL RIGHT.

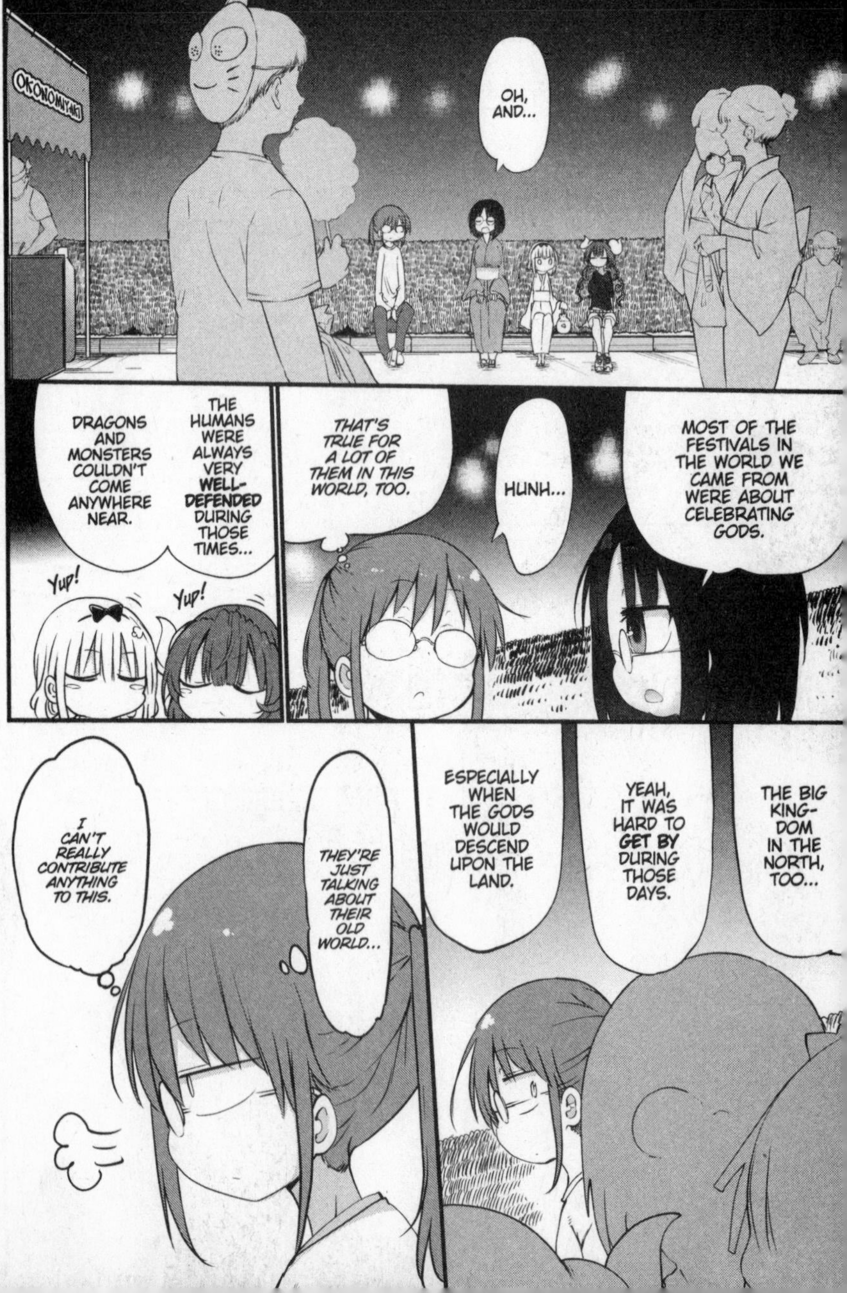
OKONOMIYAKI
OH, AND...
MOST OF THE FESTIVALS IN THE WORLD WE CAME FROM WERE ABOUT CELEBRATING GODS.
HUNH...
THAT'S TRUE FOR A LOT OF THEM IN THIS WORLD, TOO.
THE HUMANS WERE ALWAYS VERY WELL-DEFENDED DURING THOSE TIMES...
DRAGONS AND MONSTERS COULDN'T COME ANYWHERE NEAR.
Yup!
Yup!
THE BIG KING-DOM IN THE NORTH, TOO...
YEAH, IT WAS HARD TO GET BY DURING THOSE DAYS.
ESPECIALLY WHEN THE GODS WOULD DESCEND UPON THE LAND.
THEY'RE JUST TALKING ABOUT THEIR OLD WORLD...
I CAN'T REALLY CONTRIBUTE ANYTHING TO THIS.

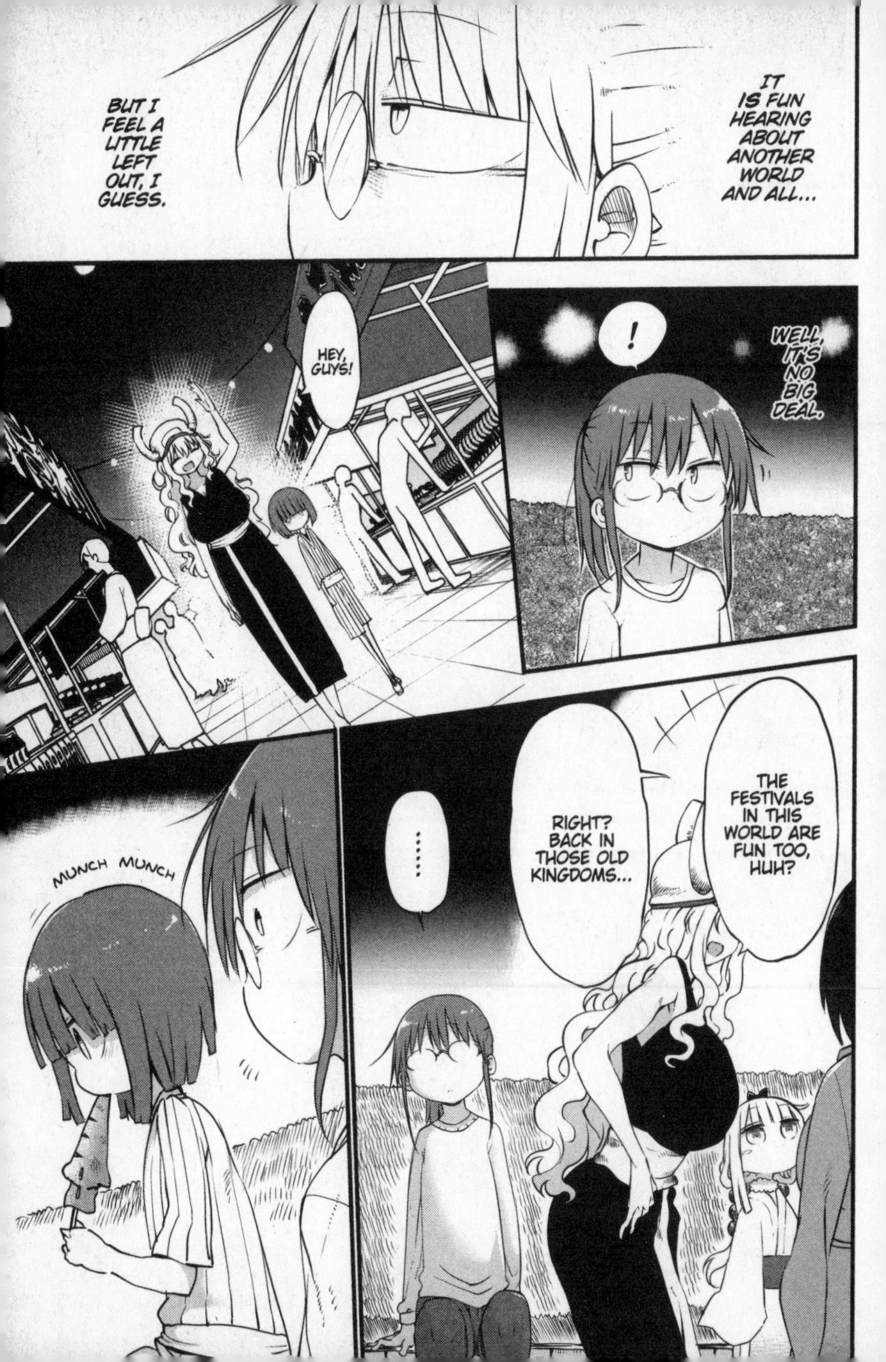
IT IS FUN HEARING ABOUT ANOTHER WORLD AND ALL...
BUT I FEEL A LITTLE LEFT OUT, I GUESS.
!
WELL, IT'S NO BIG DEAL.
HEY, GUYS!
THE FESTIVALS IN THIS WORLD ARE FUN TOO, HUH?
RIGHT? BACK IN THOSE OLD KINGDOMS...
......
MUNCH MUNCH

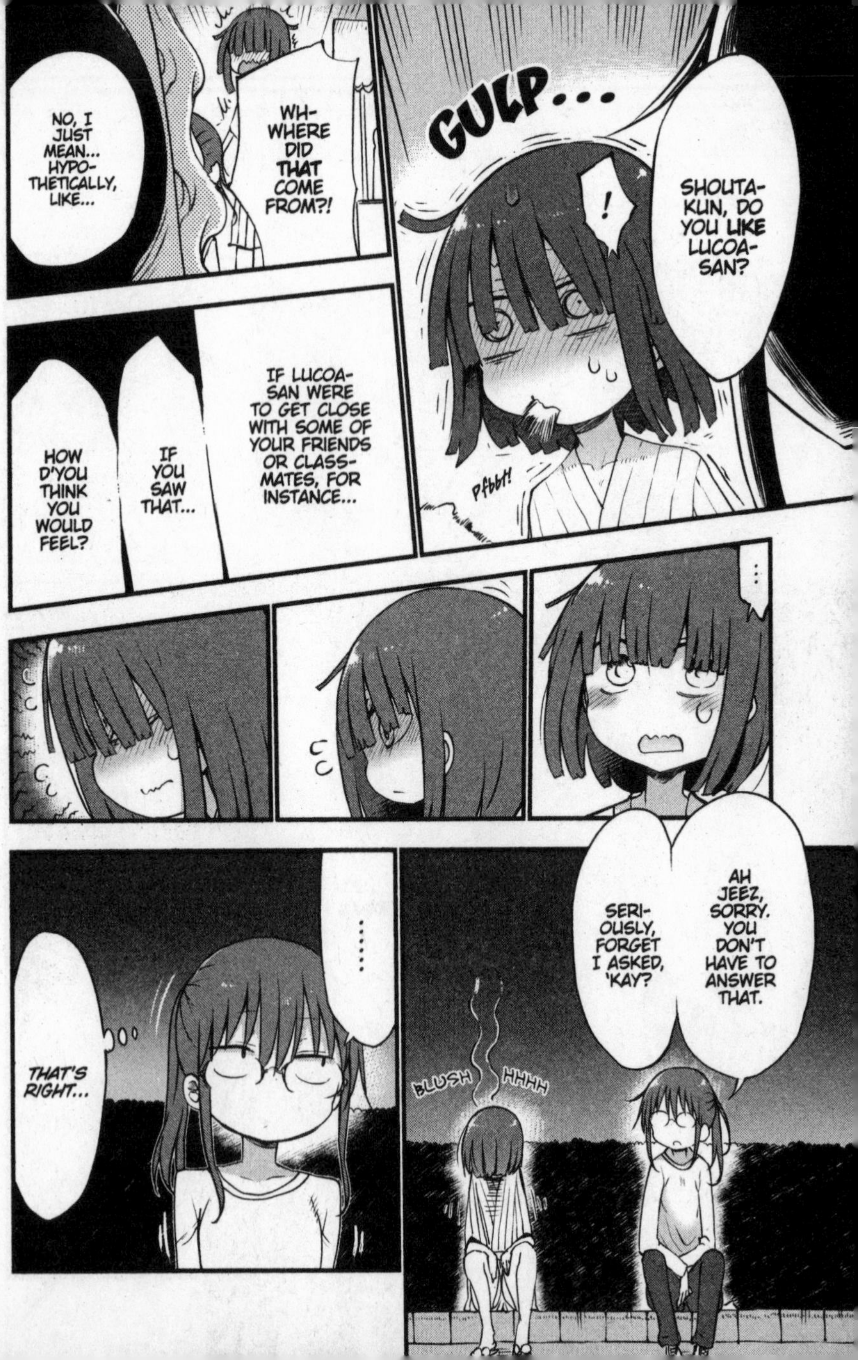
GULP...
!
SHOUTA-KUN, DO YOU LIKE LUCOA-SAN?
Pfbbt!
WH-WHERE DID THAT COME FROM?!
NO, I JUST MEAN... HYPO-THETICALLY, LIKE...
IF LUCOA-SAN WERE TO GET CLOSE WITH SOME OF YOUR FRIENDS OR CLASS-MATES, FOR INSTANCE...
IF YOU SAW THAT...
HOW D'YOU THINK YOU WOULD FEEL?
...
AH JEEZ, SORRY. YOU DON'T HAVE TO ANSWER THAT.
SERI-OUSLY, FORGET I ASKED, 'KAY?
BLUSH
HHHH
......
THAT'S RIGHT...

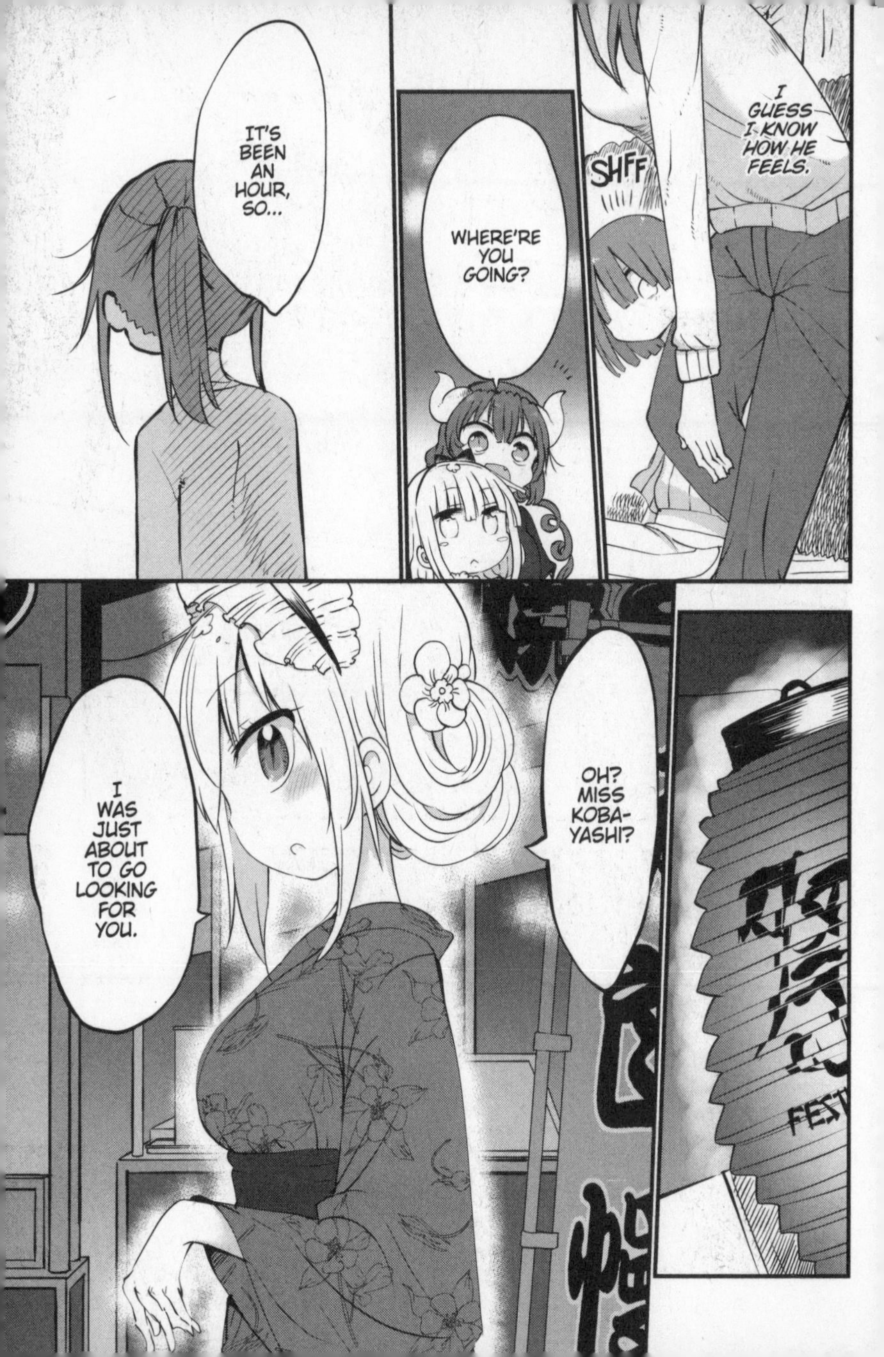
I GUESS I KNOW HOW HE FEELS.
SHFF
WHERE'RE YOU GOING?
IT'S BEEN AN HOUR, SO...
OH? MISS KOBA-YASHI?
I WAS JUST ABOUT TO GO LOOKING FOR YOU.

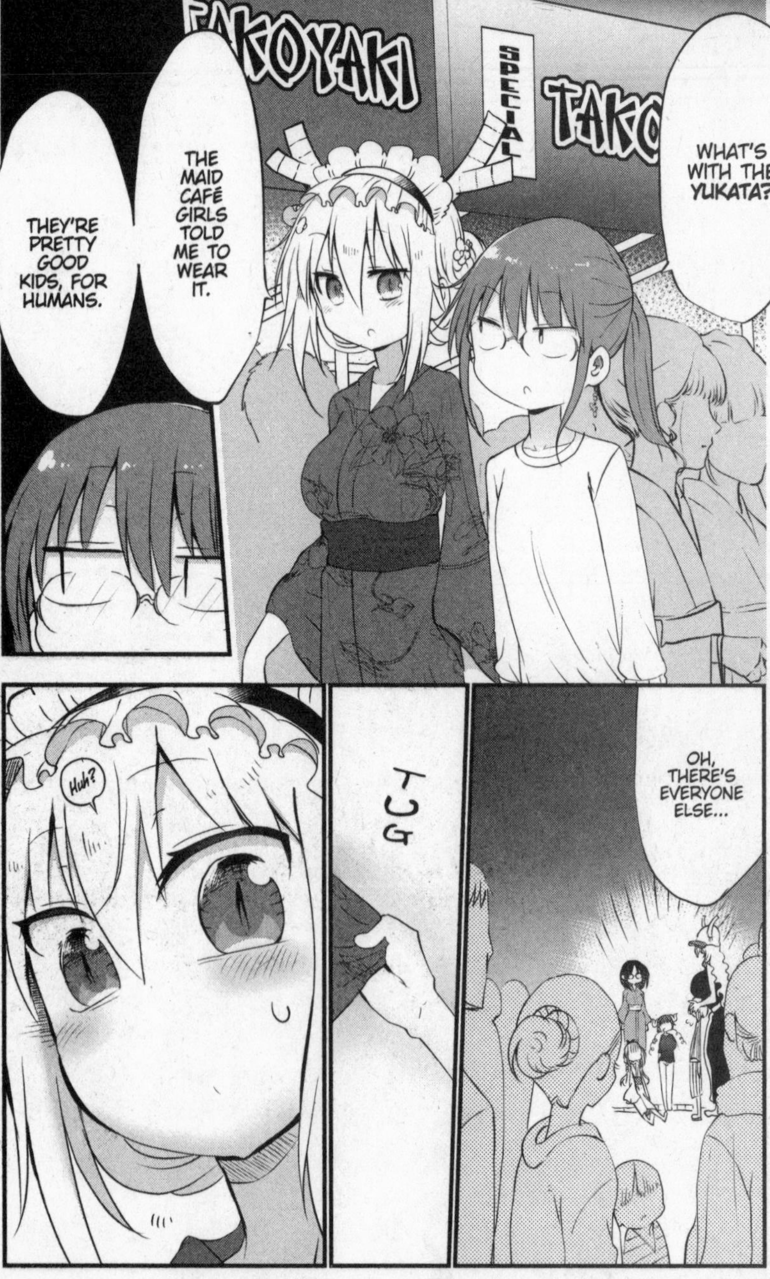
TAKOYAKI
SPECIAL
WHAT'S WITH THE YUKATA?
THE MAID CAFÉ GIRLS TOLD ME TO WEAR IT.
THEY'RE PRETTY GOOD KIDS, FOR HUMANS.
OH, THERE'S EVERYONE ELSE...
TUG
Huh?

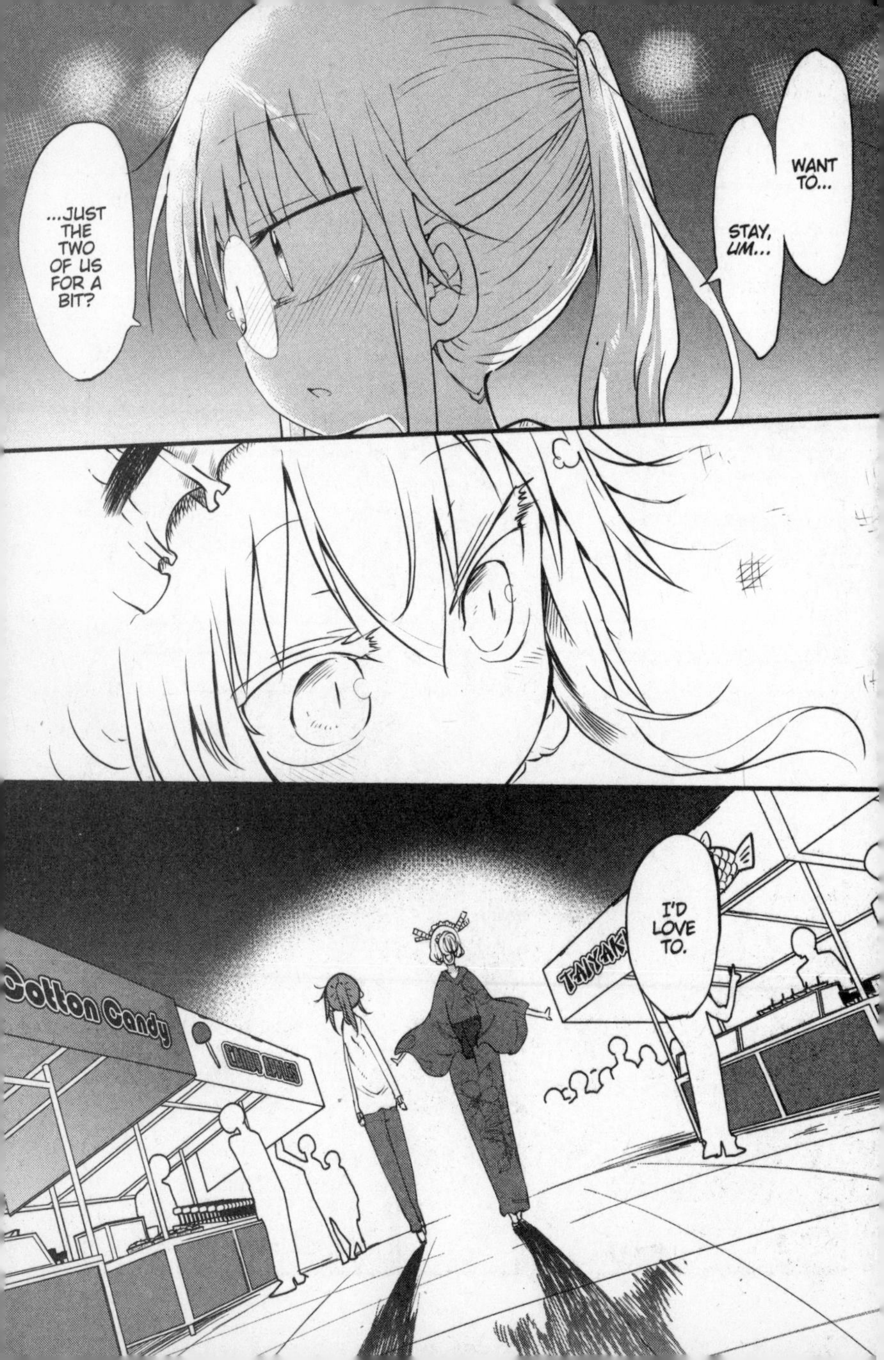
WANT TO... STAY, UM...
...JUST THE TWO OF US FOR A BIT?
I'D LOVE TO.
TAIYAKI
Cotton Candy

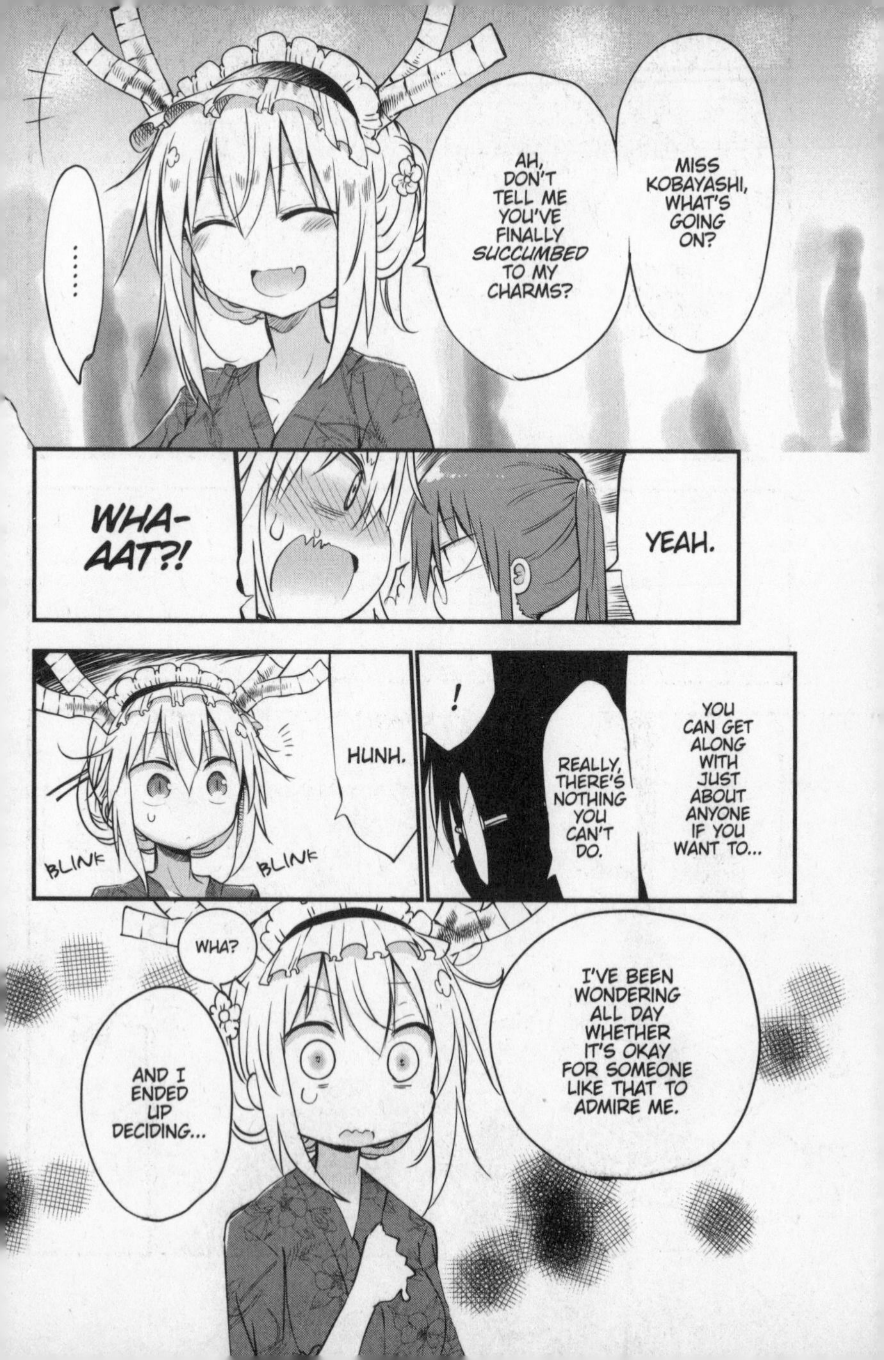
MISS KOBAYASHI, WHAT'S GOING ON?
AH, DON'T TELL ME YOU'VE FINALLY SUCCUMBED TO MY CHARMS?
......
YEAH.
WHA-AAT?!
YOU CAN GET ALONG WITH JUST ABOUT ANYONE IF YOU WANT TO...
REALLY, THERE'S NOTHING YOU CAN'T DO.
!
HUNH.
BLINK
BLINK
I'VE BEEN WONDERING ALL DAY WHETHER IT'S OKAY FOR SOMEONE LIKE THAT TO ADMIRE ME.
WHA?
AND I ENDED UP DECIDING...

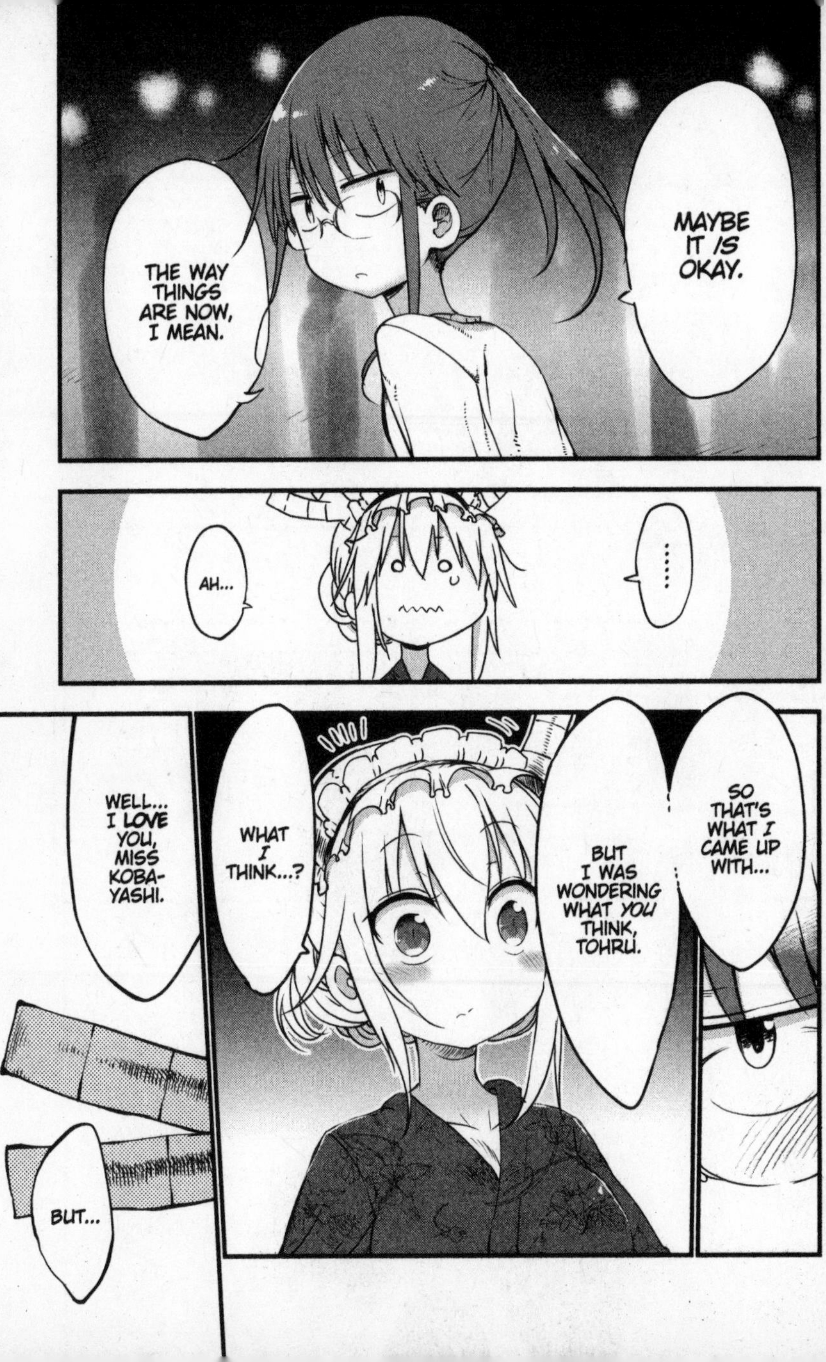
MAYBE IT IS OKAY.
THE WAY THINGS ARE NOW, I MEAN.
......
AH...
SO THAT'S WHAT I CAME UP WITH...
BUT I WAS WONDERING WHAT YOU THINK, TOHRU.
WHAT I THINK...?
WELL... I LOVE YOU, MISS KOBA-YASHI.
BUT...

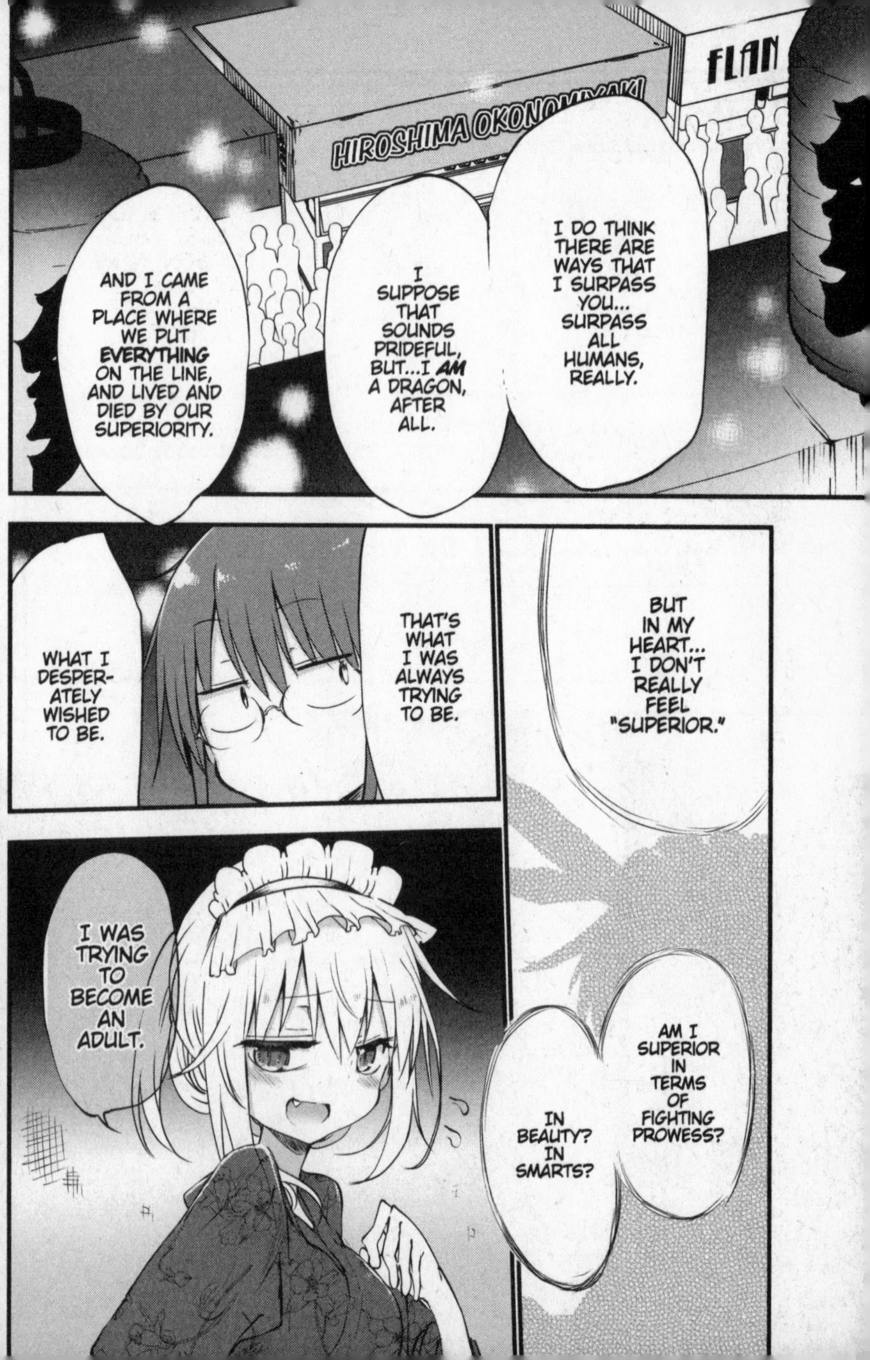
I DO THINK THERE ARE WAYS THAT I SURPASS YOU... SURPASS ALL HUMANS, REALLY.
I SUPPOSE THAT SOUNDS PRIDEFUL, BUT...I *AM* A DRAGON, AFTER ALL.
AND I CAME FROM A PLACE WHERE WE PUT **EVERYTHING** ON THE LINE, AND LIVED AND DIED BY OUR SUPERIORITY.
BUT IN MY HEART... I DON'T REALLY FEEL "SUPERIOR."
AM I SUPERIOR IN TERMS OF FIGHTING PROWESS?
IN BEAUTY? IN SMARTS?
THAT'S WHAT I WAS ALWAYS TRYING TO BE.
WHAT I DESPER-ATELY WISHED TO BE.
I WAS TRYING TO BECOME AN ADULT.

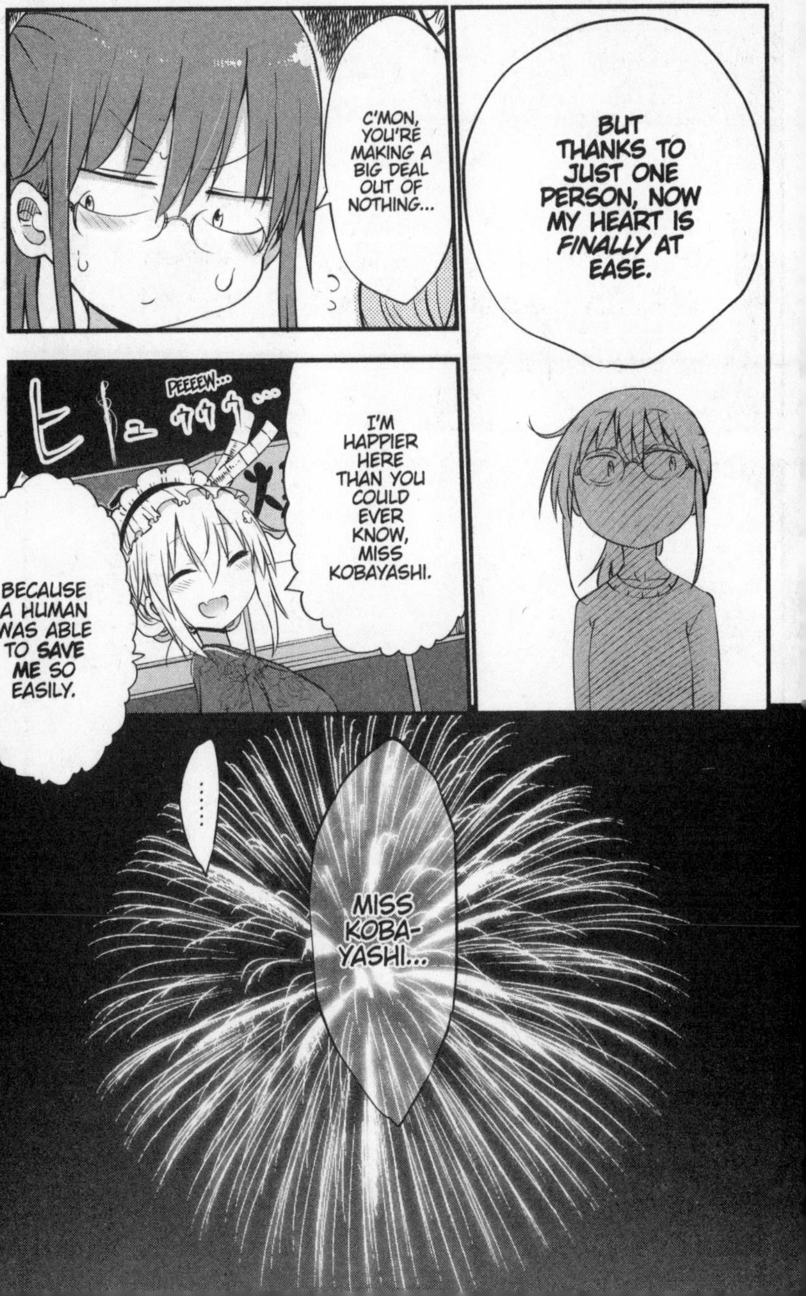
BUT THANKS TO JUST ONE PERSON, NOW MY HEART IS *FINALLY* AT EASE.
C'MON, YOU'RE MAKING A BIG DEAL OUT OF NOTHING...
PEEEEW...
I'M HAPPIER HERE THAN YOU COULD EVER KNOW, MISS KOBAYASHI.
BECAUSE A HUMAN WAS ABLE TO **SAVE** ME SO EASILY.
MISS KOBA-YASHI...
......

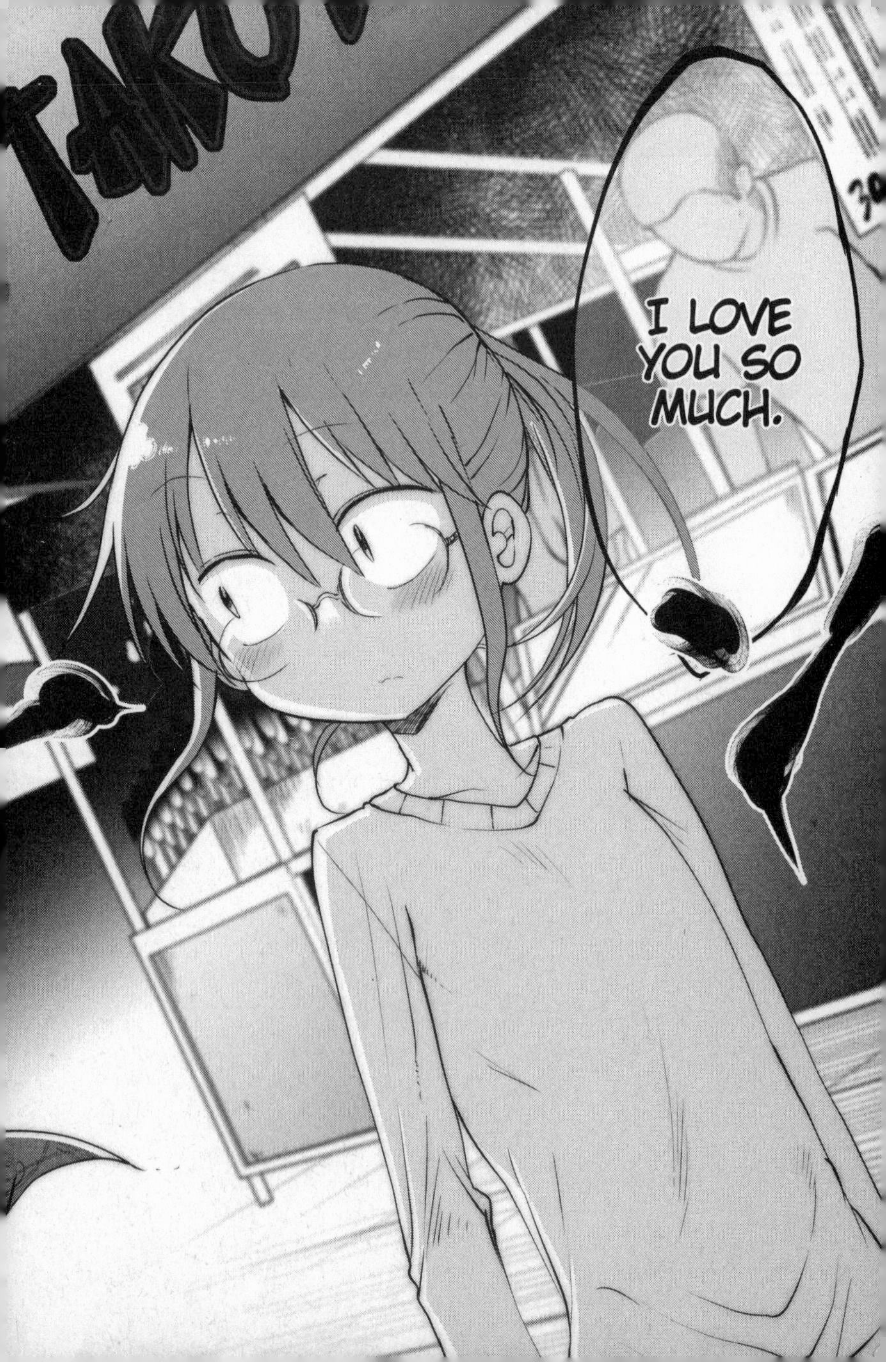
I LOVE YOU SO MUCH.

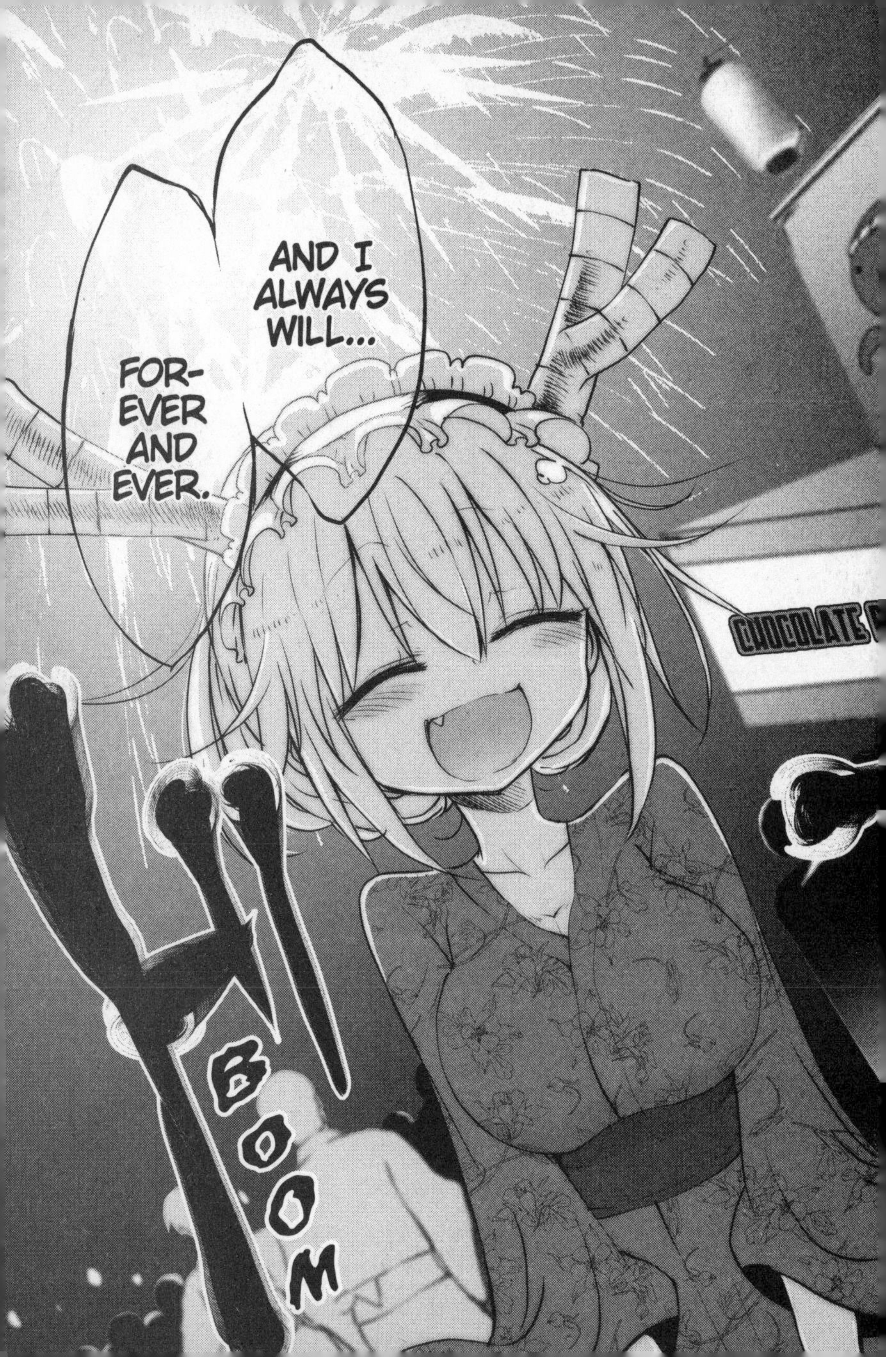
AND I ALWAYS WILL... FOR-EVER AND EVER.
CHOCOLATE
BOOM

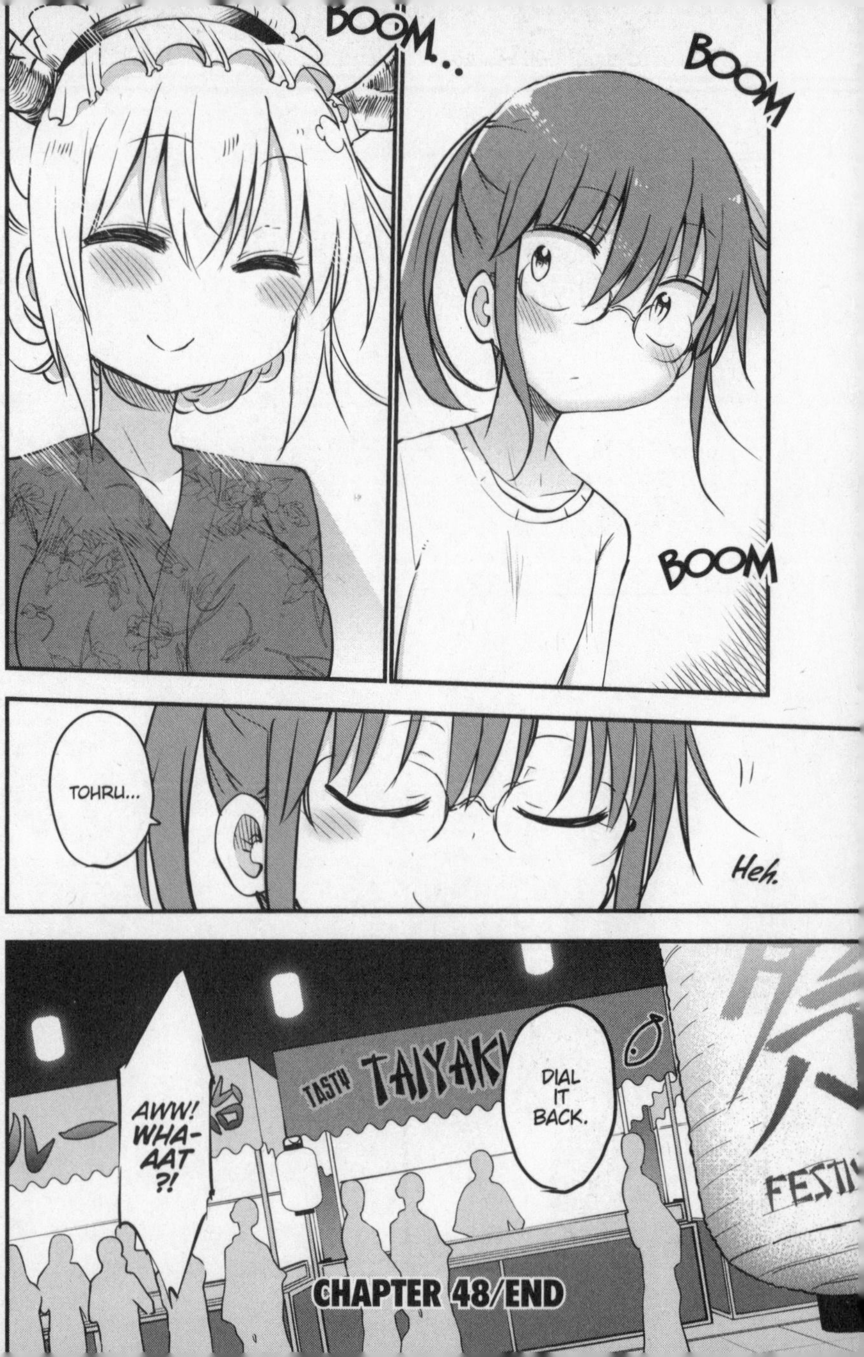
BOOM
BOOM
BOOM...
TOHRU...
Heh.
DIAL IT BACK.
AWW! WHAA-AAT?!
TASTY TAIYAKI
CHAPTER 48/END

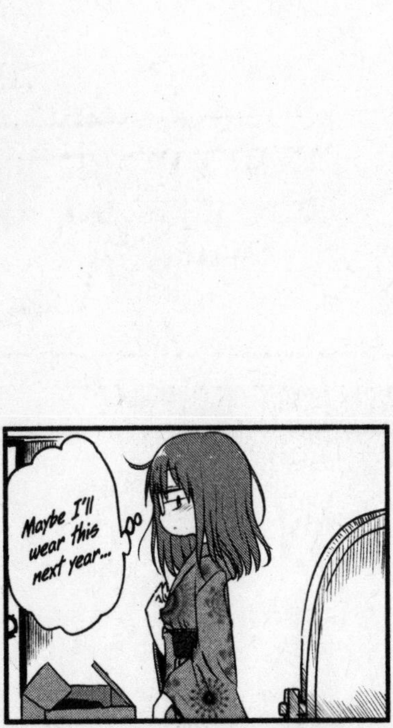
Maybe I'll wear this next year...

Miss Kobayashi's
DRAGON MAID

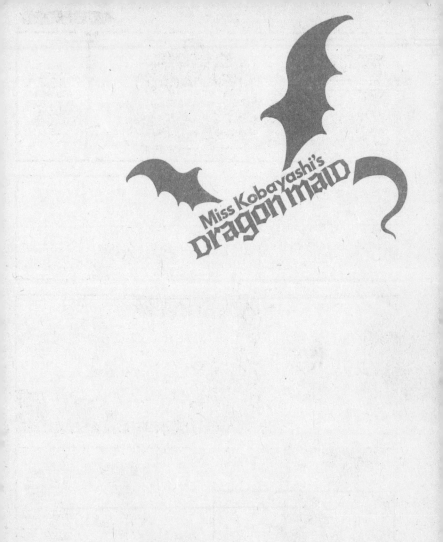